OUTDOOR ADVENTURE EDUCATION

Foundations, Theory, and Research

Alan W. Ewert

Indiana University

Jim Sibthorp

University of Utah

Human Kinetics

Library of Congress Cataloging-in-Publication Data

Ewert, Alan W., 1949-
  Outdoor adventure education : foundations, theory, and research / Alan W. Ewert, Indiana University, Jim Sibthorp, University of Utah.
      pages cm
  Includes bibliographical references and index.
  1. Outdoor education. 2. Experiential learning. 3. Adventure education. I. Title.
  LB1047.E94 2014
  371.3'84--dc23
                                                    2013026937
  ISBN-10: 1-4504-4251-X (print)
  ISBN-13: 978-1-4504-4251-0 (print)

The web addresses cited in this text were current as of August 2013, unless otherwise noted.

In the cover photo students are examining snow layers and structure to contribute to their assessment of avalanche risk. Digging snow pits is a common practice for winter mountaineering and backcountry skiing and snowboarding.

Acquisitions Editor: Gayle Kassing, PhD; **Developmental Editor:** Jacqueline Eaton Blakley; **Assistant Editors:** Anne Rumery, Casey A. Gentis, and Katherine Maurer; **Copyeditor:** John Wentworth; **Indexer:** Katy Balcer; **Permissions Manager:** Dalene Reeder; **Graphic Designer:** Fred Starbird; **Graphic Artist:** Kathleen Boudreau-Fuoss; **Cover Designer:** Keith Blomberg; **Photograph (cover):** Courtesy of Kirk Nichols; **Photo Production Manager:** Jason Allen; **Art Manager:** Kelly Hendren; **Associate Art Manager:** Alan L. Wilborn; **Illustrations:** © Human Kinetics; **Printer:** Sheridan Books

Photos on part openers and sidebar screens courtesy of Scott Schumann. Photo on chapter openers courtesy of Nate Bricker.

Printed in the United States of America   10   9   8   7   6   5   4   3   2   1

The paper in this book is certified under a sustainable forestry program.

Human Kinetics
Website: www.HumanKinetics.com

United States: Human Kinetics
P.O. Box 5076
Champaign, IL 61825-5076
800-747-4457
e-mail: humank@hkusa.com

Canada: Human Kinetics
475 Devonshire Road Unit 100
Windsor, ON N8Y 2L5
800-465-7301 (in Canada only)
e-mail: info@hkcanada.com

Europe: Human Kinetics
107 Bradford Road
Stanningley
Leeds LS28 6AT, United Kingdom
+44 (0) 113 255 5665
e-mail: hk@hkeurope.com

Australia: Human Kinetics
57A Price Avenue
Lower Mitcham, South Australia 5062
08 8372 0999
e-mail: info@hkaustralia.com

New Zealand: Human Kinetics
P.O. Box 80
Torrens Park, South Australia 5062
0800 222 062
e-mail: info@hknewzealand.com

E5853

First, we would like to dedicate this book to our children:
Alyssa, Alanna, Ava, Lily, and Mia,
who represent the future users of Outdoor Adventure Education (OAE).
Second, we would also like to dedicate this book
to all the current and future students in OAE
who serve as the stewards of both the programs and the activities.
May their devotion and passion for OAE
be as great as that of their predecessors.

Contents

PART I

FOUNDATIONS 1

PART II
THEORY 61

PART III
RESEARCH 109

Foreword

ike many of you, I was first drawn into outdoor adventure, and eventually outdoor education, by impactful experiences. On early outings, I found a new world, or certainly found a new way of interacting with the world I knew. I also discovered new physical activities that provided challenge, opportunity, exploration, and greater self-confidence. Those early activities were primarily about the "experience," which became a powerful drive to seek out further experiences and eventually a career helping others discover and pursue such experiences. I loved climbing, kayaking, canoeing, backpacking, and other outdoor activities. I knew they were somehow good for me—both for my body and soul. I assumed that if they were good for me, they must be good for everyone, so I pursued this life in outdoor adventure with great passion and drive.

Of course, from time to time we adventurers must leave the wilderness. When I returned to other circles of friends and family I often faced the question of, "Why?" Though I could describe my work and my passions, friends and family did not share my understanding of its importance or value. Some of them found my activities and career choice to be frivolous, even bizarre, especially for someone who had studied physics and math. I found that what I knew in my heart could not always be translated into understanding for others. When I was able to explain why I had chosen my career, I was often asked how I knew outdoor adventure made a difference.

I share this experience because I have witnessed parallels as I have led and watched other outdoor adventure education (OAE) organizations and businesses. Many, if not most, OAE businesses were started by passionate and active outdoors people. These founders tend to be very knowledgeable about implementation and skills and are passionate about their chosen pursuit. They also know in their hearts that what they are doing is good for them, and therefore, assume it will be good for all other participants. They are grounded in the what, usually not as clear on the why, and seldom have an interest in the evidence of outcomes.

In *Outdoor Adventure Education: Foundations, Theory, and Research*, Alan Ewert and Jim Sibthorp urge us all to evaluate and plan our programs in a way that goes well beyond the basics of operating them. This is a book that reflects the maturity of our field. Ewert and Sibthorp walk readers through and explore themes of design, implementation, and evidence. In the process, they provide an overview of the history and development of OAE, and subsequently, chart out the challenges our industry faces in the future. Certainly, it is an excellent foundation for all potential practitioners of OAE, but it is also of value to anyone currently working in or leading outdoor organizations.

It is likely all of us were drawn to this field through a powerful experience or series of experiences. In fact, we may all be a bit hesitant to attempt to evaluate that experience in an academic way. Ewert and Sibthorp take on this challenge, as both are instructors in OAE programs as well as researchers and scholars. They understand the independent nature of those who have been drawn to this field. Their approach is not dogmatic, but rather, invites the reader into the discussion and debate. It is a bit of an experiential textbook, inviting us to interact in the same way we do with our students or clients.

When I started teaching at the National Outdoor Leadership School (NOLS), I was grounded in the practice and motivated to refine my skills. As I progressed beyond the implementation, I found myself absorbing the philosophy of Paul Petzoldt, the founder of NOLS. I found great benefit in anchoring my practice as an outdoor educator to his description of program design and purpose. I also found that his descriptions of program outcomes for students and society helped me perfect my answer when justifying why I pursued my selected career.

Though I was successful in formulating my response to that "why", when I moved into leadership positions at NOLS, I found I was increasingly challenged by new questions. The foundation of design and purpose that Paul laid for NOLS is key to the many successful outcomes of our students, but when I came to the school in 1980, it was clear that we lacked discipline in collecting and using evidence of program outcomes. We had nearly infinite anecdotes illustrating success, as probably most OAE programs do, yet I became increasingly bothered by the lack of any research-based evidence on outcomes.

So in the 1980s, NOLS took a big step into research and evidence through work in risk management. We started to clearly quantify and analyze all of our incident data, and suddenly, risk management analysis was no longer driven by anecdote. These steps in quantifying and analyzing evidence helped lead to the establishment of the Wilderness Risk Management Conference in 1993.

While evidence on risk improved, NOLS' evidence on benefits was not similarly developing. How could we really address the risk/benefit equation when we only had data on risks? This dilemma prompted a significant commitment to researching NOLS programs and outcomes. The results of a collaborative effort between NOLS and other researchers and programs have helped us to understand, refine, and improve our program offerings. It brought our organization the important cycle of evidence that is essential to accompany both design and implementation. It led to organizational change and development. It has also been an essential tool in preparing for our future with students who are also changing over time.

This track is by no means unique. I believe this full cycle of program development is important for all OAE programs and is becoming increasingly pressing in our changing world. Ewert and Sibthorp reflect upon these changes in the final chapter of this book, and thus, present challenges that we all face as we create the future of OAE.

Passionate outdoor adventure educators will find great benefit in reading and interacting with this book. It is a book for the practitioner, the student of OAE, the business leader, the "fun hog," and the many passionate individuals who make up this field. It will engage your heart, your body, and your mind.

John Gans
Executive Director
National Outdoor Leadership School

Preface

A ship is safe in harbor
but that's not what ships are for.
—Anonymous

For hundreds of thousands of people in North America and elsewhere, the lure of the outdoors is irresistible. For many of these individuals, the opening quote captures their motivation for getting up out of their chairs and leaving the comforts of home to seek adventures and challenges in the great outdoors. More and more people head into nature not for the fishing, hunting, or scenery (although these are important) but for the excitement of such activities as wilderness hiking, rock climbing, and whitewater kayaking. An extensive infrastructure now caters to outdoor adventurers, ranging from facilities such as hiking chalets to floating tent platforms for canoeists. Whatever their activity or outdoor pursuit, most adventurers have gained much of their skill and expertise through organized groups, universities, guide services, or other forms of instruction. That is, they engage in some form of outdoor adventure education (OAE).

As a student of OAE, it is important to make intentional decisions about your individual program and personal practices. While there are a variety of considerations that might influence how you approach OAE, a fundamental understanding of the foundations of the field, contemporary theories, and current research will afford you a rich array of information to contemplate and apply.

This book uses three underlying themes to explore OAE: design, implementation, and evidence. We define *design* as the intentional plan that provides a structure and framework for the OAE experience. Although designs can be specific and planned in detail, others are more amorphous and emerge as a program progresses. Most good designs, however, have an end in mind and seek to address some critical questions, such as, What is the purpose of the program? What outcomes do you want participants (be they students, clients, employees, or patients) to achieve? What resources are needed to accomplish these outcomes?

Once the design is created, *implementation* takes place—that is, the program or course is actually conducted, which, in turn, leads to the creation of an experience. In this book, we define implementation as the direct application of foundational information and technique, theoretical knowledge, and evidence by OAE instructors during OAE experiences.

Evidence is the compilation of data that informs OAE professionals about the value and worth of OAE design and implementation. Evidence can be accrued through professional practice, individual observation, or the testing of theoretical propositions via research. In essence, your evidence supporting why a specific OAE process or program is effective comes through your philosophy, past history, anecdotes, lived experiences, a synthesis of disparate experiences, intuition, and logical reasoning. Experienced OAE instructors often use the multiple facets of empirically gathered evidence, personal experience, theoretical understandings, and reflection to develop a body of evidence that informs their actions and belief system. For example, do you believe that OAE programs can be valuable in promoting the growth and development of an individual or group? Whether your answer is yes or no, what evidence did you use to develop that belief? As you see, evidence often involves more than the findings of an empirical study; rather, evidence is a mosaic of information that you use to form judgments and base your decisions on.

HOW THE BOOK IS ORGANIZED

We explore OAE by examining the foundations of the outdoor adventure industry, its allied fields, history, and many divergent mediums of contemporary practice (e.g., guiding, university programs, municipal offerings, and expeditions sponsored by organizations such as the Sierra

Club). We then establish the theoretical foundations that serve to provide the guiding principles underlying this industry, such as learning theory, motivations for participation, and risk-taking behaviors. By understanding how OAE addresses these issues in general, readers can develop a better understanding of the specific roles they serve. This book is thus designed to meet the needs of a variety of readers, including the private entrepreneur, highly skilled guide, university student, academic scholar, general practitioner, and others. This book addresses the wide base of experience and application from different perspectives by providing examples, accurate and timely documentation and referencing, and a knowledge base developed over a combined 60 years of experience in working with groups in outdoor adventure settings.

We have divided the book into three parts and 12 chapters. Part I provides the foundations underlying OAE. In chapter 1, we begin with an overview of OAE by characterizing the adventure experience, presenting definitions, and introducing OAE-related terms such as outdoor education and environmental education.

In chapter 2 we summarize the history of OAE. Because many of the foundational attributes characterizing OAE experience were formed in the early history of mankind, this chapter stretches way back before moving forward to the modern day. In chapter 3 we discuss contemporary practice in OAE, including important distinctions between the OAE experience and the guided experience featuring adventure activities such as climbing or rafting. Activities commonly associated with OAE are described and components of the adventure experience explored. In chapter 4 we dissect contemporary theory on motivation and risk taking, relevant constructs to understanding antecedents to participation in OAE. This chapter also introduces the advent of research and other forms of systematic study that have been part of many programs offering OAE and related experiences.

In part II we are concerned with developing our understanding of the theoretical constructs of OAE. In chapter 5 we describe the development of theories and models commonly used in the OAE field. Much of our current understanding of how and why OAE can be effective with a variety of groups and in a variety of settings is increasingly linked to our findings in research and the development of appropriate theories and models. Whereas chapter 5 begins the discussion of theories and models, in chapter 6 we present extant theories and constructs significant to OAE. In chapter 7 we examine theories of development and how they intersect with application and practice in OAE.

In part III we focus on what current research and evaluation efforts have found in the area of OAE. In chapter 8 we look at the role of evaluation research in OAE. In chapter 9 we review documented outcomes resulting from OAE participation, with particular emphasis on outcomes related to health and wellness. In chapter 10 we continue this effort by examining the history, findings, and methods of research pertinent to OAE. Chapter 11 then focuses on how to move OAE research forward and improve its utility and relevance. The book concludes with chapter 12, in which we summarize the implications of previous discussions and present evolving trends and issues of import to OAE.

Finally, we have designed a number of features in the book in hopes of enhancing learning. These elements are present in every chapter and include, *Why This Chapter is Important, Learning Outcomes, Issues for Further Discussion*, and international or specialized sidebars in which OAE professionals offer their personal views on particular aspects of OAE.

As we mentioned at the outset, we focus on three terms throughout the book that we feel are, or should be, at the heart of all OAE endeavors. These terms are *design, implementation*, and *evidence*. We believe that design, implementation, and evidence comprise three major components of the planning, application, and evaluation processes that are so important in OAE. Doubtless there are other important duties for the OAE instructor, such as ensuring the safety of participants, but we believe that design, implementation, and evidence are at the foundation of all other issues and values pertinent to OAE.

Acknowledgments

*F*irst, we would like to acknowledge the initial conceptual work that Dr. Ken Gilbertson contributed to this project. Without his early work and involvement, this book would have languished as a neglected idea on our respective to-do lists. Second, we would like to acknowledge the work and dedication of the editorial staff at Human Kinetics, who took the time to offer their expertise to improve this book and enhance both its form and function. Third, we would like to acknowledge the students, practitioners, and scholars with whom we've worked over our respective careers. This group has continued to both improve and ground our thoughts, practice, and research, and they have inspired many of the ideas presented in the following pages. Thank you all.

AE and JS

FOUNDATIONS

. . . .

For the stone from the top for geologists,
the knowledge of the limits of endurance for the doctors,
but above all for the spirit of adventure to keep alive the soul of man.

—George Mallory

*O*utdoor Adventure Education (OAE) often serves as the gateway through which millions of people across the world experience an adventure-based activity. For a growing portion of many cultures and societies, whether this experience consists of a short endeavor lasting only a few hours or a much longer and more involved engagement lasting weeks or even months and requiring a high degree of skill, knowledge, and specialized equipment, seeking and experiencing adventure has become an important component of their lives.

Not surprisingly, whether you consider OAE a recreational and educational endeavor, a professional field, or an academic pursuit, there is a long history regarding the path our species took all the way from viewing natural challenges and environments as things and places to be avoided or conquered to now when the very things we shunned in earlier times have become attractive and compelling.

In part I of this book, we provide both a general and historical overview of OAE, starting with a description in chapter 1 of the various characteristics commonly associated with the OAE experience. For example, most OAE experiences involve a combination of specific activities within a small group context that usually includes an instructor or leader, and which are typically done in some type of natural or outdoor setting. Also common for many OAE experiences is the use of a set of specific goals or objectives that serve to guide the development and implementation of the activity.

As we shall see, it has taken a long time to evolve from a belief that nature and adventure (e.g., deliberate risk taking) should be avoided at all costs, to the current belief that these types of situations should be embraced and integrated in many education systems. Chapter 2 carries us through this evolution beginning with antiquity and progressing to our contemporary time.

In chapter 3, we continue this momentum by asking the question, What is the current practice of OAE? Beginning with a discussion of the diversity and growth of OAE, we compare and contrast some of the variety of OAE delivery systems such as Educational Adventure Programs (EAPs) and Guided Trips (GTs). In addition, other developments in OAE are described including the OAE progression and the RERAS model.

Chapter 4 lays the groundwork for Part II (Theory) by describing some of the key constructs used in OAE. In this chapter we explore the influences of motivation, risk and risk taking, and fear in the OAE setting. Describing these constructs and how they interact with OAE can help us develop a better understanding of what often occurs in an OAE program and the theoretical underpinnings of the OAE experience.

In sum, the purpose of part I (chapters 1, 2, 3, and 4) is to provide a foundation regarding OAE, its various definitions, common components, history, and where we are now relative to providing the OAE experience of modern society. Remind yourself as you progress through the chapters of the three underlying themes coursing through each chapter, namely, design, implementation, and evidence. For example, in considering the historical development of OAE, the way courses and experiences are currently designed and implemented has been influenced by the historical development of OAE.

Overview of Outdoor Adventure Education

Why This Chapter Is Important

Outdoor adventure education (OAE) combines setting, activities, staff, facilitation, and reflection to take a multidimensional approach to learning and teaching. OAE means different things to different people. For some, it involves a serious undertaking in a remote location far removed from assistance. For others, it means incorporating an outdoor expedition into an educational course or program. Despite the wide range of experiences, several common points make for a unified picture of OAE. These common points present themselves across OAE programs and include a small-group atmosphere, interaction with an outdoor or natural setting, a purpose-driven dynamic for achieving specific goals, an uncertainty of outcome, and a sense of achievement on completion of the experience.

Although definitions of OAE are varied and evolving, they nearly always directly influence the what, how, and why of OAE practices. Most components of OAE relate directly to participant learning. Understanding how these components influence educational experiences will promote an ideal learning experience for participants.

Learning Outcomes

After completing this chapter, you should be able to

- describe characteristics commonly associated with OAE experiences;
- compare and contrast outdoor education and experiential education;
- explain differences among constitutive, personal, and operational definitions of OAE;
- list three possible sources of evidence to consider in making a decision; and
- compare and contrast OAE program design and OAE program implementation.

n May of 1953, Sir Edmund Hillary and Tenzing Norgay became the first people to reach the summit of Mt. Everest. Since then, over 4,000 people have reached this goal. Many of these were not professional climbers and had only moderate or even minimal climbing experience, and have hired professional guides to help them reach the summit.

Even more astounding numbers are associated with rafting on the Colorado River through the Grand Canyon. By 1949, only about 100 people had rafted this stretch of the river. By 1961, the number surpassed 1,000. Fifty years later, about 25,000 raft this stretch of the Colorado each year.

Such numbers speak to several salient trends in the outdoor adventure industry. First, the sustained and often explosive growth of adventure activities indicates their current level of popularity. Second, this growth is accompanied by similar increases in the number of organizations, associations, and companies featuring outdoor adventure experiences. Finally, the volume and breadth of these activities suggest a mix of participant benefits and outcomes that goes far beyond photographs and memories.

This third trend is most relevant to OAE because it is the outcomes and perceived benefits of outdoor pursuits that draw people to OAE experiences. In this chapter we examine the origins of the concept of adventure and explore the characteristics, fields, and definitions commonly associated with the OAE experience.

DEFINING ADVENTURE

The English word *adventure* comes from the French term *aventure,* which evolved from the Latin term *adventurus,* which means simply "about to arrive" but which over time has come to connote an exciting event that contains elements of risk and/or danger and where the outcome is uncertain.

The term *adventure* is broad enough to cover any enterprise potentially fraught with risk, such as a business venture, major life undertaking, or even trying a new restaurant. But for our purposes in this book, and relative to OAE in general, *adventure* will imply a pursuit in an outdoor setting within an educational context.

Characteristics of adventure as generated by practitioners and scholars in OAE include the following:

- Uncertainty of outcome (Hopkins & Putnam, 1993)
- Compelling tasks primarily concerned with interpersonal and intrapersonal relationships (Priest & Gass, 2005)
- A state of mind that begins with feelings of uncertainty about the outcome of a journey and always ends with feelings of enjoyment, satisfaction, or elation about the successful completion of that journey (see Colin Mortlock's *Adventure Education and Outdoor Pursuits* [1983])
- A search for excellence, an expression of human dignity, an act of the whole person. The concept of adventure implies not only action and intensity but also returning triumphantly, coming home, re-entry. This re-entry includes a period of telling, of piecing together, of sifting the meaning of the story (Nold, 1978).

Most agree that adventure involves uncertainty. Priest and Gass focus on the nurturing and social aspects of adventure, citing how people are changed both within themselves and in their relationships with those who experienced the adventure with them. Joseph Nold speaks of the coming back, the idea that no adventure is complete without the telling of the tale. This telling, and retelling, of the story evokes the archetypal adventure story, the encountering of unforeseen events of which the outcome is uncertain, and upon return, sharing the story with others. Think of one of the first great adventure stories, Homer's *Odyssey,* a recounting of the adventurous exploits of the Greek soldier Odysseus (known to the Romans as Ulysses), and how many times this tale or similar ones have been retold.

DEFINING OUTDOOR ADVENTURE EDUCATION

Adventure has long played a critical role in human development, but only recently have adventure and outdoor experiences shifted from necessary or utilitarian to primarily recreational. Consider the risk and danger our ancestors faced in getting close enough to kill a wild animal with a spear. In many ways, as technology has allowed humans to gain greater advantage over their natural environment, the world has become a far safer place, with a greater assurance of securing food, at least for some. With the advent of mechanization, our relationship to risk has significantly evolved with most outdoor adventures usually not becoming matters of personal survival. Where we once accepted risk in order to survive, we now pursue risk in order to thrive—to feel as though we are making the most of our lives. During this shift in our perspective on risk, the field of OAE originated.

OAE has been defined in many ways, including all of the following:

- Direct, active, and engaging learning experiences that involve the whole person and have real consequences (Prouty, 2007)
- . . . education that focuses on the development of interpersonal and intrapersonal relationships while participating in outdoor activities that include attributes of risk and challenge (Wagstaff & Attarian, 2009, p. 15)
- . . . education that is conducted in a wilderness-like setting or through nature and physical skills development to promote interpersonal growth or enhance physical skills in outdoor pursuits (Gilbertson, Bates, McLaughlin, & Ewert, 2006, p. 8.)

Because it can be applied in a variety of settings and situations and because it remains true to the original concept of adventure, in this text we will use the following definition of OAE: *A variety of teaching and learning activities and experiences usually involving a close interaction with an outdoor natural setting and containing elements of real or perceived danger or risk in which the outcome, although uncertain, can be influenced by the actions of the participants and circumstances.*

Let's look more closely at our definition of OAE. First, in the teaching, learning, and experiencing that occur in OAE, education is of primary importance. Wagstaff and Attarian (2009), for example, suggest that OAE instructors serve three functions in the realm of adventure education: facilitating the experience, safeguarding the experience, and minimizing the impacts on the natural environment. Of course each of these functions

Outdoor adventure education involves direct, active learning that involves the whole person and has real consequences.
Courtesy of Dan Smith.

involves making the experience as educational as possible for all participants, taking advantage of every opportunity to teach the hows, whens, and whys implicit in each experience. In a sense, OAE instructors often strive to *explain* the adventure activity in addition to actually *doing* the activity.

Second, note the (typically) close interaction with the outdoor environment. Although some climbing walls and rope course facilities are indoors, a natural setting serves as a key component in the education process for the vast majority of OAE programs—for reasons we shall explore later.

Third, in our definition and most others, OAE typically contains elements of real or perceived risk. Risk (discussed further in chapter 4) can be real and inherent to an activity, such as a rock fall in a rock-climbing area, or can be merely (mis)perceived by participants within a safe activity. That is, instructors can manage an adventure site to make activities seem risky when in fact there is a very small chance of actual injury or loss. One example is employing a top rope in rock climbing where there is little chance of rockfall and a competent person is belaying the climber. For the participant, it often seems quite risky and dangerous when, in reality, the activity is quite safe.

Fourth, in our definition of OAE, outcomes tend to be uncertain. Such factors as weather, terrain, participant abilities and attitudes, and equipment can make program outcomes quite unpredictable. Uncertainty plays an important role in adventure programs primarily because of what it can teach participants. Although often psychologically uncomfortable, uncertainty can force participants to confront their anxieties, analyze their decision-making abilities, and assess their physical, emotional, and leadership skills.

Of course the amount of risk involved in uncertain outcomes can be significantly influenced by the skills of the participants. Participants can use their intuition, training, personal abilities, and team resources to make good decisions and take effective action to deal with uncertain outcomes.

Circumstance and luck also play roles in uncertain outcomes. The ability to make accurate decisions tends to be largely affected by circumstance. Despite ambiguity inherent to many situations, the goal is always to gather as much information as possible, analyze the situation, make an informed and careful decision, and take the best possible action given the circumstances.

In upcoming chapters we will further explore our definition and understanding of OAE. For now it should be helpful to discuss two fields inherently related to OAE: outdoor education and experiential education. Each of these fields has its own long history and philosophy.

Outdoor Education

Outdoor education can be a controversial concept in the realm of teaching in the outdoors. Although some adventure educators and environmental educators contend that outdoor education is not a part of their field, several authors write otherwise. One of the earliest definitions of outdoor education comes from elementary school teacher L.B. Sharp, who said, "Those things which can best be taught outdoors should there be taught" (1947, p. 43). Later, Donaldson and Donaldson added that "Outdoor education is education *in, about,* and *for* the outdoors" (1968).

Priest (1986) wrote that outdoor education has been described as a place, a subject, a reason, a method, a topic, and a process. He believed that all are part of outdoor education. Later, along with his colleague John Miles, he defined outdoor education as "an experiential method of learning with the use of all senses. It takes place primarily, but not exclusively, through exposure to the natural environment. In outdoor education, the emphasis for the subject of learning is placed on relationships concerning people and natural resources. Historically, two branches of outdoor education have been identified: environmental education and adventure education. Truly functional outdoor education incorporates aspects of both approaches" (Miles & Priest, 1990, p. 113).

Gilbertson, Bates, McLaughlin, & Ewert (2006) described outdoor education as being comprised of three primary components: physical skills, interpersonal growth or educational skills, and ecological relationships. The primary method of presenting education including these components is experiential education. Moreover, Gilbertson and his colleagues suggest that adventure education, environmental education, interpretation, and ecotourism are aspects taught within the realm of outdoor education (figure 1.1). In Gilbertson's model, adventure education is closely aligned to outdoor education along three dimensions: ecological relationships, physical skills, and interpersonal or educational skills. That is, where OAE and outdoor education coincide is in the areas of engaging in activities that involve the natural environment, practicing

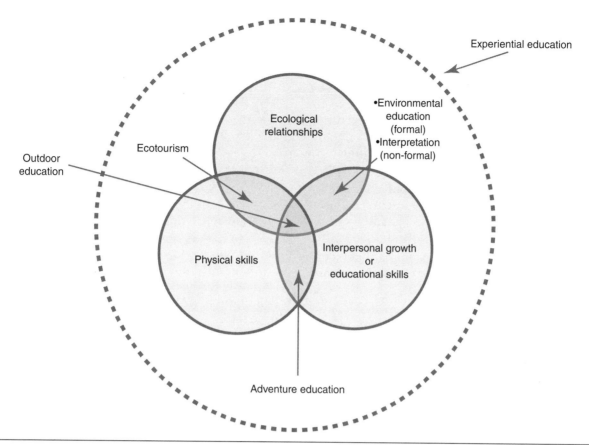

Figure 1.1   Gilbertson's model of outdoor education.

Reprinted, by permission, from K. Gilbertson, T. Bates, T. McLaughlin, and A. Ewert, 2006, *Outdoor education: Methods and strategies* (Champaign, IL: Human Kinetics), 6.

physical movement and skill development, and being part of a small group for either recreational or educational purposes. In addition, according to Gilbertson's model, encompassing the various components of OAE, environmental education, and outdoor education is experiential education.

Experiential Education

Gilbertson et al. defined experiential education as a method, a profession, and a philosophy (2006). In his work *Experience and Nature* (1938), philosopher and educational reformer John Dewey delineated the use of direct experience in education, or experiential education. According to Dewey, experiential education requires a great deal of planning, organization, and structure by the teacher. Experiential education is not merely having an experience in the outdoors; it must follow rigorous scientific principles, employing relevant learning theories based on systematic testing. Dewey claimed that the teacher's role in experiential education is to ensure that students

have an educational opportunity rather than a noneducative (having no effect on learning) or miseducative (learning detrimental) learning experience. Since Dewey's writings, experiential education has become a field of study with an international following. For example, the Association for Experiential Education (AEE) a leading proponent of international experiential education, defines experiential education as a philosophy that informs many methodologies in which educators purposefully engage with learners in direct experience and focused reflection in order to increase knowledge, develop skills, clarify values, and develop people's capacity to contribute to their communities.

Using this definition as a foundation, experiential education has a long history and is based on a number of principles including the following:

- Experiential learning occurs when carefully chosen experiences are supported by reflection, critical analysis, and synthesis.

- Experiences are structured to require the learner to take initiative, make decisions, and be accountable for results.
- Throughout the experiential learning process, the learner is actively engaged in posing questions, investigating, experimenting, being curious, solving problems, assuming responsibility, being creative, and constructing meaning.
- Learners are engaged intellectually, emotionally, socially, soulfully, and/or physically. This involvement produces a perception that the learning task is authentic.
- The results of the learning are personal and form the basis for future experience and learning.
- Relationships are developed and nurtured: learner to self, learner to others, and learner to the world at large.
- The educator and learner may experience success, failure, adventure, risk taking, and uncertainty because the outcomes of experience cannot be totally predicted.
- Opportunities are nurtured for learners and educators to explore and examine their own values.
- The educator's primary roles include setting suitable experiences, posing problems, setting boundaries, supporting learners, ensuring physical and emotional safety, and facilitating the learning process.
- The educator recognizes and encourages spontaneous opportunities for learning.
- Educators strive to be aware of their biases, judgments, and preconceptions and how these influence the learner.
- The design of the learning experience includes the possibility to learn from natural consequences, mistakes, and successes.

http://www.aee.org/about/whatIsEE

As can be readily noted, many of the principles associated with experiential education also have meaning and connections to the adventure education field. Thus it is not surprising that OAE and experiential education have common roots, values, and outcomes. Moreover, it is often assumed that outdoor education, adventure education, and outdoor adventure education

and direct experience go hand in hand and use overlapping techniques and methods within their educational approaches. Moreover, it should be noted that the design, implementation, and evidence associated with experiential education have similar or identical components in how OAE activities and programs are designed, implemented, and evaluated for evidence.

TYPES OF DEFINITIONS

There is more than one type of definition, and different types of definitions connote different levels of understanding and representation. The definitions we have summarized to this point are generally taken from published works or established sources. But these are not the only definitions of OAE. Organizations and individuals have their own working definitions, which might be one of three types—constitutive, personal, or operational—or a blend of these.

Constitutive Definitions

Although earlier in the chapter we presented a definition of OAE, this definition is not above scrutiny. It is our definition. As the definition is published in this book, it is considered a *constitutive*, or established, definition. A constitutive definition is the definition that is recognized by professionals in the field. A professional conformity can be found through the professional organization of the topic (e.g., the Association for Experiential Education for adventure education, experiential education, or outdoor education). Another source for a professionally recognized definition is the literature in the field. This literature is commonly reviewed by peers considered experts in the profession. Examples of peer-reviewed journals relevant to OAE include the *Journal of Leisure Research; Journal of Experiential Education; Leisure Sciences; Research in Outdoor Education; Journal of Outdoor Recreation, Education, and Leadership;* and *Journal of Adventure Education and Outdoor Learning.* The literature on OAE also includes scholarly books or articles by professionals in the field, including *Effective Leadership in Adventure Programming* (Priest & Gass, 2005), *Outdoor Leadership: Theory and Practice* (Martin, Cashel, Wagstaff, & Breunig, 2006), *Adventure Education: Theory and Application* (Prouty, Panicucci, & Collinson, 2007), *Leadership and Administration of Outdoor Pursuits* (Blanchard, Strong, & Ford, 2007), and

Teaching Adventure Education Theory: Best Practices (Stremba & Bisson, 2008). Examples of more general sources of definitions of adventure education are dictionaries and popular magazines such as *Outside*, *Rock and Ice*, *Paddler*, and *Climbing*.

Constitutive definitions can often vary, even within a single field of study. This might cause confusion, but there are often common themes among the variations. Finally, constitutive definitions are not static. As knowledge is gained, definitions will likely be modified accordingly.

Personal Definitions

Whereas a constitutive definition comes from an external source, a *personal* definition is held by one or more individuals. These definitions tend to be subjective and based on values gained through personal experiences; they can exist with or without formal training. Personal definitions are helpful in generating discussion but can also be barriers to deeper understanding when people become overly rooted in their own definitions and closed to all alternatives. However, it is often through a personal definition that a person is motivated to become a professional in OAE. From a personal definition of what OAE is, a person begins to explore OAE further and gains greater understanding of all that it involves.

Operational Definitions

An operational definition is typically based on a constitutive definition. Based on what occurs in common practice, an operational definition is how an agency or individual applies an established definition within their setting. For example, University of Minnesota Duluth's outdoor program uses adventure education in its Kayak and Canoe Institute to promote paddle sports through teaching the physical skills of kayaking and canoeing. In contrast, Outward Bound schools use adventure education to promote personal growth. Although both schools are providing OAE, they are educating

for a different outcome, even while using the same setting to teach their students. Thus an organization's operational definitions are often tied to its values.

As we further explore the field of OAE, consider your own personal and operational definitions for outdoor education, experiential education, and outdoor adventure education. Compare and

Personal definitions of OAE are firmly rooted in an individual's experiences, preferences, and values.

Courtesy of Nate Bricker.

Outdoor Adventure Education Down Under

Glyn Thomas, PhD—La Trobe University Bendigo, Australia

Exact definitions and understanding of OAE are not universal but tend to vary across cultures, contexts, and times. Most of my experience with OAE has occurred in Australia, where the vast majority of practice occurs in schools with students between the ages of 10 and 17. However, even within the school context there is considerable diversity of OAE within Australia's eight states and territories, and also from school to school. In some places, OAE's main focus is on personal and group development, with strong links to pastoral care programs in schools. All private schools in Australia boast some form of OAE program, and many have their own residential campsites within a few hours' drive from the school. Many private providers, companies, and not-for-profit organizations also offer both standard and customized OAE programs to schools ranging in length from 1 to 28 days.

In some Australian states, strong ties have been forged between OAE and environmental studies, and the role of adventure is deemphasized. Outdoor activities are still used as the mode of travel or exploration to learn about natural environments and sociocultural issues. In this context, students in the final three years of high school complete formal assessment tasks to measure learning that occurs on practical trips and in school-based classwork.

In Australia, there is a small but strong OAE academic community, a dedicated refereed journal (*The Australian Journal of Outdoor Education*),

and several higher education programs that prepare our outdoor leaders and teachers. Within this community there has been vigorous debate about the use of adventure and risk as pedagogical tools and the tension their inclusion creates with other program aims. Although some authors (Lugg, 2004; Wattchow & Brown, 2011) have encouraged a deskilling and reduced focus on adventure in order to restore an environmental or setting-based focus in programs, I have found this dichotomization frustrating and unnecessary. For many adolescents (not all), the inclusion of adventurous activities and the corresponding focus on skills plays an important role in engaging and motivating participation. I acknowledge that an excessive focus on thrills and skills can be detrimental to other educational objectives, but ultimately the degree to which adventure activities become "all consuming" is within the facilitators' control (Thomas, 2005). Moreover, I don't believe the unintended consequences of removing adventure from outdoor programs have been researched enough to justify these changes (Martin, 2004).

The environmental impact of OAE programs is another contentious issue in Australia. Although we do have large areas of open space, our relatively small population (23 million) creates infrastructure and management challenges in many national and state parks. Some natural environments used in

The focus and purpose of OAE programs varies across Australia.
Courtesy of Glyn Thomas.

OAE programs are being "loved to death." For this reason, many schools purchase their own campsites in rural areas to limit the impacts on natural environments open to the public. Concerned scholars and practitioners have also argued for sustainable practices that use local places, rather than far-flung, exotic locations that require more travel resources (Wattchow & Brown, 2011). This is a positive development as OAE programs in Australia embrace deeper, more ecologically aware interactions with their settings (Brookes, 2002; Stewart, 2008). Most OAE programs in Australia have a growing commitment to promote environmental sensitivity.

References

Brookes, A. (2002). Lost in the Australian bush: Outdoor education as curriculum. *Journal of Curriculum Studies 34*(4): 405-425.

Lugg, A. (2004). Outdoor adventure in Australian outdoor education: Is it a case of roast for Christmas dinner? *Australian Journal of Outdoor Education 8*(1): 4-11.

Martin, P. (2004). Outdoor adventure in promoting relationships with nature. *Australian Journal of Outdoor Education 8*(1): 20-28.

Stewart, A. (2008). Whose place, whose history? Outdoor environmental education pedagogy as "reading" the landscape. *Journal of Adventure Education & Outdoor Learning 8*(2): 79-98.

Thomas, G. (2005). Traditional adventure activities in outdoor environmental education. *Australian Journal of Outdoor Education 9*(1): 31-39.

Wattchow, B., & Brown, M. (2011). *A pedagogy of place: Outdoor education for a changing world.* Clayton, Victoria: Monash University.

contrast your definitions to the constitutive definitions presented.

EVIDENCE, DESIGN, AND IMPLEMENTATION

Regardless of your personal and operational definitions of OAE, the central purpose of this book is to improve research, theory, and practice related to OAE. To this end, we discuss three main themes throughout the text: evidence, design, and implementation. These three themes are best viewed as a cycle that begins and ends with evidence.

Evidence is a collective of indicators that professionals access to make decisions in their practice. Evidence comes from history, anecdotes, lived experiences, logic, synthesis, feelings, and thought. When decisions need to be made, people tend to turn to the accessible evidence. If they lack personal experience, people tend to consider what someone has told them or something they have read. Experts often have a wide-ranging combination of evidence on a topic that combines personal experience, theory, research, and reflection. The best decisions tend to result from a combination of sources of evidence that yield a robust understanding.

Why does OAE have value and relevance? How does OAE work? Answers to these questions require evidence. We expect our readers to be both active creators and active users of evidence. You should be able to read, think, reflect on, and, ultimately, synthesize evidence from a variety of sources to come to your own understanding of the theories, philosophies, and research presented in this text. Evidence of success, failure, effectiveness, or uselessness can all help to inform practice in OAE.

Design is the intentional plan that frames the OAE program. Just like research, a program design can be emergent, amorphous, or inductive. When designing a program, questions might include: What is the purpose of the program? What outcomes do you want participants to achieve? What activities will best elicit these outcomes? Do you have the resources for these activities? One mistake that new programmers make is to focus on the activity rather than the outcome: "I want to run a backpacking trip." Experienced programmers know that most good designs begin with a goal in mind. They view a program in terms of the problem the program might address or the need it might fill. For example, if you believe that young people in New York City do not have adequate access to nature and thus feel disconnected from the natural world, a backpacking trip to a nearby nature spot might form the framework for a program design. Design choices would likely look different for programs targeting academic outcomes, mentoring connections, or therapy, but all might be possible within the framework of a backpacking trip.

We want each of your outdoor programs to have a well-planned and purposeful design, but it is also critical that you know how to apply the content of this book during an OAE experience. *Implementation* is the application of foundations, theory, and research during an OAE experience; it can be thought of as *how* you deliver a program in the moment. Program designs are critical, but they are also inflexible and can take years to adjust. You cannot simply redesign a 10-day sea-kayaking course in Alaska targeting wildlife photography into a 14-day coastal sailing course in California targeting leadership. However, over these 10 or 14 days, you can act, respond, teach, and interact differently. That is, you can choose to apply philosophical, historical, theoretical, or research-based evidence differently at the point of service. There is no universal way to facilitate a group initiative. Many OAE decisions must be made in context when the players and parameters are clearer (though they are rarely crystal clear). Your developing the ability to apply the foundations, theory, and research of OAE across contexts is a central goal of this book.

And the cycle continues. Evidence from implementing a program feeds back into how the next program is designed and the next decision is implemented. Formal evaluation can certainly assist in this process, but the lived experience of implementing a program provides evidence for your personal perspectives on how and why elements of an OAE program succeeded or failed. This evidence is likely to shape all future practice.

SUMMARY

We have defined outdoor adventure education (OAE) as a variety of teaching and learning activities and experiences usually involving a close interaction with an outdoor natural setting and containing elements of real or perceived danger or risk in which the outcome, although uncertain, can be influenced by the actions of the participants and circumstances. This definition is a complex mix of education in a natural environment involving risk, uncertainty, and bidirectional influence involving the participant and the context. Over the next few chapters,

we will continue to explore these elements of OAE.

Outdoor education and experiential education are allied fields of OAE that have considerable overlap with OAE. Outdoor education is often viewed as an umbrella term that encompasses a large range of educational experience in, about, and for the outdoors. The Association of Experiential Education (AEE) defines experiential education as "a philosophy that informs many methodologies in which educators purposefully engage with learners in direct experience and focused reflection in order to increase knowledge, develop skills, clarify values, and develop people's capacity to contribute to their communities." In general, OAE is both outdoor education and experiential education, but it also has additional characteristics.

Whereas constitutive definitions are established by external sources, personal definitions are internal and individual in nature. They are also critical to how individuals approach practice, as they form a lens through which evidence is interpreted. Operational definitions involve application in professional practice. Different organizations approach and use OAE activities and techniques in different ways. These ways define, operationally, the OAE experience within that organization.

The concepts of evidence, design, and implementation as presented in this book are intended to help the reader consider and improve OAE theory, research, and practice. Evidence to inform practice comes from such sources as history and philosophy, theory, and research. This evidence, in turn, allows for practitioners to better design, or plan for, what they want to accomplish through an OAE experience. What are the goals and what pieces need to be in place to achieve them? Implementation is how a design is executed in the context of the experience. Like design, implementation is purposeful, but it is also highly flexible and can be changed as circumstances demand.

By understanding some basic terms and characteristics associated with OAE, it is easier to further discuss the related foundations, theory, and research. To that end, the next chapters explore the historical and contemporary practices of OAE. Later, in part II, we discuss related theory, and in part III we look at OAE research and evaluation practices.

Issues for Further Discussion

1. Discuss several terms related to outdoor adventure and describe how each affects the profession and service delivery.

2. Describe the origin of the term *adventure* and how the understanding of the term has evolved.

3. How do your personal definitions of OAE, outdoor education, and experiential education compare to the constitutive definitions presented in this chapter?

4. What are the operational definitions of OAE for some of your local organizations or organizations you are familiar with?

5. Which sources of evidence do you, personally, think are most important in informing professional practice?

History of Outdoor Adventure Education

Whether you think of outdoor adventure education (OAE) as a one-day ropes course, canoeing down a quiet river, or engaging in a weekend of outdoor activities with military veterans, the evolution of employing such experiences for human development has a similar historical background. For many involved in OAE, what began as exploration for conquest and nationalism eventually became more personal. The change from an external goal to an internal goal, one intrinsically relevant to the individual, was a crucial turning point in the development of OAE.

It is important to understand the long and winding path that led us to realize how and why exposing individuals to outdoor activities that contain elements of challenge, potential risk, and diverse demands, both physical and psy-

chological, can be growth enhancing for both individuals and groups. The path to this realization, though it began many years ago, still holds important meaning for today's designers and leaders of OAE programs.

Often intertwined with adventure are the concepts of leisure and recreation. These concepts are similar but not the same, though they are frequently integrated with each other and with OAE. For example, although OAE is strongly linked to education, it is often engaged in during an individual's leisure time or within a recreational outing. Understanding the intersections of leisure and recreation is helpful for anyone hoping to design and implement OAE experiences.

Learning Outcomes

After completing this chapter, you should be able to

* summarize how early Roman and Greek civilizations influenced the concept of adventure;
* describe several historic explorations and their influence on OAE;
* explain the development of the field of OAE; and
* identify formalized schools of OAE and their early advocates.

In the early 1900s, a notice appeared in the *London Times* seeking volunteers to travel to the South Pole. The ad attracted thousands of applicants, although the notice warned of extreme discomfort and clearly indicated that safety could not be guaranteed. A hundred years later, corporations from many countries are seeking to provide commercial space travel. Although test flights are ongoing, costs are very high, and participants undergo extreme risk, there is a waiting list of people who wish to travel into space.

Consider a group of high school students attending the Sir Edmund Hillary Outdoor Pursuits Centre of New Zealand who were about to begin their first day of leadership training. The course instructor asked them, "What is adventure?" After a moment of thought, the students struggled to answer. The instructor offered, "It's when a person takes a risk to do something they didn't know they could do. When you take that risk, you don't always know what the outcome will be." He then asked them to raise their hands in the air as high as they could reach. "Now, reach higher," he said. All hands went up about six inches higher. "Now reach even higher, yet," he commanded. Their hands went higher. "See how much higher you can reach, even though I started by asking you to reach your hands as high as you could? Now, see if you can reach even higher." Many hands rose still higher. "This is what this course is about. What will be different for many of you is that we are going to use the outdoors to learn how to reach as high as we can." The students were eager, though a bit nervous, to begin their first challenge of the day, which in this case was caving.

What is it in the human condition that makes us seek risk and adventure in unfamiliar places? Why are we willing to pay considerable amounts of money to hire people to guide us to these places? What is it that we are expecting to gain from such journeys? Does the Chinese phrase *wei xian* capture the essence of adventure in its definition "opportunity through danger"? Clearly, something inherent in the human psyche draws us toward adventure.

The beginnings of OAE are often linked to the origin of Outward Bound in the 1940s, but the history of people using adventurous natural settings to promote personal growth extends far beyond that time. Swarbrooke and his colleagues (2003) in the UK provide an extensive list of types of people who contributed to the areas of adventure and adventure tourism, including pilgrims, trad-ers, settlers and colonizers, missionaries, natural historians, and women travelers. For example, Gertrude Bell (1868-1926) did extensive travel and exploration in Greater Syria, Mesopotamia, Asia Minor, and Arabia.

Our early ancestors spent some of their recreation and leisure time playing "bone games," such as hanging a rock or piece of bone to a stick and then trying to hit the bone or rock with a pointed stick. These games were probably enjoyable, but they also had some utilitarian value, namely the development of eye–hand coordination so important for hunting and defense. Of note is that our early ancestors apparently valued cultivating individual growth and collective well-being through overcoming challenges placed before them by nature. Achieving positive outcomes through human-environment interactions, as experienced through the adventure setting, is often the very reason people choose to engage in OAE—then and now.

As we consider the history of humans and adventure, we can see how adventuring moved from a broad array of utilitarian motives, such as exploration in order to find wealth, spread religion, or claim lands, to more intrinsic motives such as personal growth, therapy and rehabilitation, and experiencing nature. Adventure has undergone many transformations both in how it has been defined and how and why it is sought and experienced. It all began with our early explorers and adventure seekers.

EARLY EXPLORERS AND ADVENTURE SEEKERS

The quest for adventure has always played an important role in man's exploration of and relationship with the Earth. Although frequently ascribed to a search for land or wealth, adventure was often the covert reason for exploring faraway lands. Adventuring was (and is) often perilous, but who can deny the magical pull of the midnight watch, the next "lead," or what lies around the next bend?

For the stone from the top for geologists, the knowledge of the limits of endurance for the doctors, but above all for the spirit of adventure to keep alive the soul of man.

Returning to early history, one written documentation of adventuring tells of a four-year expedition from Egypt to the mysterious land of Punt in 2500 BC, presumably in search of incense, gold, and dwarves (Lacey, 1978). So adventurous and thirsty for exploration were the early Phoenicians that, by 600 BC, they had sailed around the continent of Africa from east to west. Chiefly interested in adventure and exploration for the wealth that could be accrued, the Phoenicians used one of the components of the adventure sequence, retelling the experience, to frighten away rival explorers with tales of boiling seas and other perils.

One such account of adventure and exploration is that of the Phoenician admiral Hanno (figure 2.1). Although the original document describing Hanno's voyage, *The Periplus*, has been lost, the story of one of man's first great expeditions goes this way:

Originating from Carthage around the fifth century BC, Hanno's fleet sailed through the pillars of Hercules at the Straits of Gibraltar and headed south along the great bulge of Africa, sailing past the dry coastline of Africa down to a site which was probably Herne Island. It was at this point, having completed his explicit purpose of establishing colonies, that Hanno's quest for adventure came to the forefront and the journey continued to a length of the Senegal River ["Great and wide, and swarming with crocodiles and hippopotamuses"]. The journey continued down the coast of Africa to a point close to Sherbo Sound or possibly even the Gulf of Guinea. (Lacey, 1978, pp. 5-6)

The great Phoenician city, Carthage, on the coast of present-day Tunis, launched the next wave of adventurers—the ancient Greeks. It was from the ancient Greeks that the first great adventure novel appeared: the myth of Odysseus in Homer's *Odyssey* (Fitzgerald, 1963). In his book *The Adventurer: The Fate of Adventure in the Western World* (1974), Paul Zweig suggests

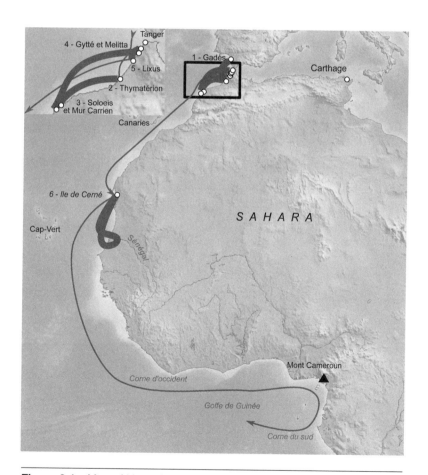

Figure 2.1 Map of Hanno's voyage.
From http://en.wikipedia.org/wiki/File:Hannon_map-fr.svg

that Odysseus (also called Ulysses) was the first adventure hero in Western literature.

Ancient Greece, however, was not just a place for storytelling. It was here, at the close of the sixth century, BC, that mountain climbing, hunting, and horseback riding became integral parts of the lives of many youths, particularly those of Sparta, the ancient city-state of Greece (Hackensmith, 1966, pp. 27-37). Once again, adventure was a means to an end, in that these activities were ways to physically and emotionally strengthen young people for their eventual roles as citizens and soldiers. Of course this parallels what has been occurring in the "new development" of pedagogy, in which adventure-based education is used to help today's youth prepare to be productive members of society.

Of course the quest for adventure is not a Western concept. The East also had its influence on adventure, including early adventurer Zhang Qian (138-115 BC), an ambassador of the Han dynasty who journeyed for 18 years and documented the Pamirs Mountain range as well as the "Silk Road." Born in China, Xuanzang (138-115 BC) was a Buddhist monk who left China to travel throughout India in search of greater knowledge. Zheng He (1371-1435), a Chinese mariner, engaged in extensive travel and exploration during the Ming dynasty. Xu Xiake (1587-1641) was among the first scientific adventurers and travel writers. As is true for the early explorers of the West, the Eastern efforts at adventuring and exploration often had economic, religious, political, or scientific motives. That said, no one doubts a sense of adventure was also a prime motivator. This sense is well captured in George Mallory's statement from a year before his last and fateful attempt on Mt. Everest in 1924.

EXPLORATION AND THE QUEST FOR ADVENTURE

From about 1800 BC until about 700 BC, a warlike tribe of people called the Etruscans settled about the Tiber and Arno rivers in Italy. Horseback riding and hunting were favorite sports of these forerunners of the ancient Romans (Hackensmith, 1966, pp. 57-58). A precursor of the modern-day "survival game" emerged, with captives given arms and loosed on each other at a burial site or other location. The only real difference between then and now is that in the seventh century BC the combatants used swords,

and now they use air-powered pellet guns loaded with harmless red-dye gelatin pellets.

Similar to the Greeks, adventure activities such as hunting, horseback riding, and backcountry travel were important avenues of training for Roman youths, particularly boys. Roman explorations served to enlarge and unify vast parts of the then-known world. It was during this era (around the third century BC) that a sailor named Pytheas completed an amazing journey to *ultima Thule* (ultimate land)—the Arctic circle. During this adventure, Pytheas may have sailed as far north as Iceland or Norway. On returning, Pytheas retold the tale of a midnight sun, ever-shining fire (volcanoes of Iceland), and water as thick as jelly. (Much later, Fridtjof Nansen (1861-1930) rediscovered the phenomena of ice sludge and ice fog and related them in his book, *The Ocean*.)

Over twelve hundred years later, on the other side of the known world, a singularly intrepid adventurer, Marco Polo, was engaging in one of the most widely known and remarkable of all journeys. Chronicled in a book titled *A Description of the World*, the twenty-four-year expedition (1271-1295) described countless sagas of adventure and exploration.

By this time, improvements in agriculture and transportation (in addition to a general decrease in invasion and warfare) led to greater urbanization, which eventually led to a greater affinity for commerce and travel (Burke, 1985). Nold (1978) in his elegant work "Profiles in Adventure" calls this the age of the Merchant Ventures. Adventurers, like many before, traveled beyond familiar surroundings for the promise of wealth and fame. But once these goals were reached, they continued their struggles in search of that elusive elixir—adventure. In a sense, adventure became *the* motivating force of explorers. As Wilfred Noyce has summed it up: "Adventure: a novel enterprise undertaken for its own sake" (Noyce, 1958, p. 16).

In 1336 Francesco Petrarch and his brother Gerado made the first recorded mountain climb (Mont Ventoux) for no other reason than to reach the top (Scott, 1974). For this feat, Petrarch is known as the spiritual father of Alpinism.

As Europe began to look cautiously beyond its immediate borders, there emerged one of the first training facilities explicitly designed for exploration and its covert companion adventure. In 1419, the celebrated Prince Henry of Portugal (known as The Navigator) established a school of navigation near Sagres, Cape Saint Vincent, the

Outdoor Adventure Education: An Eastern Perspective

Ackie Cheung, PhD—Hong Kong

OAE and experiential education had their origins in the West and have been brought to Chinese societies through colonization and further through globalization. Although its popularity still prevails in Western societies, OAE is rapidly expanding in Hong Kong, mainland China, and Taiwan, partly through Outward Bound and Project Adventure programs first introduced in the mid-1900s. The general understanding of OAE tends to be similar across regions of the globe, but its specific conception and operations vary in accordance with cultural differences.

Taking the Chinese context as an example, the Chinese words for adventure are *mao-xian* (冒險), which means "taking risk at some costs." But this literal translation cannot be found in adventure education in the regions of Hong Kong, mainland China, or Taiwan. In Hong Kong, adventure education is *li-qi* (歷奇), which means "experiencing something interesting or unknown." In mainland China, it is *tuo-zhan* (拓展), which translates to "expanding or developing." And in Taiwan, it is *tan-suo* (探索), which means "exploring or discovering." Although exploration and adventure are implicit in these definitions, suggesting a degree of uncertainty, there are not, necessarily, elements of danger or risk.

Why is the direct translation of adventure, *mao-xian* (冒險), not included in the concept of OAE for the Chinese? The answer likely involves our understanding of the term "adventure." Our translations of adventure education do not include the idea of taking risk at some costs because risk taking is traditionally not encouraged among Chinese people—although risk can sometimes be associated with the concept of crisis, *wei-ji* (危機), whereby a dangerous situation can turn out to be an opportunity. For us, risk should be taken only out of necessity, such as for survival. In comparison to the Western understanding of OAE, in which uncertainty and risk taking might be built in as part of the OAE process, the taboo of the risk-taking element in Chinese translations has deliberately been omitted. This aligns with expectations among most Chinese that education should create a strong sense of security and safety, and never danger. This explains why in our OAE programs in Hong Kong we use *perceived* risks rather than real risks. OAE activities must comply to expectations that range across educational programs.

As you see, definitions of OAE will vary depending on the values and expectations of people in different areas around the globe. As globalization continues, professionals wishing to stay current to research and develop knowledge and skills that recognize and address cross-cultural differences in OAE require cultural sensitivity and adaptive teaching and learning skills to meet the needs of all participants, including those whose values might differ from the norm.

References

Asia Association of Experiential Education. www.aaee.org.tw. (Retrieved March 16, 2013.)

Cheung, C.-K. (2013). *Experiential education and adolescents' personal and spiritual development: A mixed-method study in the secondary school context of Hong Kong*. Wiesbaden: Springer VS.

Law, W. (2004). Globalization and citizenship education in Hong Kong and Taiwan. *Comparative Education Review, 48*(3): 253–273.

Lo, S. (2011). *Adventure education and the acculturation of Chinese Canadians in Vancouver, Canada*. (Unpublished PhD thesis). New Zealand: Lincoln University. http://researcharchive.lincoln.ac.nz/dspace/bitstream/10182/3918/1/lo_phd.pdf. (Retrieved July 30, 2013.)

Luk-Fong, Y. (2001). Contexts for developing personal and social education in Hong Kong. *Comparative Education, 37*(1): 65–87.

OECD. (2011). Shanghai and Hong Kong: Two distinct examples of education reform in China. In OECD, *Strong Performers and Successful Reformers in Education: Lessons from PISA for the United States*.

Oelkers, J. (2002). Rousseau and the image of "modern education." *Journal of Curriculum Studies, 34*(6): 679–698.

Outward Bound. (2009). History. www.outwardbound.org.hk/about.html. (Retrieved March 18, 2013.)

Outward Bound China (n.d.). www.outwardboundchina.net. (Retrieved March 18, 2013.)

westernmost point of Europe (Stromberg, 1969, pp. 214-215).

It was during this Great Age of Exploration that exploration and adventure became nationalistic exploits rather than purely individual endeavors. Bartolomeu Pias, a Portuguese explorer, reached the southern-most tip of Africa, the Cape of Good Hope, in 1488. On his return to Lisbon, one of the people greeting and admiring the triumphant explorer was Christopher Columbus (Newton, 1968).

The year 1492 was momentous for several reasons. Not only did Columbus reach the North American island of San Salvador, but this was also the year in which Antoine de Ville was ordered by King Charles VIII of France to climb the difficult Mount Aiguille (ca. 6,500 feet, or 1,981 km) and to erect a cross on the summit. De Ville said the journey was the most terrifying and dangerous of his life (Scott, 1974, p. 3).

The rate of exploration and travel began to assume dizzying proportions as an era of change swept over the European continent. Indeed, the rate of change likely equaled that of our own society, a society in which change is considered the only stable condition.

In 1498, six years after the Columbus expedition, Vasco da Gama finally achieved the all-consuming quest of finding a sea route to India and beyond. Spanish exploration continued into the 1500s with the exploits of Cortés, Balboa, Pizarro, and Coronado.

Just as the Spanish sun had begun to set, other explorers and adventurers, notably English, Dutch, and French, opened up vast undiscovered areas of the New World. These explorations included the search for the Northwest Passage and led to the forerunner of the modern-day concept of adventure–exploration of the polar and subpolar regions.

It's easy to see why Antoine de Ville considered climbing Mount Aiguille the most terrifying and dangerous journey of his life!

Mont Aiguille with arch from Pas de l'Aguille, 2010. Photographer: Bdenis. GNU Free Documentation License, version 1.2.

One of the first of these journeys was led by the English explorer Henry Hudson, in search of the elusive shortcut to the Orient. Other explorations, led by Russian-born Vitus Bering (1725-30, 1733-41) uncovered vast areas of Siberia and the northern seas. On January 17, 1773, the *Resolution* commanded by James Cook became the first ship in history to penetrate the Antarctic Circle.

ADVENTURE IN TRANSITION

While the spirit of exploration for science and country was beginning to bloom, an era of recreational mountaineering was also dawning. Early mountaineering efforts, as well as an increasing number of explorations at sea, were done under scientific aegis. In 1760, the year "serious mountaineering" began (Scott, 1974, p. 3), Horace Benedict de Saussure, a wealthy scientist from Geneva, offered a handsome prize to the person who made the first ascent of Mt. Blanc. It was not, however, until 1786 that a local doctor, Michel-Gabriel Paccard, and his guide, Jacques Balmat, succeeded.

As Scott (1974, p. 4) has suggested, "the flame had been kindled and it quickly spread as mountaineering started in many alpine areas." It was a fervor pushed by a quest for knowledge, nation, and, ultimately, adventure. Starting with an early ascent of the Wetterhorn and culminating with Edward Whymper's first ascent of the Matterhorn in 1865 (Whymper, 1871), the next 30 years marked more climbs and successful summit attempts than any previous time.

During this time mountaineering began to be pursued for its own sake rather than linking adventure with the search for scientific knowledge. As described by Nold in "Profiles in Adventure" (1978), the scientific adventurer sought to bring back wealth in the form of accurate charts and maps instead of gold and spices. In contrast, the adventure mountaineer had brought back nothing but an experience and tales for the retelling.

By the 1850s it was common to see strings of "tourists" roped together on the glaciers of the more accessible peaks (Roberts, 1985). In 1857, the British Alpine Club was formed to help further the aims of mountaineering, with John Ball as its first president. This was the same John Ball who in the 1860s published some of the first guidebooks for climbing.

THE CONCEPTS OF LEISURE AND RECREATION

It is interesting to note that the concept of leisure emerged for the Athenians as a "cultivation of self" (Murphy, 1981, pp. 22-23). Athenian philosophers such as Socrates and Aristotle believed strongly in the unity of mind and body and in the importance of leisure for the proper holistic development of an individual. In *The Republic*, Plato quotes Socrates as saying, "Our children from their earliest years must take part in all the more lawful forms of play, for if they are not surrounded with such an atmosphere they can never grow up to be well-conducted and virtuous citizens" (Shorey 1953, p. 335).

The term *leisure* was derived from the Latin word "licere," which means "to be permitted to abstain from occupation or service" (Murphy, 1981, p. 24). In addition, the Greek term "schole," from which we derived the words "school" and "scholar," became aligned with leisure in the classical Greek sense as a place immune from occupational requirements and devoted to scholarly pursuits, individual freedom, and self-determination (Murphy, 1975, p. 5).

From these developments, the concepts of leisure and recreation emerged in the Western world. Leisure became a period of personal "space" free of the necessity to work or toil. It was, however, not unproductive in that while an individual was free of work, he or she was not free of activity, either physical or mental. *Schole* for the Greeks or *licere* for the Romans represented a serious way of life. Recreation, however, became more associated with activity. Thus we often speak of leisure time and recreational activities.

Here, then, we come to an apparent paradox regarding the terms "leisure" and "recreation." Although they connote periods of unobligated time or activity, these terms are not to be confused as meaning simply passing time. In fact, even contemplation was considered a productive practice. Adventure programs today have continued along this line of thinking in offering seemingly "unproductive" activities such as mountain climbing or whitewater canoeing. Today our view of these activities has dramatically changed. This is particularly true within OAE, in which the intent has been to achieve such substantial goals as changing the way people think about themselves or working together as a group.

Leisure and recreation activities are much more than a way to pass time.
iStockphoto/David H. Lewis.

THE ADVENT OF ADVENTURE RECREATION

Slowly, as all the unexplored regions of the Earth were explored, the major summits all climbed, and all the rivers run, the reason for adventuring shifted from a necessary byproduct of searching for scientific knowledge to motivations related to an individual's personal desires. The later part of the 1800s and the early 1900s saw a number of events that addressed a new awareness of the environment, the wilderness, and the emerging need for adventure. The formation of organizations such as the Appalachian Mountain Club (1876) and the Sierra Club (1892) propelled the movement toward conservation of the land and its resources. With the onset of agencies such as the Forest Service (1905) and United States Park Service (1916), the federal government became involved in land management and also, surreptitiously, the provision of adventure opportunities for an ever-growing portion of the public.

Just as Congress in 1894 funded a commission to inventory the state of outdoor recreation, the Congress of 1906 acted in a similar manner. By 1908, the report of this commission helped pave the way for the enactment of a substantial number of laws passed by both federal and state legislatures (Van Doren & Hodges, 1975). Many of the laws served to provide the settings and opportunities for future adventure recreationalists. These and other significant events and their impact on the OAE movement are listed in table 2.1. This was a time when various literature, organizations, and legislation combined in a synergistic fashion to spur the growth of adventure-based recreation. Narratives, mixed with how-to information, were the typical format of books describing some facet of adventure recreation, usually camping or mountaineering. Examples included *Deep River Jim's Wilderness Trail Book* (Deep-River Jim, *1937), Camping and Woodcraft* (Kephart, 1917), *Belaying the Leader* (Leonard et al., 1956), *Woodcraft* (Sears, 1920), *The Book of Woodcraft* (Seton, 1912), and *The Arctic Manual* (Stefansson, 1950).

This emergence of adventure as a legitimate quest for its own sake coincided with a number of broader issues. One such issue was the growing

Table 2.1 Selected Historical Events and Their Impact on OAE

Year	Event	Impact on OAE and OAE activities
1861	Gunnery School for Boys	Uses outdoor activities to build character.
1872	Yellowstone National Park	First national park; recreation an important use.
1892	Sierra Club	Protection of natural areas but also becomes an important outdoor recreation provider.
1899	Mt. Rainier National Park	Recreation becomes recognized as a legitimate leisure pursuit.
1905	USDA Forest Service	Recreation becomes a major component of the agency mission.
1910-1912	Boy Scouts, Campfire Girls, Girl Scouts	Use of outdoors to aid in the growth of young people.
1915-1916	Trappers Lake Principle/National Park Service	No development in wilderness areas.
1924	American Camping Association	Camps become a prime user of OAE activities.
1933	Great Depression leads to the development of the CCC	Constructs trails, facilities, and access to many current adventure areas.
1941	Outward Bound established in Aberdovy, Wales	Forerunner of the modern adventure movement.
1958	Outdoor Recreation Resources Review Commission (ORRRC)	Establishes the importance of outdoor resources for recreation within society.
1965	National Outdoor Leadership School (NOLS)	Becomes a major organization in OAE.
1968	Wild and Scenic Rivers	Brings protection for a number of rivers that serve as OAE locations.
1974	Association of Experiential Education	Serves a significant role in the promotion and research in OAE.
1978	Wilderness Education Association	Seeks to codify the training of OAE leaders.
1984	Development of the Association of Outdoor Recreation and Education	Focuses on delivery organization involved in outdoor recreation and OAE.
1986	President's Commission on Americans Outdoors	Reaffirms the health-related benefits of outdoor recreation.
1987	Formation of the Coalition for Education in the Outdoors (CEO)	Serves as a research and literary forum for OAE and related activities.
1987	*High Adventure Outdoor Pursuits* published	One of the first textbooks dedicated to OAE (Meier, Morash & Welton, Eds.).
1989	*Outdoor Adventure Pursuits: Foundations, Models, and Theories* published	Textbook focuses on theory and research in OAE (Ewert).
1994	Wilderness Risk Management conference	Focuses on providing best practices relative to risk management in OAE.
1997	*Effective Leadership in Adventure Programming* published	Widely acclaimed textbook on outdoor leadership (Priest and Gass).
2000	First issues of the *Journal of Adventure Education and Outdoor Learning*	One of the first journals focused on OAE and similar types of education experiences.
2003	Symposium on Experiential Education Research	Provides a research forum for experiential education research including OAE.
2008	*Journal of Outdoor Recreation, Education, and Leadership* first published	Journal with a specific focus on the areas of outdoor recreation, education, and leadership.

dissatisfaction with a vision of the world as completely explainable by either religious dogma or by social beliefs. These perspectives were becoming increasingly bombarded by assaults from reality. In addition, the image of the wilderness was changing. People were now going to the wilderness not to "conquer" it but to be mystically refreshed and re-energized. Nash believed that appreciation of the wilderness began in the cities (1967, p. 44). This appreciation was cultivated more by the writings and discussions of wilderness tourists and amateur naturalists than by actual wilderness users. Indeed, the writings of Catlin (1796-1872), Thoreau (1817-1862), Isabella Bird (1831-1904), and Muir (1838-1914) served to spur interest in the wilderness and the inescapable adventure that went with it, just as the more contemporary works of Carson (1907-1964), Abbey (1927-1989), and McPhee (1931-present) have sparked the interest of many since.

FORMALIZED SCHOOLS OF ADVENTURE EDUCATION

With the advent of World War II, the paths of three men crossed in Great Britain. This crossing led to one of the foremost organizations in the field of adventure-based education. The combination of the innovative vision of Kurt Hahn, the financial expertise of Lawrence Holt, and the energy and ability to turn vision into reality of Jim Hogan led to the formation of Outward Bound (Wilson, 1981). Since its inception as a training and educational system for strengthening an individual both physically and spiritually, Outward Bound has emerged as a leading organization in the field of adventure-based education.

It was not until 20 years later, however, that the concept of Outward Bound (by then an institution with 13 schools around the world) finally reached North America. Spearheaded by Joshua Minor and Charles Froelicher, the Colorado Outward Bound School emerged in 1962 with the purpose of

> . . . developing apparent and latent capabilities through experience, both strenuous and testing, which demand an increase of initiative, self-confidence, understanding and respect for others. Using life in the mountains as the defying force, the students are taught the importance of cooperation

and self-discipline in learning to cope with the hazards and emergencies of mountain living. They become acquainted with the great rewards of difficult and sustained efforts well done, the important spiritual value of service to others and self-respect for a well-trained body. (James, 1980, pp. 8-9)

With its motto "to serve, to strive, and not to yield," Outward Bound in the United States and Canada has grown to include a number of base camps, individual schools, and urban centers.

Three years after the establishment of the Colorado Outward Bound School in 1962, the chief instructor, Paul Petzoldt, stated he was ". . . shocked into the realization that nobody had really trained outdoorsmen in America."

> We [Outward Bound] couldn't hire anyone that met my standards. We [Outward Bound] could hire people who knew how to do one thing well: climb mountains, fish, cross wild rivers, cook plain rations, recognize flora and fauna, read topographical maps, and teach and motivate. But we could not find a person who had been trained in all those things! They didn't exist. I thought the best thing I could do for American youth, if they were going to use the wild outdoors, was to prepare better leaders for such experiences" (Petzoldt, 1974).

From this desire emerged the concept of the National Outdoor Leadership School (NOLS), with the purpose of developing skilled outdoor leaders. Interestingly, Petzoldt and the NOLS parted ways in 1975, with Petzoldt forming another outdoor adventure organization, the Wilderness Education Association (WEA). The stated purpose of the WEA is to promote the safe and ecologically sound use of the wilderness through offering the certification of wilderness users and leaders.

Outward Bound and the NOLS, along with many other outdoor adventure organizations (e.g., the Dartmouth Outing Club; Brigham Young University's Outdoor Survival program, instructed by Larry Dean Olsen; and Prescott College) emerged in the 1960s. This was the era of the "baby boomers" (large numbers of people under age 20), many of whom became affluent as adults and increasingly jaded by technology and urbanization (James, 1980, p. 5). The wilderness offered a setting to provide the emotional catharsis and physical challenge that was increasingly lacking in contemporary, urbanized society. In a sense, adventure became likened to what William James described in his essay "The Moral Equivalent of War" (Metcalfe, 1976, p. 5), a place to test and be tested, a place to nourish and solidify fundamental human virtues.

This desire for wild backcountry lands available for adventure-based activities coincided with the public's growing concern over the health of the environment and the protection of certain pristine areas. Together, these forces helped create the Wilderness Act of 1964. Land, untrammeled by man, now became a legally protected resource. Wallace Stegner, a wilderness advocate, wrote:

> . . . a headstrong drive into our technological termite life, the brave new world of a completely man-controlled environment. . . . Something will have gone out of us as a people if we ever let the remaining wilderness be destroyed; if we permit the last virgin forests to be turned into comic books and plastic cigarette cases; if we drive the few remaining members of that wild species into zoos or to extinction; if we pollute the last clear air and dirty the last clean streams and push paved roads through the last of the silence, so that never again will Americans be free in their own country from the noise, the exhausts, the stinks of human and automotive waste. (1961, p. 97)

By the very nature of wilderness, outdoor adventure activities such as backpacking and mountain climbing became accepted uses of these and other backcountry environments. This usage, combined with the phenomenal growth of organizations (e.g., Association of Experiential Education, 1974; First North American Conference on Outdoor Pursuits in Higher Education, 1974) and events (Earth Day, May 1, 1970) catering to outdoor adventure resulted in the emergence of a new genre of recreationalists, a group that deliberately sought out the trials and dangers of outdoor adventuring.

More recent events affecting the outdoor adventure scene include the first, second, and third National Conferences on Outdoor Recreation (1984, 1986, 1988) and the emergence of adventure-based magazines such as *Outside, Backpacker, Outward Bound,* and *Outside Business*. Established in 1985, the President's Commission on Americans Outdoors (PCOA), like its predecessor, the Outdoor Recreation Resources Review Commission (ORRRC) of 1962, returned its report in 1987. This report cited overused outdoor recreation resources and burgeoning demands on those finite resources. Many of these demands were in the area of outdoor adventure activities.

Into the late 1990s and through the turn of the century, OAE continued to grow and change. The Americans with Disabilities Act, which focuses on inclusion, sustainability, and social justice has influenced how and why programs are offered. Challenge, or ropes, courses have become more common, and the Association of Challenge Course Technology (ACCT) has worked to create common standards and expectations. Wilderness therapy and adventure therapy have emerged as important and powerful modalities to effect group and individual change. The OAE industry has diversified as smaller providers and organizations have filled niches in programming. The eclectic adventure and outdoor industry has come to include adventure camps, commercial guides, community recreation centers, and nature parks and has spanned across the tourism, land management, and retail sectors. We discuss contemporary approaches to the adventure industry in chapter 3.

SUMMARY

From ancient Greece to contemporary civilization, we have traced the development of humans interfacing with natural landscapes that has led us to outdoor adventuring. We have seen that adventuring moved from external quests for knowledge, spice routes, or wealth to internal searches for information on our own strength, abilities, and courage. As activities such as trail running, sailing, camping, hunting, and fishing have separated from their functional origins as necessary skills for survival, it is telling that interest in these pursuits today remains high. Indeed, when reduced to the microcosm of the individual, whether standing on the swaying deck of a small ship; peering up the white, windy expanse of a snow-covered slope; or nervously anticipating the next set of rapids on an unexplored river, what adventurer can escape these incredibly personal moments of adventure without the question: What awaits me?

Thus, in the search for something other (science, wealth, colonization, or spreading the word of God), the individual explorer of the past is linked with the adventurer of the present and future by the nature of the quest itself: a bold undertaking in which the outcome, though uncertain, can usually be influenced by the individual. In a sense, the history of adventuring represents a thread of humanity linked today with generations long past. It provides a link every bit as important as the structures, philosophies, and knowledge forged by our ancestors. As discussed in this chapter, numerous OAE organizations have provided adventure experiences for literally millions of people across the globe and constitute a major influence in the development of OAE. Through adventuring, an individual, while engaging in the activity, can *feel* the emotions, excitement, and concerns of those who have gone before.

Issues for Further Discussion

1. The implication in this chapter is that adventure seeking was the "hidden" motive underlying much exploration done by early explorers. That is, though couched within scientific or nationalistic explanations, adventure seeking was an important, if not the real, reason that many of these endeavors were actually undertaken. What do you think?

2. If "past is prologue" and knowing that the OAE movement emerged, in part, as a response to many of the challenges facing society, such as delinquency, low self-esteem, lack of trust, and others, what do you anticipate will be the role of OAE in the next two or three decades?

3. Schools such as Outward Bound and the National Outdoor Leadership School emerged in North America in the 1960s. What is emerging now, and why?

4. The "adventure for its own sake" phenomenon coincided with the growing interest in conservation in the United States during the1800s. Is there a connection between the current growth in research and design of OAE programs and recent phenomena such as No Child Left Inside?

5. How might you use the historical information presented in this chapter as evidence in designing and implementing your OAE program?

Outdoor Adventure in Contemporary Practice

Why This Chapter Is Important

The history of outdoor adventure has led us to a convergence of perspectives that today embody the field of outdoor adventure education (OAE). This convergence spans populations, purposes, social contexts, and physical spaces. OAE has become a worldwide phenomenon that encompasses a broad spectrum of approaches, methods, and organizations.

From the constitutive definition we presented in chapter 1, you might correctly assume that OAE can mean different things to different people. Operationally, OAE can look and function in many diverse ways. However, in this chapter we will see that some common elements distinguish OAE from other pursuits. We also look at the key components of OAE and explore some allied fields that work in consort with OAE.

Learning Outcomes

After completing this chapter, you should be able to

* describe the diversity, growth, and size of the outdoor adventure industry;
* compare and contrast outdoor recreation, outdoor adventure education, and guided trips;
* list the key components of an OAE experience;
* understand the OAE progression and how it affects the experience; and
* describe the RERAS model.

oday, a web search on outdoor adventure yields 55.6 million hits on a variety of topics and services, including educational programs, skills training, wilderness experiences, spiritual development, chat sites for groups with common interests, international service trips, exotic travel fishing, hunting, off-road vehicle use, snowmobiling, rock climbing, whitewater paddling, wilderness treks, nature science schools, orientation sessions for college students, workshops for development of corporate teams, and many more. More than fifty-five million!

Adventure-centered professions have grown dramatically over the past few decades, and many specializations of adventure pursuits have arisen. For example, adventure education, challenge therapy, therapeutic adventure, and challenge courses all serve diverse populations in different contexts and with different purposes. Adventure education, outdoor education, environmental education, wilderness education, adventure recreation, and adventure therapy have all become distinct aspects of a wider profession in which people are commonly taught in the outdoors and experiencing adventure can be a primary or secondary part of the learning experience. Specialty areas within OAE include therapeutic programs, programs for at-risk youth, corporate adventure training, and summer camps devoted to topics such as leadership, adventure sports, or specific skills like kayaking or rock climbing.

The professionalization of adventure has yielded a growth in training programs spanning degrees offered by colleges and universities, research units within governmental organizations, hospitals and outreach programs, the corrections system, K-12 schools, and growth of adventure programs beyond the pioneering organizations of Outward Bound schools and the National Outdoor Leadership School. The internationalization of adventure pursuits has also become quite sophisticated, and worldwide cooperation and collaboration is common. What has changed little is that people still line up to partake in adventure opportunities. Indeed, perhaps more people than ever seek an adventure experience in which they spend time in nature and struggle to learn how to become comfortable in adverse outdoor conditions while participating in activities that are emotionally and physically challenging. Data published by the Outdoor Foundation in 2010 show participation numbers in the United States (table 3.1).

The numbers shown in table 3.1 suggest that activities commonly associated with adventure education are engaged in by a substantial number of participants each year. Adventure pursuits have also grown into different forms, with each requiring different schemes of training and serving different audiences. Yet the educational backgrounds of instructors in each of these areas vary because of the skills, knowledge, and audiences. For example, instructors teaching a whitewater kayak class will focus on skill development and the kind of psychological safety that will allow participants to balance fear levels with abilities to read the conditions while practicing their physical skills to negotiate a rapid. Instructors at various types of camps may use instruments such as a ropes course to build teamwork among participants, but their primary focus might be to develop skills that help participants become better teammates and leaders in organized sports and other activities.

If you consider the term *adventure education*, a host of images might come to mind. In many

Table 3.1 Levels of Participation for Selected Outdoor Adventure Activities

Activity	Participants aged six or older (2009)	Percent of U.S. population
Backpacking	7,647,000	2.7%
Canoeing	10,058,000	3.6%
Climbing (all types)	6,148,000	2.2%
Kayaking (sea & touring)	1,771,000	0.6%
Kayaking (whitewater)	1,369,000	0.5%
Rafting	4,318,000	1.5%
Scuba diving	2,723,000	1.0%

Data from Outdoor Foundation, *Outdoor recreation participation report 2010*.

cases, these images likely involve engagement in an outdoor setting as a part of a small group while facing a set of challenges in which the group must work together to cope with the tasks at hand. Expectations often vary as well but typically focus on experiencing a challenge, addressing the challenge, reflecting on the various meanings ascribed to the challenge, and feeling a sense of accomplishment upon meeting the challenge.

PROGRAMS AND PRACTICE

Though we have discussed adventure education, outdoor education, and experiential education in chapter 1 as umbrella terms, many programs and practices intersect with OAE. Review the program types and practice settings presented in figure 3.1. Environmental education can take place in outdoor settings but also occurs in schools, environmental education centers, and urban museums. Wilderness education is always outdoors, but it is not an uninterrupted adrenaline rush, as many of the authentic aspects of wilderness education focus on living and traveling in the outdoors. Adventure therapy takes place outdoors but also indoors in inpatient and residential settings. Ropes and challenge courses are often outdoors and are typically educational or leadership based, but they are increasingly popping up at tourism destinations as high-adventure recreational pursuits. Climbing walls are similar

in this respect and continue to see a great deal of use by serious recreational climbers for practice and exercise, yet they are also becoming popular for children's birthday parties, interactive in-store attractions, and cruise ship activities. Organized camping offers a great diversity of programming, some of which is OAE. Outdoor recreation can be educational and beneficial but is not necessarily an educational setting with formal learning opportunities and curriculum. Guiding, which is a large segment of the professional adventure pursuits industry, is often educational but sometimes is simply a means of enjoying a trip down an exciting stretch of river or some backcountry powder without a real understanding of the inherent hazards of the environment. Although many of these programs and practices are primarily of interest to this book where they intersect with OAE, both outdoor recreation and guided trips are large sectors of the adventure industry and thus warrant some additional discussion.

Outdoor Recreation

Outdoor recreation, which is sometimes defined as any leisure activity taking place out of doors, typically focuses on recreational pursuits in which the outdoors and concomitant natural resources are inherently necessary. The outdoor recreation industry accounts for a notable section of the economy, especially where it overlaps with nature-based tourism, gear and equipment sales, and guiding and education programs. Current

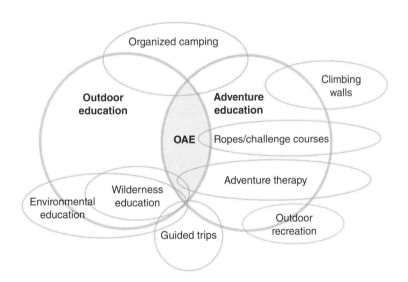

Figure 3.1 Many programs and practices intersect with OAE.

Adapted, by permission, from J. Gookin, 2011, *Development of a psychometric scale to measure challenge (stress) type and intensity in wilderness education students.* Unpublished doctoral dissertation, Prescott, AZ: (Prescott College).

Taiwan's Unique Outdoor Adventure: River Tracing

Guan-Jang Wu, PhD—National Taiwan Sport University, Taiwan

Most people view Taiwan as a high technology center in Asia. For those who have visited the island, Chinese cultural heritage and hawker stalls presenting delicious food in night markets might have left a great impression. However, still mostly unknown to the world, Taiwan has a huge potential for adventure tourism and outdoor education. Over 200 mountains taller than 10,000 feet are situated on the island, and thousands of steep rivers and canyons are available for exploration. In short, 75 percent of the island is mountainous.

In addition to having a diverse ecosystem, Taiwanese people have been changing their perception of nature from something to fear to a place that is full of possibilities. Traditionally, the Taiwanese government has restricted access to mountains and coastlines because of national security, leaving most people with a conservative view on outdoor adventure. However, Taiwan is experiencing a significant shift in the acceptance of the value of risk taking with a purpose, which matches the core values of adventure education; this is reflected in the boom of OAE in schools, adventure tourism companies, adventure race events, and youth travel programs.

Of all the adventure opportunities available in Taiwan, one activity that stands out is river tracing. River tracing (or stream walking) is a form of hiking or outdoor adventure activity that is a traditional outdoor adventure from Japan, which is rapidly gaining popularity in Taiwan. River tracing is a combination of hiking, climbing, rappelling,

River tracing provides exciting adventure as well as a rich metaphor for teaching.
Courtesy of Guan-Jang Wu.

jumping, and swimming along the river, somewhat similar to canyoneering. Specialized equipment is used: a helmet, wetsuit, life jacket, harness, and felt-bottom shoes. River tracers simply follow a river up the side of a mountain while wading through small rapids, climbing over rocks, and venturing into pristine territory. People can choose from a one-day program to a weeklong expedition into high mountain creeks.

Although it started as mostly adventure recreation, river tracing is gradually becoming used in OAE, corporate team building, environmental education, and adventure therapy. Organizations taking advantage of this activity include university programs, youth-at-risk programs, outfitters, and travel agencies. It is becoming a favorite activity of outdoor educators because river tracing has all the elements a ropes course has to offer—novelty, excitement, challenge, teamwork, and much more. The river changes every time people visit, and close interaction with the natural environment—water, vegetation, and wild animals—provides psychological benefits as well as experiential learning opportunities. Journeying up the river, participants are encouraged to choose their own path (challenge by choice), and they naturally help each other over rocks and other obstacles. Similar to a salmon trying to return home, river tracing presents a rich metaphor for facilitators to lead a deep and meaningful reflection.

The popularization of river tracing, akin to other outdoor activities, has consequences, such as risk-management issues and environmental impacts. Drowning accidents and injuries have increased significantly because of unprofessional leadership and inappropriate equipment. Comprehensive national standards for guides need to be established. Environmental concerns, such as Leave No Trace (LNT) principles, have been commonly practiced since a nationwide LNT campaign was conducted in Taiwan in 2006. However, for outfitters, profit margins may take priority over environmental protection. Thus, inexperienced leaders guiding large groups might damage natural resources and place participants at risk.

It is projected that Taiwanese society will continue to embrace adventure, both in variety and depth. Certification and accreditation of leaders and programs will gain attention from the outdoor community, and government agencies will take advantage of this niche market and promote Taiwan as an adventure tourism destination to attract people from all over the world.

estimates suggest that the outdoor recreation industry generates almost $650 billion in annual consumer spending in the United States alone (Outdoor Industry Association, 2012). However, outdoor recreation does not have to involve travel and tourism, education, organized guides, or special equipment; a simple day hike to observe wildflowers is outdoor recreation. Despite the enormity of outdoor recreation and its ability to foster an array of personal, environmental, community, and economic benefits, many initial forays into lifelong outdoor recreational pursuits begin with formal educational programs or guided experiences. Activities such as whitewater boating, ski-mountaineering, scuba diving, and ice climbing are rarely learned today without formal education.

Guided Trips

Another large and important sector of the adventure field is guided trips. Some of these are primarily recreational in nature, such as when a raft guide helps a group of novices enjoy a float down a three-hour stretch of river. Other guides are highly technical and offer educational or consultative services whereby they provide expertise, education, and leadership necessary to safely and successfully summit a peak or complete a multiday sea-kayaking expedition. In practice, programs may require staff to seamlessly move between these roles given the program's needs. According to Ewert and Wu (2007), educational trips and guided trips differ on a number of variables including types of clients, client expectations, levels of risk, and technical skills (figure 3.2). Educational adventure programs (EAPs) can be thought of as structured excursions typically conducted through education-based organizations such as schools or universities, or interna-

tional organizations such as the National Outdoor Leadership School (NOLS) or Outward Bound (OB). EAPs often include structured activities such as group initiatives or similar experiences that promote team building, trust, personal growth and maturity, and the development of individual decision making and judgment. In contrast, guided trips (GTs) can be defined as the process of providing services or assistance (e.g., training, equipment, food, route information) to individuals or groups who are engaged in an outdoor activity; the orientation is typically commercial in focus and involves financial incentives for the guide. Table 3.2 illustrates the common differences between the two approaches to outdoor adventure education.

Varying Applications of Adventure

At the center of these divisions is the difference between using adventure for recreation, education, or therapy. Many activities such as trekking, climbing, caving, or ropes courses can be recreation, education, or therapy, but the inherent way they are designed and implemented varies immensely. Educational and therapeutic programs are typically goal oriented, intentionally designed, implemented with a guiding purpose, and based on a semblance of evidence. In contrast, recreational pursuits, though often driven by an individual's goals, vary widely. Recreational rafting trips down the Colorado River range from family float trips and party floats to technical and arduous personal tests. Educational or therapeutic OAE trips are, in contrast, more organized and structured with a defined leader or instructor team.

Consider the elements of a high-quality adventure experience displayed in figure 3.3. Similar to frameworks posed by psychologists interested

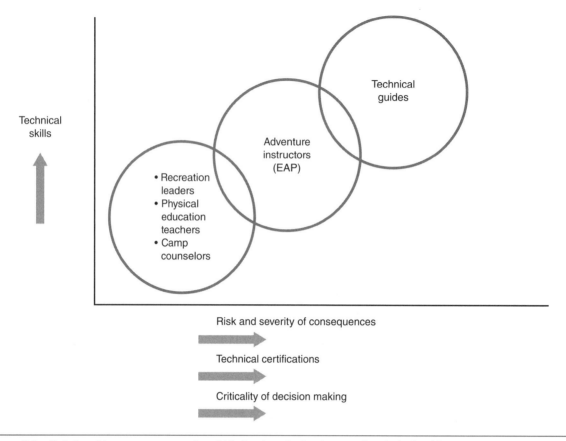

Technical skills

Technical guides

Adventure instructors (EAP)

- Recreation leaders
- Physical education teachers
- Camp counselors

Risk and severity of consequences

Technical certifications

Criticality of decision making

Figure 3.2 Relationships among recreational trip leaders, instructors, and technical guides.

Sense of freedom and choice	Autotelic experience
• Type of experience • Extent of the experience • Components of the experience • Level of engagement	• Intrinsic motivation • Activity done for its own sake
Competence and effectiveness	Optimal arousal
• Feelings of mastery and skill sufficient to be successful • Sense of effectiveness in the selected environment • Reliability and consistency of one's skills and abilities	• Sufficient complexity • Challenges matched with demands • Cognitive dissonance

Figure 3.3 High-quality adventure experiences generally include four major characteristics.

Table 3.2 Comparison of Guided Trips and Educational Adventure Programs

Issues	Guided trips	Educational adventure programs
PROGRAMMING ISSUES		
Goals/objectives	Delivery of quality experience	Facilitation of learning experience
Focus of program	Outcome	Process
Motivation	Outcome	Process
Locus of decision making	Guide	Instructor, then student
Judgment	Mountain sense (intuition)	Linear process
Risk	Higher	Structured
Clientele	Exclusive/affluent thrill seekers	More inclusive
Leadership composition	Lone, independent	Instructor team
Group size	Small	Medium
Environmental impact	Considerable (i.e., expedition guiding)	Small
Environmental ethics	Minimum impact	Leave no trace
Types of activities	Diverse	Diverse
Locale	International/national/local	Local/national
Access to natural resources	Permit/concession	Permit
Programming evaluation	Informal	Formal
PROFESSIONAL ISSUES		
Leadership training	Implicit/apprentice	Explicit/leadership curriculum
Technical training	Advanced	Intermediate to advanced
First aid/SAR training	WFR	WFR
Internal regulation (certification)	AMGA, IFMGA	WEA
Internal regulation (accreditation)	UIAGM, AMGA	AEE, WEA
External regulation	Laws and regulations	Laws and regulations

Reprinted, by permission, from A. Ewert and Guan-Jang Wu, 2007, "Two faces of outdoor adventure leadership: Educational adventure programs and guided trips," *Journal of the Wilderness Education Association* 18(1): 12-18.

in high-quality leisure experiences (Iso-Ahola, 1980; Mannell & Kleiber, 1997), a high-quality adventure experience consists of four major components:

1. A sense of freedom to choose the adventure experience in terms of variables such as type, extent, and level of engagement

2. An autotelic experience—that is, an experience done for its own sake or because it has intrinsic value to the individual participant

3. A sense of competence and effectiveness (having the skills to be successful and effective in a particular environment)

4. Optimal arousal (complexity, challenge, and cognitive dissonance)

Although all four components need not be present in equal doses or intensity, having these components can be theoretically linked to high-quality adventure experiences.

These components all make sense in adventure recreation, but they are not always realized in OAE. Some elements of OAE are not completely volitional and intrinsically motivated. Although recreation is inherent in most OAE programs, demands from the group, instructor expectations, program structure, and peer pressure can combine to shift an OAE experience from a purely recreational pursuit. However, these demands are not without value. People often grow and develop because of these demands, expectations, and coerced experiences. Growth and development occur in OAE in a variety of domains, including the physical, psychological, spiritual, cognitive, and social. Ideally, OAE programs are designed and implemented with the primary goal of achieving targeted outcomes.

Therapeutic programs are another derivation of the OAE experience, but with some important differences. In addition to programmatic processes similar to OAE programs, therapeutic programs are rarely freely chosen. Participants are typically enrolled because of therapeutic needs and the associated external pressures. Parents, counselors, or the courts can exude considerable pressure on participants to attend, contribute, and change.

Being aware of programs and practices related to OAE is important in understanding the development of OAE because though there has been a great deal of overlap between approaches there are also significant differences. The field of OAE has been built by EAPs, GTs, and other related fields, and how individuals view and personally define OAE often depends on their experiences with segments of the larger outdoor adventure industry.

COMPONENTS OF THE OAE EXPERIENCE

Using our discussion of different outdoor adventure programs and practices as an organizing framework, what types of experiences can be categorized as OAE? As shown in figure 3.4, OAE experiences generally include a setting, a set of activities, instructional staff and leaders, a processing and facilitation of the experience, and a personal interpretation of the knowledge realized from the experience.

Setting

The setting often provides OAE participants with a juxtaposition of beautiful and aesthetically pleasing scenery combined with a challenging and demanding physical environment combined with a critical and novel social environment.

Be it a river, ocean, cave, snow slope, rock face, mountain, or rainforest, setting is often a hallmark of an OAE experience. Moreover, these places can provide not only challenge and excitement but also connections to nature, places for reflection, and quiet solitude. They thus become important from perspectives of both design and implementation.

From the perspective of evidence, however, the story gets more complicated. One of the major issues that arises in terms of OAE experiences and subsequent outcomes involves the effect of simply *being* in a natural or outdoor environment versus *doing* structured activities in these environments. Several researchers have proposed that a major factor in the efficacy of OAE programs is simply being in *contact* with the natural environment (Bardwell, 1992; Mitten, 1994). It has also been suggested, however, that structured programs work to "focus the power" of nature, and that highlighting this relationship can further enhance health-related outcomes (Mitten, 2009).

Natural environments can promote positive outcomes for participants in many ways. For example, they can often provide the setting for physical activity, with numerous studies reporting the beneficial effects of "green" exercise (Driskell, Johnston, & Salas, 2001). Natural environments have been linked to the attention restoration theory (ART) in which these settings have a particular set of properties that promote restoration from attention fatigue (Kaplan & Kaplan, 1989; Kaplan & Berman, 2010). Such properties include being away, degree (diverse enough environment to hold attention), fascination, and compatibility (that is, the abilities of the individual are equal to the demands of the new environment) (Felsten, 2009, p. 160). Similar to ART, the psychoevolutionary theory (PET), proposed by Ulrich (1984), posits that natural environments are effective at reducing stress levels because they offer attributes that our species views as having inherent survival qualities, such as water and spatial openness. Hartig, Mang, and Evans (1991) integrate these two theories by suggesting an "intertwining of the mechanisms" whereby the degree to which people are attracted to and use a natural environment depends on how restorative that environment is for them. Thus through the mechanisms of PET and ART, benefits from OAE may be, in part, a result of being exposed to a natural environment (e.g., wilderness). That is, simply being in a natural setting such as a wilderness creates the potential for a positive outcome.

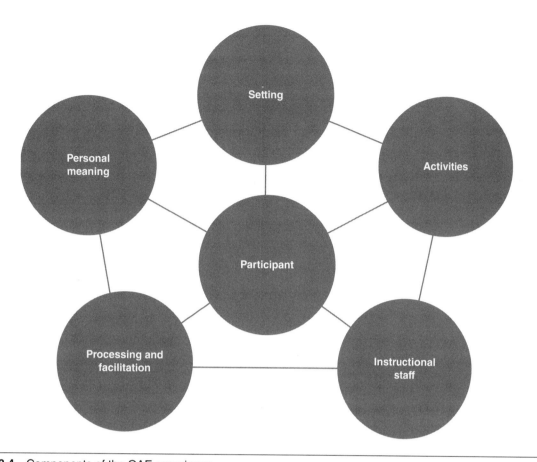

Figure 3.4 Components of the OAE experience.

In the case of OAE, however, one consistent finding from research tends to complicate the importance of the setting issue just discussed. Beginning with salient works such as Shore (1977), results from an extensive body of research and other evidence points to positive outcomes being achieved through participation in OAE no matter the environment or setting. Clearly more is at work in OAE than a mere change of scenery or immersion in a natural setting (not to deny that these can play important roles in OAE). At this point, evidence brings us back to design and implementation with the concept and use of intentionally designed experiences (IDEs) (Sheard & Golby, 2006). Similar to Mitten's (2009) idea that wilderness programs can serve to focus the benefits of nature, IDEs are purposeful in their planning and implementation to achieve specific benefits.

The idea of the IDE posits that the purpose, type, and specifics of a program, as well as the client, all affect the outcome. The IDE is an active mechanism that, depending on its design, incorporates many of the theoretical underpinnings of

the human-nature benefit interaction involving constructs such as ART and PET into a program or experience that ultimately contributes to personal growth and development. Thus combining the theories of the psychological and physical benefits of nature through ART and PET, with the use of IDEs, OAE programs become a means of acquiring wide-ranging positive outcomes—often far beyond what could be accomplished through mere immersion in a particular setting.

Activities

Similar to setting, OAE activities play a central role in intentional program design. Typically, OAE programs include activities and experiences that entail action, high energy, and meaningful consequences; strenuous and kinesthetic behaviors; and small groups of participants. OAE activities frequently include the following:

- Rock climbing
- Caving
- Ice climbing

- Whitewater boating
- Canyoneering
- Canoeing
- Wilderness trekking
- Ropes courses
- Climbing walls
- Bicycle touring
- Sea kayaking
- Mountaineering
- Snow sports
- Sailing
- Horse packing

Instructional Staff

Instructional staff play many roles in any OAE program. Often they are asked to be part coach, part instructor, and part risk manager. They are responsible both for working within the program design and for making necessary adjustments based on issues such as weather or changing situations (e.g., a participant gets ill). They are asked to balance a complex set of variables including environmental conditions, program goals, needs of individual participants, needs of the small groups, and sometimes needs of fellow

staff members. The OAE challenge they face typically contains uncertainty and includes logistical and structural barriers ranging from location and equipment to group ability and individual motivations.

Processing and Facilitation

Opportunities for processing and reflection are inherent in OAE experiences. Many times these are facilitated directly by the staff. They might also be designed into a program via structured activities, such as journaling, or formal down time, such as a solo experience. Often the inherent interest in and excitement about the activities elicits a degree of reflection and dialogue among participants so that experiences are cognitively processed without formal debriefing or framing by staff members.

Personal Meaning

Despite the importance of program design and implementation, the participant remains central to the OAE experience. Each participant brings his or her own experiences, opinions, and characteristics into the OAE experience. How participants cognitively and affectively integrate the experience within their own understanding

Opportunities for processing and reflection are inherent in OAE experiences.
Photo courtesy of Scott Schumann.

constitutes what they learn and take away from the experience. The success of even the most targeted and best designed and implemented program depends on how the experience is interpreted by participants.

PHILOSOPHICAL BASIS

Using the philosophical framework of Kurt Hahn, Outward Bound opened its first school in the United States in 1962 under the leadership of Josh Miner and the early involvement of Paul Petzoldt. This is widely considered the beginning of contemporary adventure education. Petzoldt, like Hahn, believed that learning about self and environment through nature and natural consequences was very important for all people, and especially young people. This ideal of personal growth and development through authentic challenge remains at the core of OAE philosophy.

Another central aspect of OAE philosophy involves risk and safety. Although OAE programs always seek to minimize the risk of catastrophic injuries, uncertainty of outcome is also part of the adventure philosophy. In essence, OAE programs try to maintain a balance of uncertainty of outcomes with appropriate levels of risk. This balance provides opportunities for OAE participants to engage in experiences that require perseverance, decision making, and skill acquisition with no guarantee of success.

No matter the level of success participants have in a particular experience, OAE always involves reflection and meaning making. This is why facilitation and processing are critical to the OAE structure in helping participants gain learning and meaning from their adventure experiences. Nearly always, to fully meet the goals of OAE programs, this learning and meaning must also be useful to participants later in life. The importance of this transfer of meaning cannot be understated—it constitutes a major part of the OAE philosophy.

OAE programs typically construct experiences based on several key principles:

- Experiences are supported by reflection, critical analysis, and the transfer of things learned to other aspects of an individual's life.
- Learning is personal and provides a foundation for developing meaning and relevance.

- Participants are encouraged to examine their own values and behaviors during and from the OAE experience.
- Participants are engaged at the physical, emotional, cognitive, and intellectual levels.
- Outdoor adventure educators are active learners and engage in a process that parallels that of participants.

Relative to this last point, parallel learning processes imply that educators, as well as participants, are learning as OAE unfolds. For example, while program participants are trying to navigate to a particular location, instructors might be assessing the suitability of that location as a place to camp or to engage in an activity. The essence of parallel learning in OAE is that all parties are dealing with uncertainties that can influence decision making.

One example of how components in an OAE experience can come together is presented in the RERAS model (figure 3.5). RERAS stands for restoration, empowerment, resilience, and social support (Ewert & Voight, 2011). In this model, the type of outcomes that result from participation in an OAE experience (using an intentionally designed experience, often in a natural setting) can be separated into three levels, or orders. First-order benefits can be considered the "gateway" outcome variable through which subsequent variables occur. In the case of OAE, this variable is sense of achievement. That is, to gain subsequent positive outcomes from an experience, participants must feel they were at least somewhat successful and sense they achieved something worthwhile. As we have noted, these experiences are not solely a result of being in nature but also require cognitive and evaluative processes from participants (McIntyre & Roggenbuck, 1998). Second-order outcomes include restoration, empowerment, resilience, and social support. Similar to the "broaden and build" theory originally advocated by Fredrickson (2001) in which positive psychological emotions help individuals expand their physical, social, and psychological resources, second-order benefits lead to the acquisition of third-order benefits, which include a wide range of outcomes such as those related to self-systems (e.g., esteem, concept, awareness, efficacy), stress reduction, identity formation, and social support, among many others. The concept of RERAS and the use of intentional design propose that the purpose, type, and specifics of an OAE experience can profoundly influence the outcome. Just as the

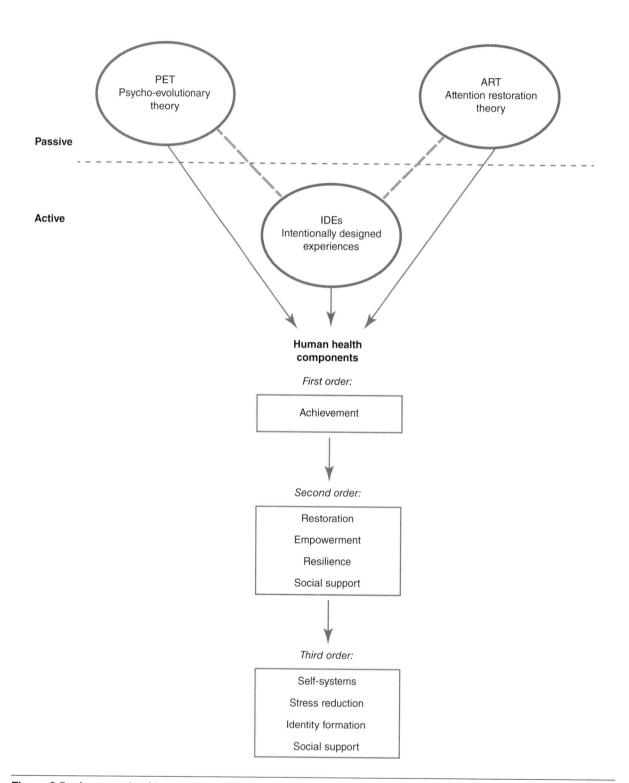

Figure 3.5 An example of intentionally designed adventure experiences and outcomes—the RERAS model.

Introduction to an adventure activity → Low levels of competence

Basic skill acquisition → Low levels of competence

Skill and experience acquisition → Attention to standards associated with the activity

Need to develop new experiences with skill base → New levels of arousal and competence

New expressions of competence and effectance → Instructing, foreign travel, increased difficulty

Figure 3.6 The OAE model of progression.

natural environment can significantly create a sense of well-being and restoration, the active use of intentionality in design and implementation tends to promote the development of a wide range of outcomes (see chapter 8).

THE ADVENTURE PROGRESSION

The adventurer typically engages in the adventure experience in a somewhat fluid and multidimensional progression. For example, as people gain skill and experience in an activity, they tend to increase the complexity or demands of that activity. As we have discussed, OAE experiences involve participants, settings, activities, instructional staff, processing and facilitation, and personal meaning. This complex is seldom static but often changes in predictable ways. Thus adventurers will often increase the difficulty of a particular adventure activity. Examples include climbing a more difficult mountain, going on a deeper scuba dive, or whitewater boating in a kayak rather than on a large raft. Of course progressions can also occur in interpersonal skills, such as when a participant moves from active follower to leader or from participant to teacher. As shown in figure 3.6, the concept of progression suggests a sequential set of behaviors, though this is not always the case. The ability to progress both in skill level and experience is often paramount in importance for individual participants. In terms of the adventure experience, however, this progression is part of a larger picture.

As we have mentioned, the retelling of the tale is associated with some modern theories regarding people engaging in outdoor activities. Clawson and Knetsch (1966), for example, suggest that the outdoor experience involves four phases:

1. Anticipation—the participant imagines an activity and considers pursuing it.
2. Planning—this often exciting and educational phase involves preparation, gathering information, and making arrangements.
3. Participation—this phase involves actually performing the activity or engaging in the experience. This phase extends from the time of departure to the time of return.
4. Recollection—in this phase the tale gets retold. This phase often involves memories, photographs, mementos, videos, and artifacts. Perhaps most important from the perspective of OAE, there is no time limit on this phase—it can last a lifetime.

SUMMARY

The programs and practices of the contemporary adventure industry are large, diverse, and growing. Challenge courses, climbing walls, and emerging forms of adventure are complementing traditional activities commonly associated with adventure education and serve to diversify the OAE program mix. Related fields such as outdoor recreation, guided trips, and therapeutic programs vary in purposes but share some common components and principles, such as settings (e.g., natural landscapes) and concern over the stewardship of those natural landscapes.

A key component of OAE is its educational focus, which places a premium on a progression that fuels personal growth, an intentional design and structure, and high-quality implementation and facilitation by trained instructors and leaders. That said, it is often the combined effect of outdoor setting, adventurous activities, instructors, processing, and personal interpretation that defines an OAE experience for an individual or group. OAE can thus be regarded as a holistic educational experience. It can be a powerful teaching tool that combines the multisensory input of the natural and outdoor setting with the cognitive, sociological, and psychological nuances of dealing with uncertainty, risk, and a small-group environment. Through OAE, participants are often forced to step outside of their comfort zones and *do* something rather than simply watch something happen. Thus learning within the milieu of OAE becomes more action centered, participant based, and holistic than most traditional classrooms.

In the next chapter we look at some important variables common in OAE programs and explore how understanding these variables can be integrated within a framework of design, implementation, and evidence.

🌿 Issues for Further Discussion

1. Explain how outdoor adventure has changed over the past 20-plus years, both in numbers of participants and types of activities engaged in. Describe the key components of an OAE experience. Do you think these key components will change in the future? How so?

2. How will technological innovations influence adventure activities?

3. In what ways can we measure the influence of an outdoor natural setting on the outcome of an OAE experience?

4. Some researchers have called the adventure experience a "state of mind." How might you test the accuracy of this claim?

5. Has the growth of adventure programs and opportunities resulted in increased involvement and broadened support by the public for the outdoor environmental resources including wilderness areas, land acquisition for parks and forests, and the acceptance of adventure activities, such as rock climbing, as legitimate leisure pursuits? What responsibility does the OAE industry have in this area?

Managing Motivation, Risk, Fear, and Stress

Why This Chapter Is Important

Knowing why people choose to engage in OAE can be extremely useful to instructors and adventure-based organizations, particularly in the areas of design and implementation. Knowing why your participants have come to your program and how they deal with issues such as risk, fear, and stress might significantly enhance the meaning they take away from the experience.

Thus, providing useful techniques for dealing with fear, anxiety, and stress can have profound implications for participants both during and after adventure experiences. The carryover from effective OAE leaves participants with valuable skills to deal with situations that occur later in their lives.

Learning Outcomes

After completing this chapter, you should be able to

* identify the motivations involved in participation in OAE experiences,
* justify how and why risk is used in OAE,
* discuss the role of fear in OAE programs,
* examine and contrast differing techniques for dealing with fear and anxiety, and
* compare and contrast stress with fear and risk and explain how stress influences decision making and physiology.

*O*f *the many* variables associated with OAE experiences, four are most pertinent to this chapter:

1. The motives for participating in OAE experiences
2. The role risk plays in OAE experiences
3. How OAE experiences deal with fear and anxiety
4. How stress-management skills can be learned from OAE experiences

These four are important because they apply to most OAE experiences, and to a certain extent they can be accounted for in the design and implementation phases of a program. In addition, although these variables are separate, they are usually interwoven with one another and must be considered carefully by instructors as they seek to provide high-quality OAE experiences.

Thus in this chapter we explore motivation for participation, risk and risk taking, and ways of dealing with fear and stress. We conclude with an overview of the critical roles these concepts play in the overall OAE experience. But before going further, we should be clear on definitions of key terms in this chapter:

- *Motivation* is a process that initiates, guides, and helps maintain a goal-oriented behavior. Three primary components of motivation are activation, persistence, and intensity. For example, an individual might take an OAE course in caving and like it (activation). That person might then continue to develop caving skills over a period of years (persistence) and visit different cave systems or types of caves many times a year (intensity). In this example, the individual might think of him- or herself as a caver and incorporate regular caving into his or her life. We call this "enduring involvement."

- *Risk* involves exposure to danger, harm, or loss. *Risk taking* is engaging in a behavior that might be harmful or dangerous but that might also provide an outcome perceived as positive. Murray-Webster and Hillson (2008, p. 5) point out that risk has two sides: uncertainty and consequence. Slovic (2006) refers to the "affect heuristic" of risk, in which the perception of risk is highly intuitive to

the individual and subject to emotion and other affective processes (e.g., how much control you have regarding the risky situation).

- *Fear* refers generally to an unpleasant emotion caused by a belief that danger, pain, or threat might be imminent. Dozier (1998, p. 3) calls fear the quintessential human emotion because no one escapes the experience of fear.

- Defining *stress* is often more difficult than observing or feeling its symptoms. In this text we are talking primarily about psychological stress and define it as a psychological and physical response of the body that occurs whenever we must adapt to a changing or threatening situation. The problem with defining stress involves the complexity of people and their backgrounds, perceptions, skill levels, and other factors. In addition, some researchers distinguish *eustress* (good or helpful stress) from *distress* (bad or harmful stress). A great deal of evidence now exists to indicate connections among perceptions, performance, and stress (Olpin & Hesson, 2007).

MOTIVATIONS IN OAE

Beginning with important works such as Wilfred Noyce's *Springs of Adventure* (1958) and Samuel Klausner's *Why Man Takes Chances* (1968), numerous explanations have arisen addressing the reasons why people engage in activities containing risk and danger within an educational or recreational setting. Theories describing motivations for risk taking in these types of settings include instinctual drive (Noyce, 1958), arousal seeking (Berlyne, 1960), flow experiences (Csikszentmihalyi, 1990; Fave, Bassi, & Massimini, 2003), sensation seeking (Slanger & Rudestam, 1997), and developing a sense of control amidst uncertainty (Lyng, 2005). A growing body of research suggests that level of experience plays an important role in the adventure recreation experience and in motivations for participation (Creyer, Ross, & Evers, 2003; Galloway, 2012; Todd, Anderson, Young, & Anderson, 2002). There has also been discussion regarding differing motives across activities (rock climbing, whitewater paddling, mountaineering, etc.) In addition, gender is considered an important variable of study because research (Estes & Ewert, 1988; Thapa, Confer, & Mendelson, 2004) has found motivational differences between female and male participants.

Not surprisingly, many approaches have been taken to investigate why people engage in both outdoor recreation and, more recently, adventure activities. For example, why does one individual prefer whitewater canoeing while another would rather rock climb? Are the motivations of instructors and leaders similar to those of participants? Does experience level play a role in what motivates individuals to participate in OAE?

Being "close to nature" is often cited in the literature as an important motivating force for participation in OAE. However, as we have seen, setting cannot entirely answer the motivation question, as multiple activities can occur in a common setting. Thus we need to examine motivations from a more comprehensive perspective, including such factors as being with friends or family, developing an image of oneself, and developing outdoor skills. Motivations for participation have also been linked to desired or realized outcomes associated with an activity or experience (Buckley, 2012; Ewert, 1994; Ewert, Gilbertson, Luo, & Voight, 2012).

Related to outcomes, research into motives for participation has also evolved into understanding what benefits an individual is trying to achieve or realize. These benefits might include personal, social, economic, or environmental perspectives. For example, individuals might engage in wilderness backpacking because of the exercise (personal), to do something with friends (social), or because doing so is part of their job (economic).

The benefits-based approach to understanding motivations is linked to the concept of need satisfaction. Manning (2011) suggests that the most widely recognized expression of the concept of need satisfaction is that of Maslow's (1943) hierarchy of needs. Participation (behavior) is a result of a desire to obtain a psychological or sociological outcome. Thus, as Manning suggests, people select and participate in particular types of recreation to meet certain goals or to satisfy certain needs. These goals and needs can be considered satisfactions (or desired outcomes) and can include settings, experiences, and benefits. These levels are hierarchical in the sense that each level becomes more complex and somewhat more abstract than the previous one.

Motivations for engaging in outdoor adventure are clearly diverse. A typical methodology for generating possible motivation factors includes questioning users regarding the importance they place on various motivations and then combining these factors into underlying "dimensions" through factor and cluster analysis techniques. Of additional importance to the generation of various underlying dimensions, or clusters, is the linking of these clusters with user groups and specific activities. As illustrated in table 4.1, different types of activities are often associated with varying motivations, although there are also a number of commonalities in these sets of motivations.

One inherent characteristic separating adventure from more traditional outdoor recreation often lies in the inherency of challenge and risk. That is, people seeking outdoor adventures through recreation are specifically interested in participating in activities that feature risk and potential danger. This danger, as mentioned earlier, can be translated into actual or perceived threats of physical or emotional harm. Though the outdoor recreationalist might occasionally experience similar circumstances, these types of occurrences are usually not deliberately sought out. In addition, the settings of the outdoor

Table 4.1 Motivations Associated With Outdoor Rec and Adventure Activities

Ewert et al., 2012	Ewert et al., 2008	PCOA, 1986	O'Connell, 2010
Adventure activities	Adventure education	Outdoor recreation	Sea kayaking
• Social • Sensation seeking • Self-image	• Challenge and achievement • Personal fulfillment • Social aspects • Image	• Excitement seeking • Escapism • Fitness • Sociability	• Achievement and stimulation • Learning • Escape from personal, physical, or social pressures • Enjoy nature • Be with similar people

adventurer and outdoor recreationalist often differ, with the former seeking out settings such as whitewater and steep cliffs and the latter looking for a lake, quiet stream, or scenic camping spot.

Many studies have examined motivations underlying participation in outdoor activities. For example, Alexandris and Kouthouris (2007) looked at the reasons for alpine skiing and found that motivations for skiing depended on the types of constraints that people experienced (bad weather, expensive equipment, etc.). Focusing on outdoor education, Festeu (2002) identified five motivational categories: to have fun, to meet new friends, to escape daily routine, to enjoy nature, and to explore unknown areas.

Looking more closely at the connection between motivations to participate and adventure activities, some commonalities have begun to emerge. For example, Whisman and Hollenhorst (1998) found that river boaters participated primarily because of the excitement and to test their skills. Similarly, Ewert (1994) found that people climbing Mt. McKinley (Alaska) did so because of the exhilaration, social aspects, image, climbing skill development, and catharsis or escape. The strength of these factors changed depending on level of experience of the individual climber.

Several models have been developed in an effort to conceptualize motivations in the adventure and risk recreation experience (Celsi et al., 1993; Martin & Priest, 1986; Robinson, 1992). Among these is the adventure model (Ewert & Hollenhorst, 1989; Ewert, Shellman, Yoshino, & Gilbertson, 2008; Todd, Anderson, Young, & Anderson, 2002). Ewert, Gilbertson, and Luo (2012) examined the connection between specialization and motivations to pursue adventure activities. Employing both confirmatory factor analysis and logistic regression, four adventure-based activities were examined: rock climbing, whitewater kayaking, canoeing, and sea kayaking. Findings suggested that motivations could be categorized into five basic categories: social, self-confidence, sensation seeking, self-image, and escape. Other significant findings included gender differences, differences across activity types (rock climbers, kayakers, canoeists, and sea kayakers), and differences caused by level of experience.

Moreover, O'Connell (2010) has identified associations between motivations for sea kayaking and ambient temperature, as well as gender and age of participants. Thus it seems increasingly clear that motivations for participating in adventure activities vary based on several factors,

For the one engaged in outdoor adventure pursuits, achievement is often associated with intangible accomplishments.
Courtesy of Scott Schumann.

including experience level and gender, but that they generally involve challenge and excitement, desired personal image (e.g., being seen by others as a mountaineer), and social aspects.

Once again, motivations are based on a number of factors such as activity type, gender, and level of experience with the existing literature revealing similarities and differences across a broad range of adventure activities, people, and settings. For instance, the desire to escape from crowds and everyday routine and to be alone is often expressed as an important consideration for adventure seekers (Ewert, 1985b; Knopf & Lime, 1984). For some adventure seekers, the absence of other people provides a chance to escape something (e.g., a sense of being crowded), whereas for others being alone provides a potential increase in the risk of the activity. Thus solo rock climbers might be engaged in the same activity but for fundamentally different reasons.

Also commonly overlooked, or at least under-considered, is the achievement factor in outdoor recreation. Achievement in this context often means catching a fish, bagging a deer, spotting a bald eagle, and the like. For the individual engaged in outdoor adventure pursuits, achievement is more often associated with less tangible accomplishments, such as climbing a mountain, rafting down a class IV river, or practicing good technique while engaged in these types of activities. Thus while both groups usually report achievement as a motivating factor, achievement for the outdoor adventurer is associated more with the completion of a self-imposed, personal goal than with a tangible outcome. It is the seeking of the less tangible and more implicit goals of outdoor adventure pursuits that often creates confusion and misunderstanding, especially when compared to more traditional forms of outdoor recreation. Of course the same could be said of less traditional forms of outdoor recreation that are also intrinsically motivated but with less tangible goals, such as birding, enjoying the serenity of a setting sun over a lake, or climbing a tree. The difference, once again, becomes one of deliberately accepting risk and challenge, which leads us naturally into a discussion of risk and risk taking.

RISK AND RISK TAKING

The concept of risk has a long history that illustrates how civilization evolved in its thinking about the idea. In Greece, around 140 BC, the term *peirao* was used to convey an attempt at an endeavor, to try to do something, to try one's fortune, or to make an attempt by sea. By AD 109, the Latin term *perîculum* (the root of *peril*) was used to mean "to run the risk of one's life, to get into danger, to release from danger, to do a thing at one's own risk." By 1598, the Italian term *riscare* captured the contemporary meaning most of us ascribe to the term with its definition, "to hazard, to adventure, to jeopardize, to endanger."

Risk is often inherent in adventure activity. This risk can be real or perceived, based on the perceptions (including misperceptions) of the participant and the reality of the situation. In other words, the risk of an activity is often based on participant perception rather than on the actual degree of danger. But for the participant, the perceived risk is *felt* as real, so it can be as significant to stress levels and behavior as real danger is. In fact, because of the increase in stress levels, misperceived risk can sometimes be even more dangerous than real risk, even when the real risk is underestimated.

Fave, Bassi, and Massimini (2003) report that risk taking is essentially an autotelic (personally meaningful) experience that changes as an individual's experience level changes. In the outdoor adventure setting, most risks are attributed to physical risks, such as falling, fast water, or cold temperatures. Some scholars suggest that social risks, such as appearing incompetent to one's group or experiencing conflict or confrontation within the group, are also significant (Carney, 1971). How participants deal with the risks often inherent in adventure activities involves several variables:

- The amount of interest and time necessary to learn the prerequisite skills needed to engage in the activity
- A knowledge of the equipment and other materials needed for the activity
- The elements of instruction and leadership
- The relative need for physical strength and personal abilities

Meier (1977) suggests that "when the terms risk and recreation are combined, most people visualize a broad array of leisure activities which provide exposure to physical danger" (p. 3). Other authors claim that emotional danger is also important in the overall assessment of risk (Mitten, 1992). We are now distinguishing between emotional risk, such as realizing you don't have the level of skill you thought you did, and social risk, such as appearing incompetent to peers. Though somewhat different in nature, for our purposes we will include social risk under the umbrella of emotional risk.

Several general assumptions underlie the use of risk in OAE:

- With very few exceptions, OAE programs do not result in serious injuries. For example, based on accident and incident data, Bird and Germain (1992) developed the accident ratio triangle as a way to estimate injury and accident rates in a variety of fields (figure 4.1). These data suggest that accidents and injuries rarely occur in OAE and when they do they are not serious.

- Risk is often based on the perception of the participant and organization; these perceptions are relative in that they are influenced by variables such as level of experience and skill, age, background, comfort level, and trust. Differing perceptions of risk can lead to situations in which participants believe an activity such as rock climbing is more dangerous than the instructor believes.

- In OAE, appropriate risk-taking activities are often an integral part of the experience, and are included in the curriculum for a purpose. For example, one pur-

pose of OAE is perhaps most elegantly summed up in the idea that youth crave adventure, and if adventure is not made available to them, they will seek it out, sometimes in illegal or immoral ways. Of course recognizing risk and making the decision to cope with it successfully is also part of the maturation process. If we withhold all risk from young participants, we thereby do them a disservice. Thus appropriate risk taking is one part of the adventure experience and can be a powerful tool for the instructor when used judiciously and competently.

In attempting to explain risk seeking, Allen (1980b) developed a conceptual framework of risk in OAE (figure 4.2). Within this model, the antecedents (predispositions), behaviors, and consequences are interlinked so that risk-taking behaviors and potential consequences are easily recognized. Within the antecedents are the components of demographics, personality, experiences, attitudes and values, and self-efficacy. Research findings suggest that the outdoor risk taker is usually relatively young, middle class, and male. As for personality, Allen (1980a) reports that findings are relatively consistent, with risk seekers scoring consistently higher than nonrisk seekers in the areas of confidence (Cober, 1972), need for achievement (O'Connor, 1971), sensation seeking (Zuckerman, 1979), and risk-taking propensity (Allen, 1980b). A note of

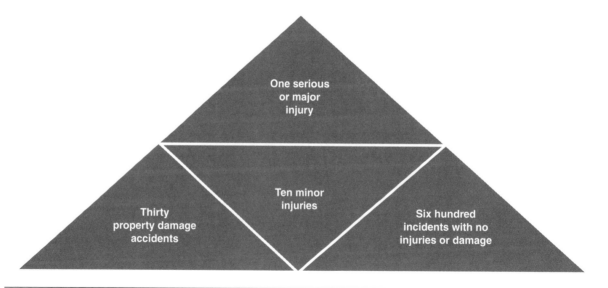

Figure 4.1 Bird and Germain's accident ratio triangle.

From F. Bird and G. Germain, 1992, *Practical loss control leadership* (Loganville, GA: International Loss Control Institute).

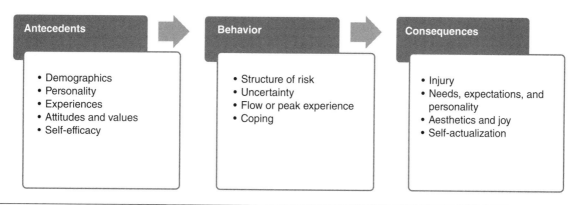

Figure 4.2 Conceptual framework of risk in OAE.

Reprinted, by permission, from S. Allen, 1980, Risk Recreation: A literature review and conceptual model. In *High adventure outdoor pursuits*, edited by J. Meier, T. Morash, and G. Wellon (Salt Lake City, UT: Brighton Publishing), 52-81.

caution, however—it should not be assumed that risk taking in activities such as adventure education is uniform among personality types across populations or that risk taking in one activity automatically leads to risk taking in another. We should also point out that no matter what their personality type, the ability to accurately assess risk level and the consequences of failure is an essential attribute for OAE instructors.

Note that although figure 4.2 presents a linear progression, when linked to benefits, risk is sometimes not a linear function, as shown in figure 4.3. Figure 4.3*a* illustrates a situation in which risk and benefits are linear but inversely related; that is, as risk increases, perceived benefits decrease. In figure 4.3*b*, we see a positive and linear relationship in which, as risk increases, so do the perceived benefits. Conversely, in figure 4.3*c*, we see the benefits increasing with increased risk but only up to a point. Once this point is reached, the potential benefits quickly drop off. It is likely that figure 4.3*c* most accurately represents the reality of the risk-benefits relationship. In any case, OAE instructors should strive to be sensitive to differing thresholds among participants regarding at what point perceived risk overrides potential benefits.

Although the benefits of enhanced self-confidence and need for achievement are self-evident, sensation seeking and risk taking are of particular importance to researchers in adventure education. Sensation seeking as described by Zuckerman (1985) refers to a need for varied, novel, and complex sensations, along with a willingness to take physical and social risks for the sake of the experience. Closely linked to optimal arousal, the concept of sensation seeking is of obvious relevance in outdoor adventure pursuits.

Research indicates that the high-sensation seeker might be less fearful than the low-sensation seeker (Zuckerman, 1979). An interesting theory of sensation seeking has been suggested by Frank Farley (1986), titled the Big T, Little T theory of thrill seeking. Farley suggests that personality can be categorized along a continuum anchored by Big T and Little T types of people. Individuals with a Big T personality deliberately seek thrills and novel sensations. In contrast, Little T personalities seek to avoid risks and overt stimulation. Farley suggests that the Big or Little T personality is partly determined by genetic makeup and early experiences. He explains that Big T personalities can make either a constructive or destructive contribution to society. Constructive Big T personalities usually seek their stimulation through outdoor adventuring or physical risk taking, and may often become scientists, entertainers, or artists. Destructive Big T personalities seek out sensation through antisocial activities such as delinquency and may often become criminals, schemers, or con artists. Although Type T personality research is in its infancy, the concept is not new to OAE. Indeed, most outdoor adventure educators have long recognized that young people will generally seek adventure one way or another.

Thus far it appears that the willingness to take risks is both an inherent aspect of OAE and one often structurally built into adventure activities. Allen (1980a) suggests that risk-taking propensity is strongly related to a preference for uncertainty. This search for uncertainty might result from an innate drive to acquire knowledge about interactions with the environment. Though it would seem reasonable to assume that adventure risk takers would also be risk takers in everyday

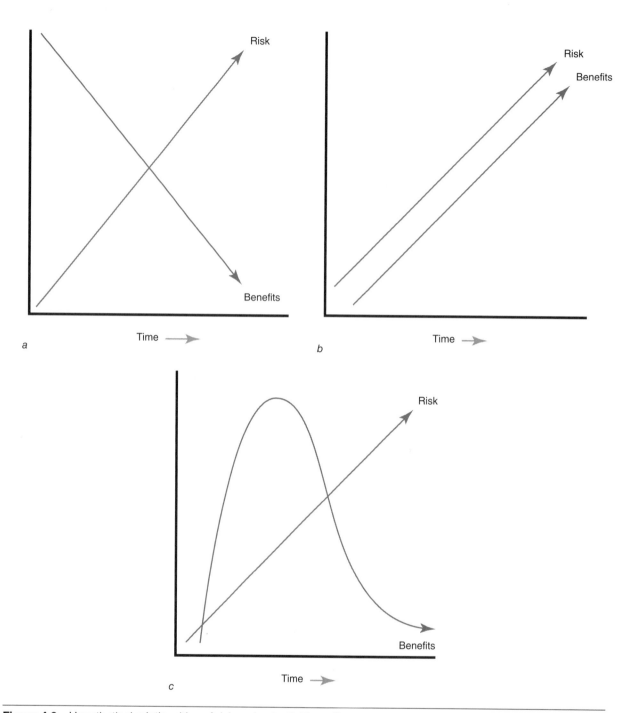

Figure 4.3   Hypothetical relationships of risk and potential benefits.

life, Slovic (1972, 2010) and Zuckerman (1979) suggest this may not always be the case. That is, although an outdoor adventure pursuit such as mountain climbing might seem risky, even foolhardy, to some, the mountaineer will often view it as a highly controllable situation. Carney (1971) describes the propensity of risk taking as "risk hunger" and distinguishes between level I and level II risk taking. This classification is

based on level of fear. Level I risks are described as highly stimulating, often physically dangerous, exciting, and usually very intense but of short duration. Level II risks tend to last longer, have lower intensity, and involve risk to the ego rather than the body.

For example, a level I risk might entail entering a cave environment where the terrain and attendant risks are unknown. From the perspective of the participant, important questions arise regarding what challenges lie ahead and if the situation will be dangerous or threatening. A level II risk might involve an instructor taking a group into an unfamiliar cave in which the instructor knows about the cave features from another source but either does not like cave environments or is unsure about his or her skill level and does not want to show that uncertainty in front of others. Thus while the physical risk involved is relatively small, the emotional risk is larger and longer lasting—that is, the instructor might avoid caving whenever possible. Although outdoor adventure pursuits have traditionally been associated with Carney's level I risk taking, fear in the recreation setting involves both physical and emotional risks, as we will soon discuss.

Lyng (2005) supports the desire for risk taking by arguing that people engage in risk taking through experiences such as OAE primarily as a way to establish personal identity and as an escape from social conditions that provide few opportunities for personal transformation. In addition, research is fairly consistent in demonstrating that perceptions of risk change as an individual becomes more experienced in an activity and acquires a higher sense of competence (Morgan & Stevens, 2008).

Several authors have suggested that individual propensity for risk taking might be influenced by exposure to risk and challenging situations. Some have suggested that individuals take risks in an adventure setting because they have gained enough experience, skill, and experience-use-history (EUH) to create a decreased perception of risk (Demirhan, 2005). Others claim that the propensity for risk taking can be transferred to other life situations (Breivik, 1996; Whitacre, 2011). Once again, like the perception of risk,

risk taking is not static but depends largely on the individual and the situation.

Throughout this section we have presented ideas and information regarding the concepts of risk and risk taking. In large measure, OAE uses risk and appropriate risk taking to achieve program goals and outcomes that are desirable for a majority of OAE participants. The evidence regarding the use of risk also points to several other issues:

- Perceptions and acceptance of risk are rooted in social and cultural factors such as background, family, and friends and are both inherently objective (e.g., a rock fall) and subjective (e.g., going out on that glacier feels risky).

- Both experts and nonexperts are prone to heuristics (mental strategies or beliefs) regarding risk that may or may not be grounded in reality. Moreover, they view different OAE activities as more risky or less risky. See table 4.2 for how people view the risk involved in certain adventure activities.

- A balance exists between the perceived risk in an adventure activity and the perceived level of capability a participant possesses to deal with that activity. OAE instructors should be sensitive to this internal psychological balancing process.

- In assessing risk, experts often use technical information (e.g., the Bird and Germaine triangle shown in figure 4.1), whereas nonexperts tend to use hazard characteristics (how steep, how high, how difficult) to ascertain the danger of a situation.

Table 4.2   Risk Assessment Relative to Outdoor Adventure Activities

Activity	Overall risk	Physical	Psychological	Sociological
Parachuting	6.8	6.4	4.4	4.2
Climbing	6.4	5.9	4.0	3.5
Rafting	5.5	5.5	3.5	2.3
Caving	4.8	4.3	3.4	2.0
Hunting	4.6	4.4	3.2	2.9

Based on a 0-8 scale, with 8 = extreme risk.

Adapted, by permission, from L. Brannan et. al., 1992, "Public perceptions of risk in recreational activities," *Journal of Applied Recreation Research* 17(2): 144-157.

Participants often experience a sequence of changes as they approach, engage, and move past an activity featuring risk (figure 4.4). Referring to figure 4.4, let's look at a rappelling activity. The rope is set up over a cliff, but you are well behind it in a *safety zone*. Participants are beginning to rappel, and your turn is coming; as you move closer to the rope, you experience the *anticipation zone*. It is now your turn to rappel. You get hooked up into the rappel system. Your heart and respiration rates increase as you approach the edge of the cliff for that famous first step—you are in the *risk zone*. Finally, you are on the ground. You unhook from the system and step back to a safe area. You now have time to think about the experience and what it meant to you. You are in the *reflection zone*.

Hand in hand with risk taking are the emotions fear and anxiety. Participants in OAE tend to exhibit a wide range of fear and anxiety levels. In the next section we discuss fear and explore ways of dealing with it.

FEAR IN OAE

Because of the inherent nature of OAE activities, many of which contain perceived or real levels of risk and the presence of fear or anxiety, OAE instructors must become well versed in dealing with participant fear. Fear, in fact, can sometimes be used as a learning tool. That said, using fear in an educational setting poses questions of both function and form, not to mention ethics. OAE

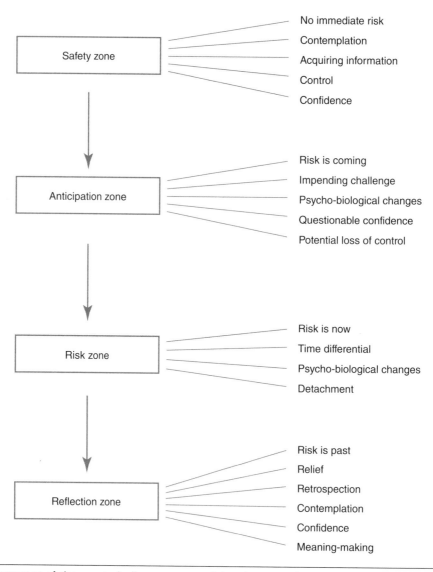

Figure 4.4 A sequence of changes typically occurs as participants approach, engage, and move past a risky activity.

instructors must ask themselves what can be gained by including activities that might be frightening for some participants. If these activities are used because they produce desirable outcomes, how can they be structured to be effective and ethical?

The Concept of Fear

Fear has been with us since humans first walked the Earth. In early times, fear was an essential survival mechanism, helping to protect people from imminent danger. Today, many acute fears such as fear of pain, starvation, or disease have been replaced by a more subtle but sometimes chronic level of unfocused fear that some term as *anxiety*. Many people have varying levels of anxiety over matters ranging from nuclear holocaust to financial disaster. Levitt (1980) reports that "anxiety is the most pervasive psychological phenomenon of our time."

Fear has not totally lost its survival instinct, as it can impel us toward self-improvement and achievement that help us not only to survive but to thrive. A term closely related to fear is stress. Similar to fear, stress can elicit different affective stages in people, including precognition, warning, impact, and recoil. We will discuss stress in greater detail later in the chapter.

One measure of progress in any civilization is the ability to insulate itself from both environmental (e.g., cold, dark, hunger) and societal (e.g., confrontation, alien cultures) fears when the sources of these fears cannot be reduced or eliminated. Societies and individuals have learned to adapt to fearful situations. This adaptation has been considered a hallmark of successful life (Seyle, 1950). Periods of fear and anxiety often proved to be catalysts for significant change. World Wars I and II and the Great Depression are examples of this influence. Paradoxically, as our societal institutions have sought to counteract fear, many of our educational and recreational systems have sought to provide opportunities for people to experience fear, or at least the illusion of fear. Some suggest that using fear and stress in outdoor programs enhances decision making, discipline, and personal awareness (Emerson & Golins, n.d.). Of course an underlying assumption of such thinking is that dealing with fear in an educational or recreational setting will transfer to better handling fearful experiences in other contexts. This transfer has been described in various ways, including freeze-thaw-refreeze (Rhoades,

1972), adaptive dissonance (Walsh & Gollins, 1975), attractive enemies (Kleinman, 1984), and trans-derivational searches (Bacon, 1983). To understand how this transfer works, one must first understand the nature of fear.

We all have firsthand experience in feeling fear. However, feeling fear and being able to define fear operationally are two different things. We know fear through biophysical responses such as sweating palms, rapid heartbeat, and "butterflies" in the stomach. We also know fear through the anticipation of certain experiences or social situations. Fear is both caused by and affects emotions, perceptions, and feelings. This "affectiveness" of fear tends to blunt the sharp measuring instruments of science. Rachman (1974) reports that subjective reports of fear are often quite different from the observed physiologic responses. Studies using written instruments or interviews suggest that people will usually underestimate their courage. Conversely, their behaviors will generally underestimate the fear they have for a particular activity. In other words, participants will be more likely to say they are more fearful than they actually are and engage in activities in which they are more afraid than they appear.

According to Rachman (1978), fear is made up of four components: the subjective experience of fear, associated physiological changes, outward expressions of fear, and attempts to eliminate the source of the fear. A few years earlier, Ratner (1975) proposed four responses to fear: freeze, fight, flee, or feigning death. We have all heard the cliché "frozen with fear," and this sometimes happens in OAE. But other responses occur more often. If OAE instructors are to effectively use activities that might evoke fear in participants, they must be able to recognize the range of responses. Fortunately, despite media reports to the contrary, panic is not a typical group response in most adventure settings (Abraham, 1970; Resnik & Ruben, 1975), just as being paralyzed with fear is not the norm. More likely responses to fear include talkativeness (or, on the flip side, extreme introversion), irritability or increasing hostility, inability to concentrate (flighty behavior), forgetfulness, or detachment (table 4.3). Instructors should also watch for any participant behaviors that appear unusual.

Research on Fear

Fear is one of the most powerful emotions known to both humans and other animals. Although

Table 4.3   Behavior Components of Fear in Outdoor Adventure Activities

Physiological changes	Expressions of fear	Resolutions
Perspiration Increased heart rate Muscle tension Elevated respiration Elevated blood pressure Hypoglycemia Pupil dilation Increased temperature Gastromotility	Talkativeness Irritability Lack of focus Hostility Overly precise Forgetfulness Unusual behavior Pointless activity Seeking reassurance Rationalization for inaction Diminished performance	Participation • Freeze • Flight • Nonparticipation Alternatives Inhibitions

animals are faced primarily with environmental dangers, people face both environmental and social perils. Epstein (1976) has claimed that fears in animals are related to life and limb, but fears in people are primarily linked to threats to ego. Hauck (1975) suggests that the most common types of fear in humans are related to rejection and failure. In contrast, Coble, Selin, and Erickson (2003) found that for women hiking alone, their most prominent fears included getting hurt by another individual, accidental injury, getting lost, wild animals, and theft of belongings left in the car.

Specific to OAE programs, Ewert (1985a) cites an analytic study of outdoor participants that isolated six underlying factors surrounding the concept of fear: lack of control, personal inadequacies, personal skills, homeostasis (state of physiological equilibrium), level of comfort, and program inadequacies (table 4.4). On examining the individual factors, items deemed to be particularly important in terms of causing concern were not getting enough to eat, keeping others from reaching their objectives, not fitting in with the group, and not getting their money's worth from the course. Mean scores suggest that many of the fears expressed by the participants were centered on social and program concerns. Further observation of the data yields that social fears, rather than situational fears, are of greatest concern for most individuals in OAE settings. This finding supports Hauck's (1975) contention that social fears are of paramount importance to individuals in contemporary society. It should be noted, however, that Bixler and colleagues (1994) reached a different conclusion in a study that found snakes, insects, plants, getting lost, and dirt or mud as provoking the most fear.

Abusing the Presence of Fear

Because fear can be such a powerful emotion, the potential for abuse is immense. Imagine, if you will, a first-time rock climber. What might at first appear to be a relatively straightforward situation can be immensely complex if one considers that a variety of fears might be involved. These fears might include obvious ones such as falling, being struck by rock fall, or being injured, or more covert fears such as lack of ability, appearing foolish, or being singled out as the one person who is afraid. No matter what the particular fear involves, the fear can be exacerbated if it does not receive a proper response. One improper response to fear (of many possible ones) is to pay no attention to it, but more likely, the fear will be discounted, as if it can be easily overcome. The cliché, "no problem, you can do it," spoken to someone who truly *has* a problem and doesn't think he or she *can* do it is, to say the least, limited in its effectiveness.

Inciting fear or stress unnecessarily is an example of fear abuse. OAE instructors who lead OAE programs involving risk must have a thorough understanding of when and why fear is useful. A participant's degree of fear must not exceed the stated objectives of the program. If it does, the participant's fear has been abused. In addition, if instructors cannot or do not connect the use of fear with the desired result of the imposed fear, the trust between participants and instructors will be compromised, perhaps to the point of program failure. As previously stated, the social aspect of fear is made up primarily of rejection and failing. To avoid abusing the concept of fear, it is vitally important to separate success or failure and personal self-worth. Establishing this separation is an often-stated protocol within OAE programs, but problems arise when instructors

Table 4.4 Means of Fear Items

Item	Mean (0-5)	Item	Mean (0-5)
Not getting enough to eat	3.53	Being uncomfortable	2.37
Keeping others from reaching objectives	3.31	Imposed beliefs	2.29
Not fitting in with group	3.06	Emergencies	2.28
Bothered by insects	3.04	Becoming physically entrapped	2.26
Not getting money's worth	3.00	Venomous animals	2.06
Falling	2.92	Lack of privacy	2.04
Being isolated	2.88	Forced to interact with group	2.04
Not being recognized by the group	2.86	Tasks too demanding	2.04
Not given enough information	2.76	Not enough strength	1.98
Making wrong decisions	2.75	Insufficient experience	1.98
Lack of sleep	2.74	Sexually harassed	1.86
Instructor being impatient	2.73	Being injured in violent act	1.86
Inadequate clothes	2.73	Poisonous plants	1.67
Inadequately trained	2.67	Constant surprise	1.66
Not being accepted by peers	2.66	Temperature extremes	1.62
Letting myself down	2.63	Sharp edges	1.57
Becoming lost	2.53	Unable to control environment	1.45
Becoming unkempt and dirty	2.49	Darkness	1.24
Confrontation with others	2.41	Deep water	1.22
Becoming bored	2.41	Fast water	0.92

Note: 0 = low importance; 5 = high importance

Reprinted, by permission, from A. Ewert, 1985, Identifying fears in the outdoor environment. In: *Proceedings southeastern recreation research* (Athens, GA. Institute for Behavioral Research: University of Georgia).

fail to recognize the latent self-perceptions of their participants.

Failing at an activity can be devastating for an individual, particularly if he or she is already prone to fear of failure. Merely telling him or her that "it is all right" does not alleviate those feelings of failure or reduce the fear of future failures. According to Bandura's social cognitive theory (1997), verbal persuasion is the least effective way for people to gain information about their ability levels. Rather, instructors should rely on actual performance-based activities to inhibit the failure cycle of one failure creating an attitude that creates more failure, and so on. Abuse can occur when instructors allow a lack of success in an activity to grow into a fear of future failure.

Fear abuse can also develop when a group is allowed to use activity failure as a basis for rejecting a fellow participant. Younger participants are particularly prone to this fear syndrome and will go to great and often dangerous lengths to avoid rejection.

No one will deny that physical danger is involved in many OAE activities; to ignore or discount these dangers would be both foolish and counterproductive. We want participants to foster a healthy respect for the environment and the activities in which they are engaged. Healthy fear is displayed when participants recognize danger but feel they have control over it. Or, if the danger is too great, to back away from the activity or modify it in some way that reduces

Fear in the Backcountry

Ken Gilbertson, PhD—University of Minnesota Duluth

Fear in a backcountry situation seems to follow something like a sine-wave progression. Even though the fear equation is important and useful for an outdoor instructor, it seems that fear and risk cannot be truly understood until participants have had direct experience with them. Fear and risk also seem to be situational. Consider the following scenario, which I have experienced annually with my students for 30 years in the same area: outdoor leadership training in the Theodore Roosevelt National Park in western North Dakota.

My class begins in March with the intention of addressing the cognitive aspects of leadership plus beginning to get familiar with the site by studying maps, field guides, and safety plans. Poisonous snakebites, scorpion stings, and bison charges seem to capture most of the students' attention, whereas steep and slippery terrain, dehydration, sunburn, prickly pear cactus, and poison ivy do not generate much interest. Obviously, these latter items do not elicit the sense of fear or risk taking that the former items do.

On entering the park, students typically see wild horses and bison as well as the steep and unstable terrain even before we reach our first night's camp. At this point, bison and snakes are clearly high on students' minds. Not surprisingly, their first response to a direct threat is often exaggerated. A first encounter with *any* snake informs them how high they can jump in a backpack, though most of the snakes are harmless green racers. The first encounter with a bison is usually a lone bull, frequently a sudden surprise around a blind corner.

Among my students, the first cognitive response to risk and fear is typically casual and complacent—probably because few of them can relate to the dangers and risks they will be encountering. It takes several discussions, but by the end of the first day the more mundane dangers and risks associated with terrain challenges, heat, sunburn, and dehydration are better understood and appreciated. As the course progresses, so many bison and wild horses are encountered that students tend to move to complacency mode around them.

Whatever responses students have to the environment, and of course they tend to vary, the OAE instructor must be in a continual state of communication and attention toward the range of risks encountered in the backcountry until direct experience by the student has developed to an appropriate level of judgment in responding to all risks and fears. Once this has occurred, the students' motivation to explore the environment more deeply is significantly enhanced.

By the end of the seven-day trip, students have developed an adequate experiential base to accurately appreciate and respond to the array of risks within the park and have developed appropriate responses to fearful encounters with various threatening elements. Also by the end of the trip, many students talk about returning. Thus it appears that through risk and appropriate response to fear, OAE participants become motivated to return for more. It might be said that the direct experience of fear and risk becomes a motivation to develop a sense of place, which can be said to be an important if not primary goal in backcountry travel.

the level of risk. Thus, perception of control is of great importance to everyone in OAE; when a participant perceives he or she has lost control of a situation, it is very difficult for education to occur. When an instructor feels like the activity is beyond an acceptable level of control, they should stop or modify the activity.

In OAE programs involving risk, instructors must take extreme care in what they say. What sounds like a joke to one participant might cause extreme anxiety for another. For instance, if when questioned whether the group can make it through a particular activity, the instructor answers something like, "Some of you will and some of you won't," he or she might be creating excitement for some participants (which is probably his or her intention), but such a comment could easily create unnecessary and unhealthy fears in others.

Fear can sometimes be manipulated through the withholding of information, as shown in the following equation:

$F = Pr(Ir{*}Is)P_c$, where

F = fear

Pr = the perceived risk or consequence

Ir = the information required to successfully engage the activity

Is = the information actually supplied to the participant

P_c = perceived competence of the individual

The greater the perceived risk, the greater the felt need for information. In practice, this means that instructors can create feelings of anxiety and fear by failing to supply enough information. Although participants can play a question-and-answer game with the instructor by creating a constant barrage of questions, usually with the hidden purpose of seeking reassurance, instructors need to recognize the tremendous power the information giver has over the information needed. An often-used technique by the instructor is the question reversal, in which the question is turned back to the participant for an answer. If this technique is used tactfully, participants can be made more aware of their own problem-solving abilities. If it is used indiscriminately, instructors can create an aura of unconcern, or worse, discourage participants from coming to them when they are having problems.

Using Fear in the OAE Setting

Although fear is a powerful emotion, and subject to abuse, it can also have tremendous value in the OAE setting. The key to its successful use is in remembering that function follows form. There are two main purposes in using fear: teaching people about themselves, and learning to overcome fear. Any use of the fear paradigm must relate back to one or both of these concepts or the activity might be ethically unsound and programmatically indefensible. Situations open to use of fear-provoking activities include personal testing, self-imagery, stress coping, optimal arousal, sensation seeking, and learning. In any of these situations several considerations must be taken into account.

First, most of the situations just listed, such as personal testing and stress coping, are subject to the Yerkes-Dodson law (Levitt, 1980; Yerkes & Dodson, 1908), which presents a curvilinear relationship between fear and the situation in question (figure 4.5). Simply stated, some fear might be useful in facilitating learning or self-concept, but too much fear can inhibit both learning and performance. Hackman (1970) reports that this inhibition can be affected by three factors: the amount of time available, the complexity of the task, and the consequences of failing to perform the task successfully.

As can be seen, fear might be either a motivating or debilitating influence, depending on the level of intensity. If the activity is designed to be

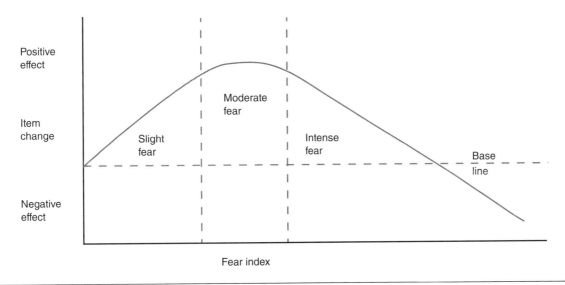

Figure 4.5 Changes in mean scores as a function of level of fear.

From J.R. Hackman, 1970, Tasks and task performance in research on stress. In *Social and psychological factors in stress*, edited by J. McGraph (New York: Holt Rinehart & Winston), 202-237.

generative, in that it will promote transferable positive behaviors or attitudes, fear can be useful.

OAE instructors should strive to understand the probable mechanisms through which fear is overcome and coped with by participants. Fear stimuli can be generalized into four categories: intensity, novelty, specific situational factors (darkness, cold, etc.), and social interaction (Gray, 1974). The individual's perception of fear is acquired through direct experience, instinct, or various methods, such as being told not to do something because something frightening might happen.

This state of mind manifests itself in a series of physical reactions, including increased heartbeat and respiration. This physical state creates a desire in the individual to do something to alleviate the fear. If its source cannot be removed, the fear creates behavior change or adaptation. For instructors to provide opportunities for participants to overcome fear, the construct must be approached from all four of these states.

In addition, Rachman (1974) suggests four techniques for modifying fear: systematic desensitization, flooding, modeling, and rehearsal. *Systematic desensitization* involves a gradual exposure to the fearful situation in which individuals attempt to modify not only their cognitive and emotional reactions but also their physical responses. OAE instructors often unknowingly use this technique when suggesting that a frightened participant relax, slow down, and take it easy. Results are not always positive because the approach can be used too abruptly. To be effective, participants must be allowed to approach the situation gradually, forming positive coping mechanisms as they proceed. *Flooding* involves a prolonged exposure to a fearful situation, usu-

ally used in connection with combat or disaster settings. OAE instructors might occasionally use flooding in a programmatic situation in which participants are constantly exposed to fear. In this setting, great care must be used in providing coping mechanisms. Without these mechanisms, participants' performances and attention to safety can drop radically. Several studies have indicated that prolonged stress and fear can have debilitating effects on individual performance (Powell & Verner, 1982).

Related to the previous two techniques, *modeling* involves the transmitting of new coping behaviors that lead to the development of new adaptive behaviors. Though modeling can present participants with new cognitive perceptions, the fourth fear-modification technique, *rehearsal*, provides participants with the direct experience necessary for effective learning. OAE instructors must show participants useful procedures to cope with fear and provide opportunities to practice these techniques. The most effective method of dealing with fear is not to isolate the modification techniques but to combine them into logical formats geared to the outdoor setting; table 4.5 illustrates these techniques.

Fear can play an important role in the OAE setting. The participant who has overcome a particular fear or learned personally meaningful information through a fear-provoking activity has had a valuable educational experience. The OAE instructor has the responsibility of providing opportunities for this type of personal growth and of monitoring the participant and activity to prevent a fearful situation that can inhibit learning. Although intuition can play an important role in this process, the efficacy of the program can be enhanced if fear theories and protocol are

Table 4.5 Fear-Modification Techniques

Techniques	Description	Comments
Systematic desensitization	Gradual exposure to source of fear	Effective but time consuming
Flooding	Prolonged exposure to fear	Can be debilitating
Modeling	Demonstrating new coping techniques	Powerful but demands instructor knowledge and expertise
Rehearsal	Practice new adaptive behaviors	Very useful but requires planning and can be time consuming

understood. Fear has been with mankind since our beginning, and our physical and sociopsychological makeup are wired for coping with fear. Only recently has civilization replaced short-term, intermittent fears with a more omnipresent anxiety. OAE programs and experiences can be effective in helping individuals deal with the characteristics of both fear and stress.

STRESS IN OAE

Several years ago one of the authors heard an OAE instructor mention that she taught a successful course because "there was enough stress in it." Although the instructor probably meant that the participants had a challenging and exciting course, her statement suggested that stress-inducing activities provided for beneficial outcomes for participants. As we mentioned in the previous section on fear, stress can be understood as a condition that arouses anxiety or fear, along with other psychological and physical symptoms. The cause of this anxiety or fear is an individual's appraisal that a particular demand is beyond his or her capabilities or threatening to his or her well-being. Like fear, stress can elicit different affective stages in people, including precognition, warning, impact, and recoil. For example, an individual might identify a situation that will be stressful (precognition), such as a change in cloud formation, or be made aware of new or changing information that indicates a potential problem and is increasing the feeling of stress (heavy rain starts to fall). The situation might change both drastically and rapidly, such as a river rising and increasing its flow rate (impact). Finally, the individual is faced with a set of circumstances that might have consequential outcomes, be time dependent, or involve complex decision making, all of which afterward lead to a feeling of exhaustion and fatigue (recoil). As a concept, however, stress is multidimensional and not always subject to easy manipulation or control. For example, stress-inducing events, often termed "stressors," might consist of changes that are cataclysmic and affect large numbers of people (e.g., earthquake, war); changes that affect only one or a few people (e.g., death of a loved one, illness); or less dramatic changes that are ongoing, often called daily hassles (e.g., pack is too heavy) (Lazarus & Cohen, 1977; Lazarus & Folkman, 1984).

To further complicate the concept of stress, stressors can also be classified into acute, time-pressure stressors, such as an avalanche, rock fall, or missing participant; sequenced stressors, such as an ongoing disagreement with another instructor about how an OAE course should be conducted; and chronic or long-term stressors, such as ongoing job stress or a permanent disability.

Not surprisingly, we see a broad variety of stressors in OAE, ranging from frozen or wet boots to issues related to post-traumatic stress disorder (PTSD). In the case of PTSD, Schiraldi (2000) suggests that OAE, or what he calls action-based programs, can create favorable outcomes because OAE can create physical arousal through activities that are surrounded by positive feelings, a safe emotional climate, and a facilitated atmosphere. This is very much in line with the concept of *eustress*, as proposed by Seyle (1950; 1978), which implies a good stress (Cherry, 1978). Eustress, however, has not gained much viability in contemporary psychology, where stress is generally considered a negative event; that is, all stress, from any source and of any duration, is considered detrimental to health (Doublet, 2000).

Herein lies the conundrum for OAE—namely, do we risk exposing our participants to stress-producing experiences that can be debilitating even while our intention is for the experiences to be growth enhancing (Templin, n.d.)? Most of us in OAE strongly believe that OAE offers beneficial experiences, but can we deny that our programs do not do occasional inadvertent harm as well? Clearly, OAE providers should always consider the risk of causing harm when they design and implement programs and experiences.

As shown in figure 4.6, after an initial assessment of a situation, people will experience stress if the demands appear greater than their skills or abilities. However, with appropriate training and protective skills, the stress can be successfully navigated. The goal of OAE programs should not be to expose our participants to stress but rather to give them tools with which they can counteract this stress, both in the present and in the future. Thus, within the context of stress, OAE programs should do the following:

- Focus on training the participant to develop an effective stress-buffer system, or "coping competence" (Schroder, 2004).

- Use the small-group atmosphere often present in OAE to promote an emotional support system that focuses on current and potential situations that act as stressors.

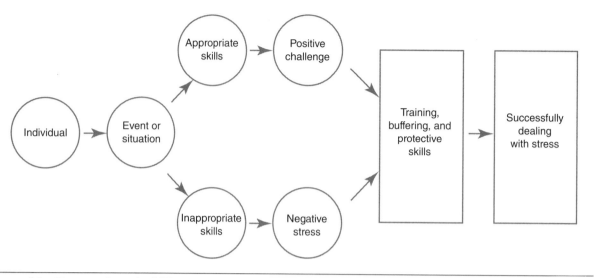

Figure 4.6 Stress pathway in OAE.

- Design the OAE experience to take advantage of down time or leisure moments to allow for a sense of relaxation and restoration (Iwasaki, 2006).
- Use the feelings of achievement, accomplishment, and success to strengthen a sense of resilience and empowerment that, in turn, will help develop participants' stress buffers and protective barriers to stress.
- Use the power and beauty of the natural environment, physical activity, and camaraderie to build the stress buffer.

SUMMARY

This chapter has focused on four important variables to consider when designing and implementing OAE programs and experiences. These four variables are motivation, risk and risk taking, fear, and stress. Though there are many variables to consider in OAE, these four were selected for four primary reasons: They are typically present in most OAE experiences; they can, to an extent, be accounted for in the design and application phases of OAE; they typically interweave with one another; and they are issues that OAE instructors should always consider as they seek to provide high-quality OAE experiences.

What does the evidence tell us regarding these four variables? First, motivations for participation in OAE seem to hinge on issues such as challenge and a sense of achievement; sensation seeking; social components, such as meeting new people or working together as a team; self-image; and escape from everyday life activities. In addition, we now know that risk and risk taking are not simple constructs but involve a broad array of psychological and physical parameters including physical skills, past experience and background, normative values held by friends and companions, perceptions of consequences, and level of uncertainty. Fear and stress influence OAE participants in a number of ways and often present a broad array of physically observable symptoms. We have discussed how fear and stress can be both observed and ameliorated, but a need for broader discussion in the OAE field remains—namely, to what extent should fear and stress be used in OAE settings? Though they might allow for several positive outcomes and benefits, fear and stress has the potential to be abused. OAE designers and instructors must only use stress and fear in programs when they are confident that the positive outcomes of this stress or fear far outweigh the possible harm that might be done. Likewise, they should cease using fear and stress when they recognize this stress or fear is serving as a debilitating factor with their students.

Finally, all four of these variables—motivation, risk and risk taking, fear, and stress—present the OAE researcher with constructs that are powerful and influential. All four variables present important opportunities for continued research and subsequent refinements in the design and implementation phases of OAE programs.

Issues for Further Discussion

1. Although motivation, dealing with risk, fear, and stress are often part of many OAE experiences, all these concepts are partly affected by the demographics of an individual program. How and in what ways should OAE instructors consider the demographics of their groups when designing and implementing a program? How should age, gender, and other background variables influence how a course or program is conducted?

2. We have proposed in this chapter that risk and risk taking are often integral to the OAE experience. After all, most definitions of adventure include an element of uncertainty or risk. Yet recent research efforts on motivation for participating in OAE have found that risk is a very low motivator for participation. This being the case, what role should risk play in OAE experiences?

3. Given the prevalence of risk in everyday life (Kanters, Bristol, & Attarian, 2002), what are some activities and processes that OAE programs could employ to deal with everyday risk?

4. What is the rationale for OAE programs to offer experiences in which participants are exposed to risk, danger, fear, or stress? Can these types of experiences be justified within the context of education? How so?

PART

II

THEORY

■ ■ ■ ■ ■ ■ ■ ■ ■ ■

Experience without theory is blind,
but theory without experience
is mere intellectual play.

—Immanuel Kant

In part II we explore the importance of theory in the OAE field. In considering Kant's quote, when one examines the theories and constructs used in OAE, two observations immediately appear. First, far from being an academic or intellectual exercise, OAE deals with real people in real situations and, as such, mandates that any theories used in the design or implementation of OAE activities be grounded in experience and reality. For example, Bandura's social cognitive theory suggests that direct experience is often the most effective way of learning about one's abilities and competencies. Within the OAE setting, however, the instructor is often faced with developing a positive experience for participants who might have low levels of skill or ability.

The second observation involves the limited number of theories that are specific to OAE. Most of our theories and theoretical propositions are borrowed from other fields, such as psychology, sociology, and education. Although often useful, this borrowing frequently leads to OAE situations and concerns being "fit" into a theory, which does not always account for various OAE implementations and values. Thus, as you read through the chapters in part II, keep in mind how the theories discussed are typically linked to actual practice (implementation) and program design.

Beginning with chapter 5, Theoretical Constructs Used in OAE, we discuss the various definitions of theories and models and explore their importance to the OAE field. Far from being simply an academic exercise, we follow Kurt Lewin's lead that "There is nothing more

useful than a good theory" and suggest that these theories and models can be critically useful in helping provide clarity and organization as we view such variables as participants' attributions (e.g., personal skill or luck) in OAE outcomes.

In chapter 6, Extant Theories and Key Constructs in Outdoor Adventure Education we discuss several theories commonly associated with OAE experiences, including expectancy value theory, social cognitive theory, and the theory of planned behavior. These and other theories presented in this chapter were selected on the basis of their widespread applicability in OAE.

Because of the emphasis on developing educative experiences that are focused on participant-centered learning, in chapter 7, Development Across the Life Span, we discuss a number of theories related to various stages of development. For example, what are the theoretical underpinnings relative to OAE programs dealing with young people compared to those developed for older adults?

Inherent in all three chapters in part II is the issue of application. We are always exploring the question, How can knowing something about theories that are applicable to a particular participant group help OAE instructors design and implement high-quality experiences? Finally, we put forward the idea that understanding the basics of the theories presented in these chapters can help provide a framework that might be useful in answering the question, How does this work?

Theoretical Constructs Used in Outdoor Adventure Education

Why This Chapter Is Important

Kurt Lewin's claim that nothing is more useful than a good theory applies within OAE. Theory underlies much of what we do in OAE program design and implementation. For example, many OAE programs promote individual growth and development based on theories concerning attribution and self-determination. A clear understanding of the connection between programs and their theoretical bases supplies an additional resource to OAE providers as they consider their programs' curriculums. Of course the goal is to develop and provide experiences that best meet the needs and goals of their participants and organization.

Models provide OAE planners with tools for developing targeted learning experiences. As we discuss in this chapter, one of the most widely emulated models in OAE is the Outward Bound process model developed by Victor Walsh and Gerry Golins in 1976. For many, if not most, OAE programs this process model guides the planner in both the design phase of the program and in the explanation of how the program works. Both theories and models, then, play an important, though often hidden, role in the development and implementation of OAE programs.

Learning Outcomes

After completing this chapter, you should be able to

* distinguish theories from models and provide an example of each;
* describe the accumulative role of research;
* explain how symbols, assumptions, and relationships fit together within a theoretical framework to provide a viable explanation of a phenomenon; and
* propose a new theory or model relevant to OAE based on the information discussed in this chapter.

ow do we know the world? How do we get a sense of cause and effect and discern what is real from what is illusion? Most of us rely heavily on intuition, observation, and trial and error to guide us through the world. Of course we also learn through secondary sources, including various forms of media provided by others. Researchers and evaluators, however, tend to be more scientific than the rest of us; they pose questions that are typically answered through systematic inquiry and testing (Bickman & Rog, 2009).

THEORY AND MODEL DEVELOPMENT

Systematic inquiry and testing often involves the use of theories and theoretical models, which aid both scholars and practitioners in their quests to understand, predict, and influence their specific areas of study. Whereas *theories* can be considered a collection of explanatory statements about observed and inferred relationships among variables (Neuman, 2007), *models* can be considered depictions or analogies that provide descriptive patterns. As Kraus and Allen (1998) have written, "A model is a theoretical abstraction or depiction of a given process or set of relationships," (p. 31) often in the form of a graphic or equation.

Of course the purpose of science is to predict and explain, and this requires the development of

explanatory theories and models. In turn, theories and models rely on the use of research questions and attendant hypotheses to investigate relationships among various factors and variables. On testing these hypotheses, the findings are used to support, refute, or redesign the original theories and models. DiRenzo (1967) suggests that the maturity of a science is reflected in the accumulation of its theory. This accumulative role of research is illustrated in figure 5.1.

With respect to OAE, the systematic development and inquiry into applicable models and theories has had a relatively short history. Nevertheless, there are a variety of theories and models that can be used to describe and characterize the adventure education experience. We will look at some of these soon, following a closer examination of the nature of theory.

DISSECTING THE CONCEPT OF THEORY

As we have noted, theory is defined as a collection of explanatory statements about observed and inferred relationships among variables, so it is not surprising that theories are often constructed around concepts, assumptions, and relationships. Let's discuss these three components a bit further. *Concepts* are the elements or components of a theory (Kane & Trochim, 2009, p. 436) that are typically based on something factual, such as

Purpose of science is the development of concepts, models, and theories

Theory is a systematic accounting of the relationships among a set of variables

Research questions, state a situation needing inquiry, discuss, and come to a solution

Hypotheses are conjectural statements about the relationship between two or more variables

Figure 5.1 The accumulative role of research.

number of people engaged in an adventure activity. In this case, participation can be considered a concept. On the other hand, when an object is hypothetical or inferential, it is considered a *construct*. For example, motivations underlying participation in OAE could be considered a construct. To avoid confusion, in this book we will generally use the term concept rather than construct. Both concepts and constructs, however, have two parts: a symbol (word or term) and an operational goal. For example, in OAE, empowerment is both a theoretical concept and an operational goal or desired outcome. That is, we often want our participants to develop greater levels of empowerment, but from a research perspective, we also need to know what we mean by that term. For instance, many OAE programs want participants to feel more empowered to make changes in their lives following participation in a program. Do these changes imply greater levels of confidence, a heightened sense of self-efficacy, or simply a willingness to try different things? These would be important distinctions if one were interested in either defining the operational goals of a program or garnering evidence that a particular program is effective in achieving these operational goals.

In the development of a theory, researchers commonly rely on initial *assumptions*, which can be defined as statements about the nature of a phenomenon that is presumed to be true, if only temporarily (Vogt, 1993). For example, two related assumptions made in OAE are that participation in a program will lead to benefits, and that these benefits will last beyond the OAE program. Wolfe and Samdahl (2005) point out that these common assumptions are not always borne out in subsequent research and evaluation studies.

Another component of theory, serving to link various concepts and underlying assumptions, is that of *relationships*, or how strongly concepts are connected to each other. For example, we know that self-concept and a sense of achievement are closely related, particularly if this sense of achievement is a result of a participant's personal initiative or skills. Thus theories can inform us on whether, and in what way, various concepts are related to one another and how strong that relationship is.

When researchers test or study a particular relationship between two or more concepts (or variables) they often use an *hypothesis*. If additional studies provide data that support the

hypothesis, the idea might then be treated as a *proposition*. Propositions tend to be developed over time, and researchers tend to have more confidence in propositions than they do in hypotheses (Neuman, 2007). An hypothesis might be that students who participate in a freshman wilderness experience program (FWEP) will have higher levels of self-efficacy in college after participating in the program (Hinton, Twilley, & Mittelstaedt, 2006). If this hypothesis is supported by subsequent studies, it might become a proposition: FWEPs are effective in enhancing levels of college self-efficacy.

Theories often operate at various ranges and levels. Range of theory can include empirical generalizations, middle-range theory, and theoretical frameworks. For example, one empirical generalization in the OAE field is that more males than females participate in high-risk adventure activities. Thus the empirical generalization refers to a pattern concerning two or more easily seen concepts (e.g., gender and level of participation). Middle-range theories are more abstract than empirical generalizations and focus on a specific and substantive topic. For example, both research and theory support the idea that empowering participants is important to their learning and development; this premise forms the foundation of a middle-range theory in OAE. Theoretical frameworks are also known as paradigms, or a general orientation or way of seeing its subject matter. Three examples of theoretical frameworks in OAE are presented in table 5.1.

Levels of theory involve the extent to which the theory is relevant. Theories that primarily deal with small time frames or numbers of people, such as an individual adventure course, are usually considered *microlevel* theories. For instance, OAE instructors may theorize that all participants in a certain course are there to learn to climb and care little about social or group-related outcomes. Theories that deal with larger groups or have a broader level of impact than microlevel theories are termed *mesolevel* theories. The previous example of college students who participated in a freshman wilderness program is an example of a mesolevel theory. Finally, *macrolevel* theories deal with larger groups or institutions. That OAE is effective in increasing self-efficacy in young people is an example of a macrolevel theory. Theory at this level applies across a wider range of participant groups (e.g., ages, motives, background) and contexts (e.g., wilderness orientations, adventure therapy programs, mountaineering courses).

Table 5.1   Selected Theoretical Frameworks in Outdoor Adventure Education

Theoretical framework	Description
Expectancy value theory	Human interactions are constructed around give and receive resources (social approval, personal approval, or material). People engage in adventure activities because they expect to get something from them that they want.
Social cognitive theory	A person, his or her behavior, and the environment are each determined, in part, by the other two. How an OAE program participant will behave is a function of both the individual and the context.
Theory of planned behavior	Behaviors follow from the combined influence of a person's intention to perform a behavior and the behavioral control (ability to actually perform the behavior). Even intended behaviors cannot be realized without the ability to perform them.

OAE programs typically focus on microlevel theories in their individual operations and only sometimes consider macrolevel theories in the broader applications of OAE to society. For example, many programs use the direct experience aspect of self-efficacy theory as a powerful way for participants to learn about their personal abilities and strengths. Similarly, the OAE field tends to adhere (often without realizing it) to the unfreezing-change-refreeze macrolevel theory of personal change originally advocated by Lewin (1951).

Finally, the primary purpose of a theory is to explain. This explanation comes in three forms: causal, interpretive, and structural. *Causal* explanation is the most widely recognized and is concerned with cause and effect. For example, did the OAE experience cause the change in the participant? An affirmative answer to such a question requires four conditions:

1. Temporal order—the cause must come before the effect.

2. Association—two or more phenomena must occur together in a systematic or patterned way.

3. Elimination of plausible alternatives— no other reasonable explanations can explain the outcome.

4. The causal relationship makes sense within a broader theoretical framework.

Consider a participant who takes part in an OAE course on leadership skills. Immediately following the course, the participant becomes involved in a leadership position in her community. Did the OAE experience cause the participant to take the position? The answer is probably, but many other variables might have also come into

play; see Ewert & Sibthorp (2009) for a discussion on confounding variables.

An *interpretive* explanation within theory provides a more subjective account of a situation or set of circumstances. For example, advocates of OAE typically believe that OAE programs create opportunities for beneficial change in participants. A number of theories—attribution theory, self-determination theory, self-efficacy theory—might explain how the OAE experience has created this beneficial change. Which theory you choose might depend in part on your interpretation of the changes, or on the values that guide your perspective. Thus, your interpretation of why and how something happens in an OAE program would greatly influence the theory.

Theories that provide a *structural* function serve to provide a mosaic of where a particular observation, or even theory, fits into a broader framework. For example, an explanation of an outcome of a particular OAE experience from a structural perspective would consider many of the characteristics and variables that might influence that outcome. That is, what are the various components that make up the structure of this experience and that contribute to the outcome? From a theoretical perspective, these components might include the personality of the individual, instructor capabilities, external influences such as weather or course activities, and how the curriculum was designed and implemented. When considered together, the causal, interpretive, and structural forms of explanation provide a more holistic approach to understanding OAE outcomes and impacts.

Now that we have discussed the components that make up a theory, in the next section we turn our attention to models and examine some examples of models used in OAE.

MODELS IN OUTDOOR ADVENTURE EDUCATION

As previously stated, models serve as a theoretical abstraction or depiction of a specific relationship or process (Kraus & Allen, 1998). Developing and testing models can result in powerful insights toward explaining or predicting a particular phenomenon. Although the terms "models" and "theories" are often used interchangeably, they typically represent different constructs. Theories tend to be propositional or abstract, whereas models are often used in more operational terms. In addition, models might be process or theoretical. Process models typically depict the sequence of events that takes place, whereas theoretical models tend to reflect what was realized from, say, participation in an OAE program and how components fit together to achieve the end result.

Process Models

As an example of a process model, consider figure 5.2, in which adventure activities and behavior are sequenced along a chronological continuum. That is, individuals are introduced to an adventure activity, in part, because of its novelty. If

they continue to participate in the activity, they may alter the activity in ways that require more skills or raise the standards. As can be seen in the figure, if participation continues, rewards move from being essentially intrinsic to being more extrinsic. For example, a person engaged in adventure recreation may move from going to different places and adventuring with a variety of people to a situation where the adventure activity becomes his or her job or profession. Or, the person engages in the activity for competition and winning awards. Thus, and as illustrated in figure 5.2, a typical sequence of behaviors and actions on the part of the adventure recreationist is to move from more intrinsic to extrinsic rewards as they gain experience, skill, and competence in the activity.

As shown in figure 5.2, adventure recreation often follows a sequential process that begins with an introduction to an activity, such as rock climbing. As a participant gains in skill and experience, he or she generally seeks out more difficult climbs and includes what we call artificial constraints. In rock climbing, artificial constraints might be to stay on route, avoid driving in pitons, or lead climbing instead of always top-roping. The participant might also engage in rock climbing in different settings or with different people, or

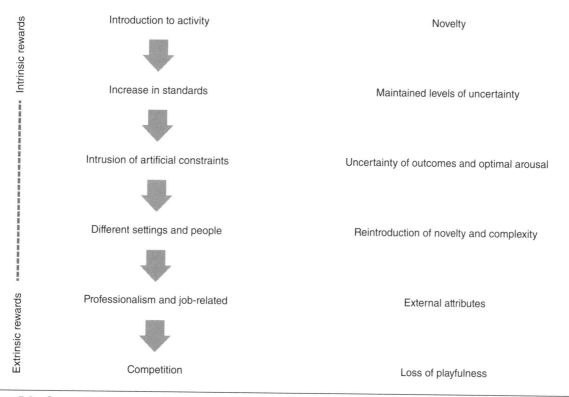

Figure 5.2 Sequential process of adventure recreation.

What's in a Theory?

Karla Henderson, PhD—North Carolina State University

Theory is the basis for all research regardless of the topic. Unfortunately, theory sometimes gets a bad rap when it is dichotomized as theory versus practice. Further, when I teach research methods class and tell my students they need to have a theoretical foundation for their work, they sometimes struggle. One frustrated student joked one day, "Isn't there a website I can go to, like Ineedatheory.com?" But theory need not be an evil or a mystery to anyone when it is understood related to its importance and purpose.

Theory's different connotations somewhat depend on discipline as well as culture. A traditional sociological view of theory, for example, might be described as "pure idea uncontaminated by mundane facts." But the way scholars in North America tend to define theory is as "a systematic explanation of recurrent phenomena based on evidence (i.e., data or facts)." Most agree that theory gives insight into what might be or has been observed, and provides a systematic explanation for describing data and interpreting behaviors. Although postmodernists adamantly insist that no one theory can exist related to a topic, some means must exist to explain events and occurrences. Regardless of one's philosophical stance, theory is contextual, dynamic, and ever evolving. The process of research should create the body of knowledge that professionals need to build theories; theories should then be used to promote quality of life and best practices.

Sometimes fields such as OAE or recreation services are criticized as atheoretical. "Practice trumps theory," some critics say. But I think a problem exists when theory and practice are viewed as dichotomous. For research to be useful in OAE, it must address theory and practice together. When theory is defined most broadly, it can range from formal scientific explanations of facts to explanations used by individuals to account for their own personal experiences.

Some scholars talk about the notions of public and private theories, which corroborate how theory is ubiquitous in both research and practice. Common sense is the basis for private or personal theory; data are the basis for public theory. Most people have theories related to how they live their lives whether they express them as theories or not. Further, data can be collected based on no apparent theoretical foundation because implicitly personal theory underlies everything that humans undertake. Differences between public and private theories seem to lie in the nature, soundness, and source of people's experiences whether related to previous research or to individual interpretations of experiences. Further, practice often is an expression of personal theory, which can be referred to as reflective practice. OAE practitioners might have personal theories about their work, but the language of practitioners might not always fit with the researchers' explanations of behavior through public theories. Thus the value of theory in OAE lies in wedding the roles and use of public and personal theories.

Nothing is permanent in society; knowledge is always limited, and change is continually occurring. Further, beliefs about theory are constantly evolving. Both practitioners and researchers seek to explain empirical data as well as experiential behaviors. Theory can lead to new answers to persistent questions regardless of how private or public explanations are employed. Further, no theory is total and absolute. The future of a field such as OAE will necessitate continually assessing change as well as constancies through theory as an instinctual process of explanation. Research is about developing ideas rather than completing explanations, and theory enables the asking of questions as well as improving the quality of experiences for all individuals.

---

if skill and confidence levels are high (and accurate) enough, he or she might try solo climbing. For some, rock climbing can lead to a profession, such as a guide. Moreover, in the case of many adventure-based activities, such as rock climbing, organizations like the American Mountain Guides Association (AMGA) provide certification for different levels of skill and expertise. A few rare rock climbers develop enough skill and expertise that they take part in rock climbing competitions throughout the world.

In figure 5.2, the right column indicates a personally felt or psychologically based reason for following the sequence. For example, as participants gain skill, they need to try more difficult climbs to continue to test themselves. Likewise, changing setting adds a degree of novelty and possibly complexity. Similar to what we saw in chapter 4 regarding risk and motivation, this sequential process demonstrates that motivations and behaviors associated with OAE activities are typically not static but change over time and within individuals.

In the next section, we progress from how the process of change proceeds from an individual's perspective (e.g., figure 5.2) to occurring within a broader OAE perspective.

One of the most widely ascribed process models in OAE is the Outward Bound process model (OBPM), first conceptualized by Walsh and Golins (1976). The OBPM has served as the basis for designing programs for literally hundreds of adventure programs and, not surprisingly, has been the subject of many research efforts (McKenzie, 2003; Sibthorp, 2003). In part, the OBPM is such a widely emulated model because it provides program designers with a concise set of program goals and structure. As shown in figure 5.3, the OBPM combines the variables of learner, physical environment, social environment, tasks, individual changes, and desirable end product.

Each component represents a different programmatic issue and set of opportunities. For example, the *learner* is an individual who brings in a set of experiences, past history, expectations, and a readiness to learn or undergo different experiences. In part, these different experiences are epitomized by a *unique physical environment* that is stimulating, novel, and presents natural consequences (e.g., if you don't set the shelter up properly, you might get wet). In addition to the unique physical environment is a *unique social environment* typically consisting of a small group of relative strangers placed together within a small-group context and faced with a set of increasingly more complex tasks that necessitate both individual commitment and working together as a team. These *problem-solving tasks* are typically prescriptive (i.e., a part of the program), incremental (i.e., they build on one another), and are progressive (i.e, they become

Figure 5.3   Outward Bound process model.
Adapted from Outward Bound.

more difficult and complex, often involving factors not easily controlled by the participants or staff, such as the weather). Engaging in these problem-solving tasks often precipitates a sense of *adaptive dissonance* (i.e., finding ways to deal with uncertainty and discomfort) which, if successful, leads to a *sense of mastery and competence*. In turn, this mastery and competence helps the individual *reorganize the meaning and direction* of his or her learning (e.g., if I can climb that mountain, maybe I can achieve other goals and aspirations). The instructor serves as an important catalyst in this process, not only directing the activities but facilitating, translating, and mentoring throughout the experience.

From this process, the instructor (or program designer) can alter the activities and tasks, the physical environment, and the social environment to achieve specific goals and outcomes. These goals and outcomes can also be realized through implementation adjustments such as types of facilitation, experience or activity processing, activity sequencing, transfer exercises, and helping participants develop their own meanings from the experience.

Ewert and Voight (2007) have developed a process model for OAE based on stages of a course. The adventure-based experience and personal change (AEPC) model features five stages that are linked to distinguishable times typically seen in an OAE course, such as precourse, start of course, in-course, and course closing. The five stages are self-determination, placement and commitment, task–activity, planning and change-out, and change and maintenance. The model is loosely based on the transtheoretical model of behavior change as proposed by Prochaska, DiClemente, and Norcross (1992). Figure 5.4 illustrates this model and the accompanying attributes associated with each stage. As can be seen, this process model is based on the assumption that participation in an OAE program is strongly linked to emotion, affect, and social cognitive variables (Armitage & Conner, 2000; Ulrich, 1983; Zajonc, 1980). Thus, while the OBPM focuses on the sequence of course components that lead to participant outcomes, the AEPC model is designed to identify attributes that an individual is experiencing at each stage of an adventure course.

Theoretical Models

As stated earlier, theoretical models generally seek to provide an understanding of how something occurs; by their very nature, they are typically more abstract and comprehensive than process models are. They are also more useful in developing an understanding as to *how* something works and how to predict future outcomes using the model. Underlying many theoretical models are connections to constructs or theoretical frameworks. For example, figure 5.5 illustrates Robinson's (1992) risk recreation model. Here certain individuals are attracted to risk (as exemplified in the types of risk taken in adventure activities such as mountaineering, rock climbing, and whitewater boating). Following this attraction, an individual makes a cognitive appraisal of the risk (e.g., what knowledge and skill do I have? how much risk is there? what do I think the outcome will be?). The individual makes a decision whether to engage, disengage, or modify engagement. Following this engagement, he or she reflects and appraises the experience with the outcome being to continue engagement in similar-risk activities and a new awareness of self.

Some models are developed around theoretical frameworks. Two examples seen frequently in the OAE literature are the adventure experience paradigm (Priest, 1999) and the outdoor adventure recreation model (Ewert & Hollenhorst, 1989). The adventure experience paradigm is strongly linked to the concept of flow, as first described by Csikszentmihalyi (1975). The concept of flow involves the relationship between the level of skill a person has in a particular activity and the demands of that activity placed on the person. When skills match demands, the person might enter a state of flow. When skills exceed demands, the person might experience boredom (see chapter 6 for additional discussion of flow). When demands exceed skills, the person might experience fear or anxiety. The adventure experience paradigm (figure 5.6) imitates the flow model by comparing an individual's level of competence with the level of risk associated with an activity. If competence sufficiently matches level of risk, an individual will probably experience *exploration and experimentation, adventure,* or a *peak adventure.* But if the level of risk exceeds the level of competence, he or she might experience a *misadventure* or *devastation and disaster.* As Priest (1999) points out, the adventure experience paradigm can be useful in matching the level of uncertainty and type of facilitation needed in a given situation.

While the adventure experience paradigm is based on the flow model, the outdoor adventure recreation model is constructed from Bryan's (1979) theory of specialization. In this theory, Bryan suggests that as individuals gain experience in an activity, they tend to seek other activities that demand higher levels of skill, specialized equipment, and more specific locations. In figure 5.7, consider the levels and types of skills, equipment, and locations an individual would evolve into as they move from rowboating to whitewater kayaking. Despite the exceptions to Bryan's theory, the theory has assumed the status of a theoretical framework because of the numerous studies and research efforts that consistently support the theory.

As shown in the outdoor adventure recreation model (figure 5.8), the variables of type of risk, social orientation, locus of control, and motivational factors can be considered functionally related to level of experience. In turn, as individuals gain experience in an activity, they evolve from an introductory stage, to a skill-development stage, and finally to a commitment stage. Each stage is associated with its own set of social orientation, locus of control, type of risk, and motivating factors.

Each of the models discussed thus far uses its own framework to represent a particular

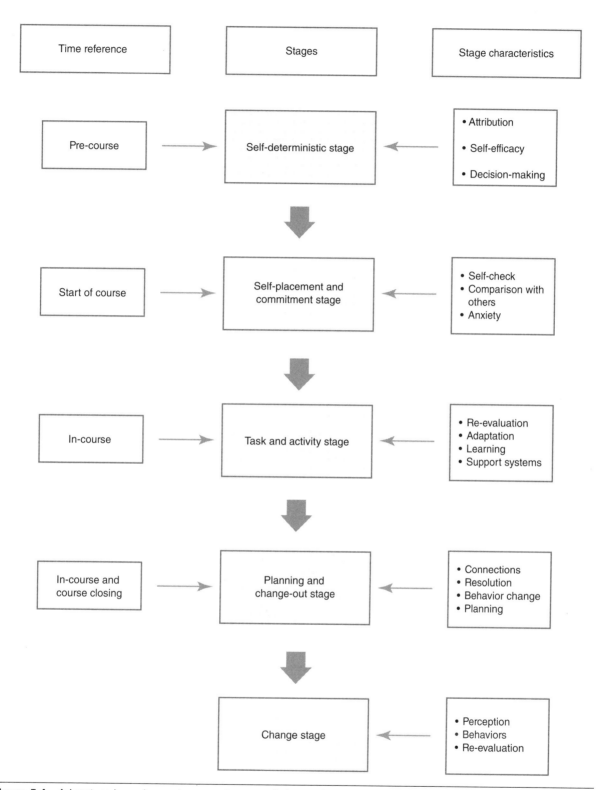

Figure 5.4 Adventure-based experience and personal change (AEPC) model.

conceptualization of the adventure experience. None of these models, however, have captured all the components and processes of the overall OAE experience. In fact, a comprehensive model encompassing all necessary components of OAE has yet to be developed. Such a model would require accounting for numerous variables involving many of the factors discussed in this chapter

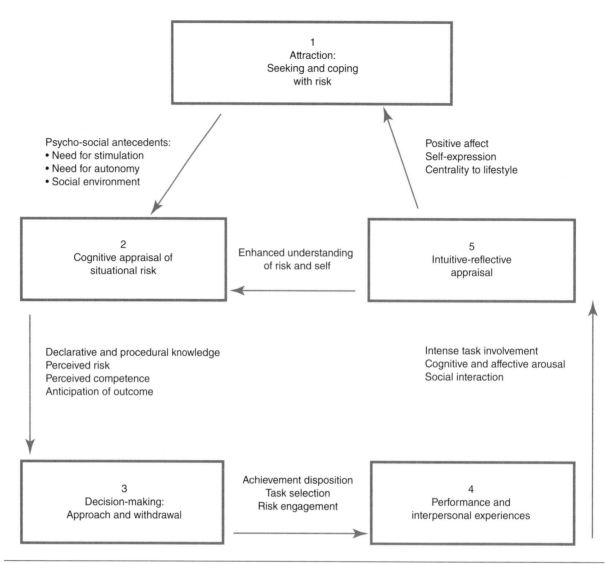

Figure 5.5 Risk recreation model.

Reprinted, by permission, from D.W. Robinson, 1992, "The risk recreation experience: Subjective state dimensions and the transferability of benefits," *Journal of Applied Recreation Research* 17(1): 12-36.

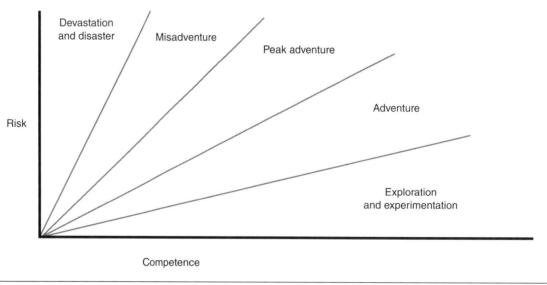

Figure 5.6 The adventure experience paradigm.

Reprinted from S. Priest, 1999, The adventure experience paradigm. In *Adventure programming,* edited by J.C. Miles and S. Priest (State College, PA: Venture Publishing), 159-168. By permission of S. Priest.

and elsewhere (Kiewa, 1994; Ewert & Garvey, 2007), such as who *is* the participant, who *are* the instructors, *what* activities are planned, *how* are the activities sequenced, *how* are the experiences facilitated, and so forth. There are also other considerations, such as antecedent conditions (conditions an individual brings to a course or program), internalities (situations and conditions within the program), externalities (situations and conditions outside the program), and outcomes. Consider the model shown in figure 5.9, which is just one example of how OAE might be conceptualized.

In this model, the OAE experience begins with the characteristics and attributes that an individual brings to a course or program (antecedents). These antecedents are coupled with items such as current events, participants' home life, and previous information they may have heard regarding the program or course. Because these factors are usually outside the organization's ability to exert much control over, they are collectively termed externalities. In turn, these antecedent and external factors influence and create attitudes and beliefs concerning the OAE experience. On entering the program or course, participants are introduced to a set of internalities (conditions within the scope of the program), such as type of course, program goals, instructor and staff expertise, environment they will be operating in, and behavior of the group (e.g., communication, normative behaviors, expectations). Participants are then introduced to various program components, including activities, framework of the course (such as sequencing and progression), level and type of risk, and exposure to uncertainty.

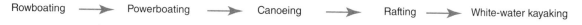

Figure 5.7 This progression demonstrates one example of Bryan's theory of specialization.

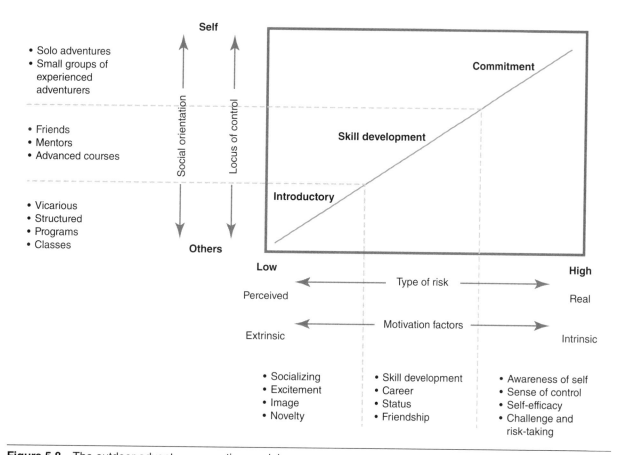

Figure 5.8 The outdoor adventure recreation model.

Reprinted, by permission, form A. Ewert and S. Hollenhorst, 1989, "Testing the adventure model: Empirical support for a model of risk recreation participation," *Journal of Leisure Research* 21: 124-139.

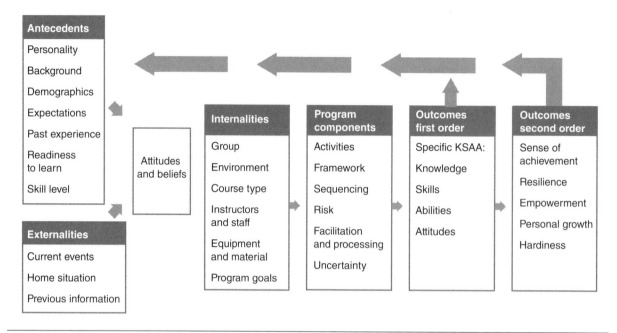

Figure 5.9 Conceptual model of OAE.

Finally, participants typically experience outcomes from participating in a program or course. In the model shown in figure 5.9, outcomes are at two levels. First-order outcomes deal primarily with knowledge, skills, abilities, and attitudes (KSAAs) learned on the course. Second-order outcomes involve more personal growth issues, namely, a sense of achievement, resilience, hardiness, empowerment, and other self-related outcomes (Sheard & Golby, 2006). Whereas the OAE model shown in figure 5.9 looks at the overall process and various components of OAE, it does not consider how the components interact with or affect each other. For example, what effect does an individual's attitude and belief system have on the ultimate outcomes realized from an OAE experience?

As of this writing, the following question remains to be answered: What theories and models must yet be constructed and tested in order to best understand the overall OAE experience? Developing our understanding of the theoretical structure of the OAE experience and being able to construct models that accurately depict that process will be of tremendous value in making adventure a more effective form of education.

SUMMARY

We started this chapter by establishing the importance for fields such as OAE to develop constructual models and theories. Models and theories, if used appropriately, are extremely useful in explaining and predicting behaviors and other phenomenon in OAE. We have noted that models and theories are often hypothetical constructs that can be useful in guiding or organizing but that they are often only partially accurate.

Although theories and models might not be able to fully explain or predict reality, they play important roles in the accumulative function of research. Often, they provide building blocks with which a base of knowledge can be constructed. A key role of research lies in the development of different levels of theories (e.g., micro, meso, macro) as well in the construction of relationships, symbolic representations, and underlying assumptions. All of these constructs and more serve to provide a foundation for understanding our world, as well as OAE's place in the world.

We have examined the concept of a process model as opposed to a theory and how we can or cannot make causal inferences based on what we see or the data that we have available. Finally, we hope the information presented in this chapter provides a foundation for others to continue developing and refining the body of knowledge we have in OAE, often through new models and theories.

In the next chapter we examine theories commonly associated with OAE and how they can be used to increase our understanding of the OAE process.

Issues for Further Discussion

1. If the primary role of research is to develop theories and models associated with a particular phenomenon or experience, develop a list of theories and models that have been used in OAE that you think are most important. What components of the OAE experience do they describe? Does that description make sense from your perspective?

2. Models and theories serve as organizing forces in how we conceptualize and think about phenomenon associated with OAE. What theories and models still need to be developed? In your opinion, what do we still need to know about how the OAE process works?

3. Using personal experience and information provided in this chapter, develop your own model of how OAE works and what changes it promotes for participants.

Extant Theories and Key Constructs in Outdoor Adventure Education

Why This Chapter Is Important

OAE is chaotic. There is a lot going on, and it remains difficult, if not impossible, to dissect an OAE experience into a sequence of discrete events. Considering OAE's complexity, are theories really of much use? Theory can only approximate reality, and OAE's reality is both messy and unpredictable. Although there is no one "theory of OAE" we can point to, many theories are relevant to OAE. These theories provide tools and explanations that can clarify why and how certain strategies work well or fail to work.

As a discipline, researchers in OAE tend to use theories and models developed by other academic disciplines; we eagerly borrow from the parent disciplines in the social and behavioral sciences. These theories are more robust, well tested, better vetted, and generally have demonstrated evidence of utility. Likewise, we often adopt existing constructs, because most of the more robust constructs, ones that remain im-

portant beyond an OAE experience, are already being studied and examined in other contexts. As we do research, we need to position our studies to be useful beyond our samples. Because most of our studies are not randomized or highly controlled, we are often better off arguing for conceptual generalization—that is, generalizing from our study findings back to a theory. The theories with the greatest, and widest, applications are typically existing theories from parent disciplines. These theories, which have been frequently used, are widely endorsed and robustly tested; they provide conceptual level guidance to practice. They represent a distillation and interpretation of data into a cumulative body of evidence. As you read this chapter, try to determine how you might use existing theories to improve your own professional practice or research.

Learning Outcomes

After completing this chapter, you should be able to

* describe implications of constructivism for OAE;
* explain how the sources of self-efficacy development fits with a typical OAE program;
* compare and contrast influential elements of the systems of influence while on an OAE expedition and at home;
* identify applications for expectancy value theory, attribution theory, theory of planned behavior, and attention restoration theory for OAE practice; and
* summarize the concepts of learning taxonomies, optimal arousal and flow, learning styles, and multiple intelligences.

Masters of their craft are purposeful in what they do. They are able to adeptly apply the skills necessary to reach optimal performance. To accomplish this, they blend skills with experience. Their experience allows them to use the correct skills at the right time with the right materials. They use the most appropriate methods to apply techniques to suit the demands of the situation. Whether one is building something or teaching someone, the same principles hold true. Masters of their craft also understand *why* they are applying particular methods and skills to accomplish their goal. In education, the "why" is recognized as theories that guide practice.

A good theory provides guidance to inform decision making. People familiar with OAE programs have many so-called theories on how and why these programs effect change. But some of these "theories" are overly reliant on personal experiences and have little or relatively weak broader evidence to support them. In contrast, existing theories from parent disciplines such as psychology, sociology, and education have proven useful in a range of settings and with a variety of populations.

In this chapter, we present several salient theories to help you better understand why OAE programs can effect change. Although it is impossible to cover all the relevant theories, some of the most promising explanatory frameworks are discussed in detail, including constructivism, social cognitive theory, and systems theories of development. These were selected because of their consistency with OAE philosophy, their macro perspective, and their rich historical backgrounds in social and behavioral science. Other foundational theories and constructs, or those central to specific aspects of practice, are then introduced.

You might have heard the adage, "If your only tool is a hammer, then all the world is a nail." In this chapter, we want to give you more than just a hammer. We hope to develop your tools so they are there for you to use when you need them. In a system as complex as OAE, many theories are at work simultaneously, so it is handy to have a variety of useful tools.

PROMISING EXPLANATORY FRAMEWORKS

Of the many existing theories, or frameworks, some fit better than others with the history, philosophy, and practice of OAE. Others are applicable in specific cases or applications, but do not provide broad support. Constructivism, social cognitive theory, and systems theories of development work well as large-scale frameworks within the field of OAE.

Constructivism

Constructivism is an epistemology—that is, a belief about how people come to know. Constructivism is the notion that what and how a person learns is based on their previous knowledge and experience. Thus learners are *building* knowledge and skill based on what they already know. This approach to education and learning places a premium on the participant experience and the ability to interpret, mediate, and influence learning.

The learner is an active agent in learning and, although influenced by external stimuli, actually constructs knowledge internally through mental processing. Reflection and other internal cognitive processes allow learners to create and reinforce connections that generate pathways for more complex learning. Constructivism is consistent with and inclusive of general approaches to experiential education (e.g., Dewey, 1938; Kolb, 1984).

Constructivism is often broken down into cognitive approaches and social approaches. Jean Piaget's work takes a cognitive approach to constructivism, in which individual learners construct meaning in their minds. New information is either assimilated into an existing schema or mental model, or the new information (and the associated mental processes it provokes) requires accommodation, or adaptation, in the existing schema or model. In the cognitive approach to constructivism, learning occurs in the mind and is subsequently expressed outward by individual learners.

In contrast to cognitive constructivism, social constructivism posits that learning and understanding are products of social influence. Lev Vygotsky is generally considered the architect of social constructivism; his sociocultural theory is one of the most influential and important theories within constructivism (1978). Vygotsky posits that the social environment shapes learning and development. Social language, cultural objects, institutions, and norms are all components of social interactions that shape and influence how people learn and develop.

The role of the OAE instructor is to structure learning situations, provide lesson-appropriate equipment, and guide social interactions to provide active involvement with the content of the lessons.

Photo courtesy of Curt Davidson.

Although Vygotsky's sociocultural theory is generally about the broad social and cultural influences on learning, one central aspect of his theory is the *zone of proximal development*, which is the difference between what someone can learn on his or her own and what he or she might be capable of learning under the guidance of another person who is more knowledgeable or experienced. In Vygotsky's words, the zone is "the distance between the actual developmental level as determined by independent problem solving and the level of potential development as determined through problem solving under adult guidance or in collaboration with more capable peers" (Vygotsky, 1978, p. 86). This premise fits well with contemporary educational theory involving techniques such as reciprocal teaching (peers teaching each other), scaffolding (temporary learning supports and structures provided by more knowledgeable others that can be later removed as content is mastered), peer collaboration, and mentoring. The premise also fits well with contemporary OAE practice.

The small-group, collaborative learning model employed in most OAE programs is well suited to engage more knowledgeable or experienced participants in teaching and mentoring others. Likewise, instructors live and work in close prox-imity with participants, which allows for frequent and individualized coaching and mentoring. Teaching and learning occur both formally and informally, and assistance is generally accessible from knowledgeable, experienced peers or course leaders.

Despite the centrality of the zone of proximal development, Vygotsky's main point is that learning is mediated by culture. Learning culture and environment are shaped by the nature of OAE programs. The role of the instructor is to structure the situations, provide the lesson-appropriate equipment, and guide social interactions to provide active involvement with the content of the lessons. As we have mentioned elsewhere in this book, the remoteness of OAE programs and their separation in time and space provide exceptional opportunities to create, influence, and experience a social environment that is smaller, more responsive, and more manageable than opportunities experienced elsewhere.

In OAE, constructivism can be applied by the instructor in several important ways. First, it is valuable for the instructor to appreciate participants' perspectives of the event that is about to occur. In this way, the instructor can guide participants toward appropriate learning that occurs in an appropriate sequence. Assuming

Bridging Extant Theory to OAE Research: The Example of Emotional Intelligence

■ ■ ■ ■ ■ ■ ■ ■ ■ ■ ■ ■ ■ ■ ■ ■ ■ ■

Aya Hayashi, PhD, Associate Professor—Biwako Seikei Sport College, Japan

Emotional intelligence (EI) has become an increasingly visible construct for both identifying potentially effective leaders and as a tool for developing effective leadership skills (Palmer, Walls, Burgess, & Stough, 2001). EI is "the subset of social intelligence that involves the ability to monitor one's own and others' feelings and emotions, to discriminate among them and to use this information to guide one's thinking and actions" (Salovey & Mayer, 1990, p189). EI can contribute to effective leadership by focusing on essential elements of leader effectiveness, such as the development of collective goals and objectives; instilling in others an appreciation of the importance of work activities; and generating and maintaining trust. Thus emotional intelligence can be considered an important component for dealing effectively with people in naturalistic settings, such as those often inherent in OAE.

Hayashi and Ewert (2006) conducted surveys of outdoor leaders and found that leaders who had higher levels of outdoor experience, including personal and professional experience, showed higher levels of emotional intelligence and transformational leadership. Based on these findings, they conducted a quasi-experimental study with college students about emotional intelligence and outdoor leadership experience. They found that emotional intelligence could be developed or enhanced through an outdoor leadership program, especially the intrapersonal aspect. Furthermore, students who showed higher levels of leadership also had higher levels of emotional intelligence. According to the qualitative part of the study, students per- ceived that the leadership opportunities, reflective experiences, decision-making experiences, and wilderness environments contributed to their development of emotional intelligence and leadership, and felt that their learning within the course transferred to their daily lives. Most important, the developmental stage of emotional intelligence along with an accompanying level of outdoor experience and leadership was discussed. The knowledge derived could be applied to leadership training programs in which the design is based on the experience level of participants. For example, participants who have a low level of outdoor experience could be initially led to obtain skills of adaptability and stress management as part of a leadership-training-through-OAE phase. Then, gradually, they could learn intrapersonal and interpersonal aspects of emotional intelligence, which would constitute their adaptation-and-practice-of-leadership-development phase. During this phase, instructors could provide participants with challenging opportunities to cultivate and reflect on their developing leadership abilities.

OAE provides opportunities to deal with various emotional situations, including situational, intrapersonal, and interpersonal relationships, which could lead to the development of enhanced emotional intelligence and leadership skills. Such training could also be useful for other audiences, such as business corporations, and in conventional school settings. However, much more empirical and theoretical work is needed to allow for effective

OAE provides opportunities to deal with various emotional situations, which could lead to the development of enhanced emotional intelligence and leadership skills.
Courtesy of Aya Hayashi.

programming that develops emotional intelligence in OAE participants.

References

George, J. (2000). Emotions and leadership: The role of emotional intelligence. *Human Relations 53*(8): 1027-1055.

Hayashi, A. (2006). *Leadership development through an outdoor leadership program focusing on emotional intelligence.* (Doctoral dissertation). Indiana University.

Hayashi, A., & Ewert, A. (2006). Outdoor leaders' emotional intelligence and effective leadership. *Leadership & Organization Development Journal 22*(1): 5-10.

Palmer, B., Walls, M., Burgess, Z., & Stough, C. (2001). Emotional intelligence and effective leadership. *Leadership & Organization Development Journal 22*(1): 5-10.

Priest, S., & Gass, M. (1997). *Effective leadership in adventure programming.* Champaign, IL: Human Kinetics.

Salovey, P., & Mayer, J. (1990). Emotional intelligence. *Imagination, Cognition, and Personality 9*, 185-211.

that a participant is starting with no knowledge or experience in an activity can be a mistake. Although participants might be new to an activity, constructivist approaches suggest that they do bring a depth of perspective based on their prior experience, knowledge, and skills and that they will, ultimately, take lessons from the experience over which instructors have a degree of influence but lack control. Second, instructors need to match the education content to the educational approach; constructivist educational philosophy is not the same as constructivist teaching practices. Educators with constructivist philosophies often choose to teach certain content in more didactic ways. Constructivist practices, such as discovery learning or collaborative problem solving, generally work well for divergent or process-oriented content, where there is not a single approach or correct answer. However, it would take a long time for participants to discover the correct way to belay a climber, and the risk during the discovery phase would likely be unacceptable. Likewise, it would be a mistake to ignore participants' past experiences in communication, leadership, or working together on a team.

Social Cognitive Theory and Self-Efficacy

Social cognitive theory (SCT) is attributed to the work of Albert Bandura (1977; 1997). This theory posits that a person, his or her behavior, and the environment are each determined, in part, by the other two. A person and his or her behaviors help shape an environment. Similarly, a person is shaped by his or her behaviors and the influences of the external environment. When consider-

ing this work, remember that the environment includes many aspects, including social, cultural, and physical elements. SCT considers learning a social phenomenon that comes from a person's interaction with others through watching and observing.

Self-efficacy is the central construct of SCT. Self-efficacy is one's confidence in his or her ability to perform a certain task. According to Bandura, "perceived self-efficacy refers to beliefs in one's capabilities to organize and execute the courses of action required to manage prospective situations. Efficacy beliefs influence how people think, feel, motivate themselves, and act" (1995, p. 2). A person is influenced by an efficacy expectation, which leads to a specific behavioral choice, which leads to an outcome (Bandura, 1977; 1997). Outcome expectations and perceptions of efficacy both influence decisions an individual will make in an attempt to reach a specific outcome.

Although self-efficacy has been linked to performance in a number of studies, it is generally mediated by outcome expectations. Efficacy expectations are based on whether or not an individual feels he or she can perform a task; outcome expectations refer to what an individual expects the reward or benefit to be if the task is completed and the outcome is realized. Learning can be latent, in that it exists in the mind but not in behavior, often because of the lack of a positive outcome expectation. However, the learning might be performed in the face of motivation, interest, social pressure, or a perceived need.

Peoples' convictions in their own effectiveness, or efficacy, is a major determinant of choice of activities, how much effort they will expend, how long they will attempt to deal with the situation, and whether they will even try to cope with a given situation. However, expectations alone will not produce the desired performance if capabilities are lacking. People might choose, for other reasons, not to change a behavior or perform in a certain manner (Bandura, 1977). Despite these limitations, self-efficacy has repeatedly proven to be an accurate and superior estimate of performance, with higher task specificity being superior to more general predictions.

Self-efficacy has three principal dimensions: level, strength, and generality (Bandura, 1997). *Level* refers to the depth of one's efficacy perceptions regarding a particular domain of functioning. For example, a person's confidence in his or her ability to climb an easier route will generally be higher than to climb a more difficult one. *Strength* of the efficacy belief refers to the perception of one's confidence in the ability to function in the specified domain. This is generally measured from 0 to 100 percent confidence. A climber might be 75 percent confident she can climb a specific route, suggesting she is fairly certain she can climb the route but understands she might be wrong. *Generality* refers to the breadth of the domain. Does the person consider himself only good at climbing, or does he consider himself generally competent in the outdoors?

Sources of Efficacy Beliefs

According to Bandura (1995; 1997), the four main sources of efficacy information are mastery experience, vicarious experience, social persuasion, and physiological and emotional status.

Mastery experience refers to the successful completion of a task; it is widely considered the most influential source of self-efficacy development. Not all successes affect efficacy perceptions equally. Success based on skill and ability rather than perseverance provides a stronger reinforcement of efficacy. To succeed at easy tasks provides little new information. Additionally, "after strong efficacy expectations are developed through repeated success, the negative impact of occasional failure is likely to be reduced" (Bandura, 1977, p. 195).

Through *vicarious experience* people can increase their own self-efficacy by watching others successfully complete a task. This is commonly referred to as modeling. Pintrich and Schunk (1996) define the two most common forms of modeling as coping and mastery models. Coping models are seen as peers struggling through a process and overcoming hardships and

barriers. Mastery models are used to demonstrate the ease with which a challenge can be handled. A leader who easily demonstrates how to communicate with a group is using mastery modeling. A peer struggling, learning, and succeeding with a task serves as a coping model.

Much of the contemporary work on modeling is directly applicable to OAE. Competent, high-status models and models that can help participants achieve a goal or desirable outcome tend to be the most influential (Schunk, 2004). Outdoor leaders tend to be admired and emulated by participants, and they are commonly helping program participants achieve goals and outcomes. Also, multiple models are best for learning. By watching multiple leaders and participants perform a task, self-efficacy accuracy and strength generally increase.

Social persuasion is essentially external encouragement provided by another in an attempt to convince someone that he or she has the ability to accomplish a task. This is most effective if the source of persuasion is trusted, respected, and perceived as a competent judge. Social persuasion is common in instructional settings for correctional purposes and might lead to successful performance, which further increases efficacy (Bandura, 1977; Pintrich & Schunk, 1996). Unrealistic or false verbal persuasion can increase self-efficacy, but if appraisals are genuinely inaccurate, performance failures will quickly erase any temporary boost in self-efficacy (Oettington, 1995).

Physiological and emotional status also influences perceptions of self-efficacy. Generally, increased emotional anxiety or physiological pain, fatigue, or aches reduce levels of efficacy, but this effect depends on how the emotional status is interpreted. A participant might interpret nervousness before a big performance as either a heightened excitement that indicates readiness or as a nagging doubt of ability.

Bandura's sources of self-efficacy mesh well with critical components of OAE. In OAE, a learner is immersed in a novel physical and social environment and faces challenges to overcome, or master. Vicarious experiences are provided through both mastery models by instructors and coping models by other participants. Social persuasion is provided by both peer and staff through encouragement and feedback provided in the supportive group environment. Additionally, these new skills are often emotionally involving because many include an element of perceived risk. These circumstances combine to make an OAE experience ideal for self-efficacy development.

Because misjudgment of personal abilities can produce adverse consequences, accurate appraisals of one's abilities (self-efficacy) are generally advantageous (Bandura, 1982). However, there are some advantages to inaccurate self-appraisals if these appraisals are slightly higher than actual ability. Higher self-appraisals tend to allow people to try new activities they might otherwise avoid, learn from their failures, and progress to greater achievement. Inaccurate self-appraisals that are lower than actual capabilities are usually detrimental because they tend to discourage the undertaking of new and challenging tasks (Flammer, 1995; Pintrich & Schunk, 1996). Obviously, grossly optimistic perceptions of ability can be detrimental as well as dangerous (e.g., trying to climb a mountain without the necessary skill). We see this increasingly in adventure-based locations such as Mt. Everest, where many climbers have low levels of climbing skills and experience. The demands of the terrain and altitude of Everest often far exceed their abilities.

General Efficacy Versus Task-Specific Efficacy

Most studies using efficacy measures have used task-specific self-efficacy scores to predict task performance. However, a few researchers, including Bandura, propose that some people have a general or personal efficacy level that relates to most, if not all, aspects of their lives. Others argue that this general state is merely an increased coping efficacy, and that all efficacy measures are really task specific with spillover to related skills. Bandura predicted early in his social learning theory (1977) that generalization of efficacy effects should occur in which high levels of efficacy would carry over to similar tasks or tasks requiring similar skills. Bandura also posited that even more general skills could be derived from successful task completion. He wrote:

> Occasional failures that are later overcome by determined effort can strengthen self-motivated persistence if one finds through experience that even the most difficult obstacles can be mastered by sustained effort.... Participants acquire a generalizable skill for dealing with stressful situations, a skill that they use to overcome a variety of dysfunctional fears and inhibition

in their everyday lives. Having a serviceable coping skill at one's disposal undoubtedly contributes to one's sense of personal efficacy (Bandura, 1977, pp. 195-196).

Most authorities at least acknowledge academic, social, and physical domains of competence (Pintrich & Schunk, 1996). Although self-efficacy and social cognitive theory have been studied extensively in OAE settings, this focus largely remains on the intrapersonal gains of the participant. In contrast, systems approaches to development take a broader approach to growth and change.

Systems Theories of Development

Systems theories of development fit well with the complex and multifaceted nature of OAE. At the most basic level, systems theories of development posit that development is a complex, bidirectional, and dynamic process that occurs as individual characteristics and factors engage with contextual factors. These approaches to development embrace the complex and individual nature of development and contrast with more deterministic or reductionist approaches to development and growth. Examples of this theoretical approach can be found in dynamic systems theory (e.g., Thelen & Smith, 2006), developmental systems theory (e.g., Ford & Lerner, 1992), and ecological views of development (e.g., Bronfenbrenner & Morris, 1998).

Although the specifics of each framework vary, these interrelated theories share a common core. In their influential text, Ford and Lerner (1992) clarify the basics of systems theories of development as they explain their developmental systems theory (DST). DST is a combination of life span, life course, and ecological views of development. Life-span approaches tend to focus on the biological impacts of aging—a 5-year-old is different from a 45-year-old. Life-course approaches recognize the influence of life events. Personal experiences such as marriage or living through a depression affect how people develop. Ecological views focus on dynamic interactions among levels of spheres of influence. Ford and Lerner outline some of the main tenets of most systems approaches to learning and development: Various levels of spheres of influence act on individuals; dynamic interaction occurs in the levels of influence; all people are different (e.g., biologically),

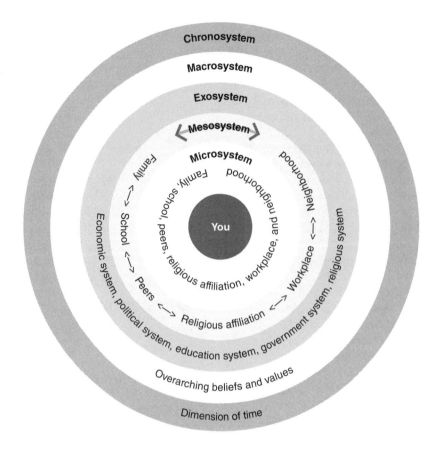

Figure 6.1 Bronfenbrenner's ecological model of human development.

Reprinted from U. Bronfenbrenner. Available: http://faculty.weber.edu/tlday/human.development/ecological.htm. By permission from the Bronfenbrenner family.

which affects how they interact with levels of influence (thus many different developmental paths are possible for each participant, who is an active agent of influence him- or herself); and individuals are constantly striving for a good fit of their own traits, preferences, motives, and needs with their contextual influences.

Visually, systems are often represented by concentric spheres or circles of influence, such as in Bronfenbrenner's ecological model of human development (figure 6.1). These spheres both influence and are influenced by the individual actor. In Bronfenbrenner's model, the microsystem consists of immediate and proximal influences to which the individual actor is known and influential (e.g., peers, family, school contexts). The mesosystem is when microsystems interact (e.g., parents speak with teachers about the individual). The exosystem consists of larger influences to which the individual actor is not known and has little voice (e.g., the local government or public education system). The macrosystem is largely beyond the influence of the individual yet has an influence (e.g., cultural beliefs or customs).

Finally, the chronosystem represents change over time (e.g., living during a recession or through a divorce).

One of the central points of systems theories of development is the premise that organisms, or individuals, self organize. Self-organization is the distillation of numerous and often competing stimuli into a complex organized system. There is no one single causal aspect; rather, the influence of the context and stimuli is mediated by the individual, who must create some new more complex organization from the situation or milieu. Concepts such as equifinity and multifinity are embraced (equifinity is the same outcome being reached through different processes or paths; multifinity is the concept that the same external experience or event can trigger far-different outcomes in different individuals); in other words, systems theories of change posit that development is often nonlinear. Development can be sudden, unexpected, and unanticipated. "Developing organisms do not know ahead of time where they will end up. Form is a product of process" (Thelen & Smith, 2006, p. 271). Thelen and Smith introduce the metaphor of a mountain stream to represent an individual. Many forces and factors come together to make each stream unique, but fundamental similarities are shared by all streams.

Consider an outdoor educator's role in changing a stream's path and trajectory. Each stream is dynamic, different, and subject to the influence of the surrounding topography. A large rock thrown into a wide, deep section of a stream will have little influence on the water flow or stream trajectory. The same rock thrown into a wide but shallow section might force the water to diverge from its original path, but it will soon return to its previous course. However, if the rock is thrown into a narrow section of a shallow stream, the stream's course might be permanently diverted. As the metaphor pertains to educators' roles, although instructors might make an educated guess about the downstream path, the specifics of the path the stream might take are ultimately unknown.

In order to change, systems need disequilibrium, or "noise." Disequilibrium dislodges behavior patterns from their attractors (an environment that promotes a specific behavior) and creates potential for changes in complexity, or growth. In another of Thelen and Smith's metaphors, they explain how disruption and change in a system are needed to foster development. Sometimes a person, like a ball at the top of a hill, is primed for change (figure 6.2a). A small push or nudge creates movement in the ball, which will stabilize when it finds a need or reason to stop. A ball in a shallow well or dip might also be moved, but it will require more energy and effort to dislodge it (figure 6.2c). This ball, too, might find a new resting place (figure 6.2d), or it might return to its previous resting spot, drawn by its natural tendency to stop in a low spot, at an attractor. A ball resting in a deep ravine (figure 6.2b) will be difficult to move, and even if dislodged, it will have a strong tendency to return to its initial resting place.

These theories of development fit well with most of the foundational and philosophical underpinnings of OAE. Most OAE professionals readily agree that there are multiple sources of influence and context matters. Each participant needs and warrants individualized attention; there is no single universally powerful developmental experience in OAE.

Another application of systems theories of development to OAE involves OAE's remoteness, which can make certain influences more proximal (stronger and more relevant) and others more distal (weaker or less important). For instance, in programs that do not run intergenerational trips, parental influence becomes more distal as students are separated from their parents. Religious affiliation and neighborhood influences also tend to become more distal in OAE programs and expeditions. In contrast, a participant's peer group and course instructors tend to become more proximal and hold greater influence in the remote and sequestered environment. This makes OAE a fertile environment for participant development (figure 6.3). The immediate on-course microsystem becomes the focus, and, for the duration of the course, the meso-, exo-, macro-, and chronosystems in Bronfenbrenner's model (figure 6.1) exert less influence.

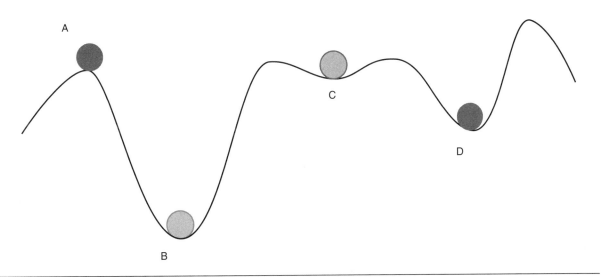

Figure 6.2   Illustration of dynamics of personal change.

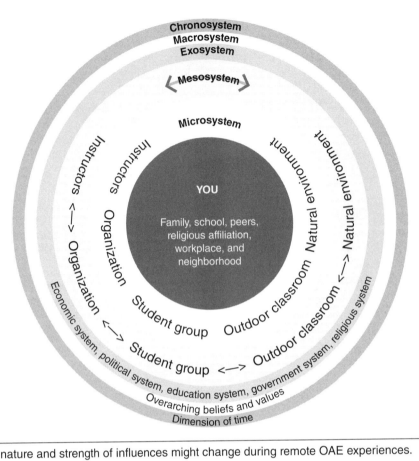

Figure 6.3 The nature and strength of influences might change during remote OAE experiences.

Systems theories of development might also prove useful in OAE research. Consider that earlier rock thrown into a mountain stream. That rock might have negligible, latent (hidden), temporary, or immediate results, depending on the stream, the rock, the topography, and other factors. Now throw that rock into a laboratory beaker—you will find the results are much more overt than latent, much more permanent than temporary. It is much easier to study, and predict, the effects of throwing a rock into a laboratory beaker than it is to study, or predict, the effects of a rock thrown into a stream; this illustrates a primary difficulty for researchers in OAE. A lack of laboratory-like, highly controlled environments continues to hamper OAE investigation. However, some of the approaches used in naturalistic systems theory research might prove useful as they make their way to OAE.

KEY THEORIES

OAE is highly complex and involves many moving parts. Subsequently, a single, overarching, and universally useful theory for OAE does not exist.

The wise practitioner is familiar with theory and knows when to judiciously apply what is known about human behavior when participating in or leading an OAE experience. Several theories are central to specific aspects of, or approaches to, practice. Other theories are widely referenced as critical to the OAE experience. We will look now at some of the more useful theories as they apply to OAE.

Expectancy Value Theory

Fishbein and Ajzen's (1975) expectancy value theory posits that behavior is a function of how much individuals value an outcome and their expectation of attaining the desired outcome through performance of a behavior. The theory assumes that people are goal oriented and will attempt to maximize the combination of expected success and value. The theory is often represented by the equation

$$B = f(E \times V)$$

where *B = behavior, f = function of, E = expectation, and V = value.*

This theory can be applied to behavior in OAE in many ways. In an effort to maximize the product of expectation and value, behaviors will change. If participants expect they can summit a peak and value the benefits associated with summiting, they will attempt to reach the peak. If an organization values conserving resources, they might promote other modes of transportation for their members rather than driving automobiles. If a family has the resources to go camping, but no family members value the benefits of the camping experience, they will not go camping. The expectancy value theory, though useful, has been expanded and combined with other theories and constructs by Ajzen (1988) to propose the theory of planned behavior, which we will look at soon.

Attribution Theory

Attribution theory is concerned with how individuals perceive the causes of outcomes. Most of the defining work on attribution theory is attributed to Weiner and colleagues (Weiner, 1985, 1992). According to Weiner (1992), when an outcome is achieved, the attribution of success or failure can be categorized among three dimensions: locus of causality, stability, and controllability. Locus of causality ranges from internal attributions, such as inherent ability or individual effort, to external attributions, such as luck or task difficulty. Unstable attributions, such as effort, vary across time. Stable attributions, such as teacher difficulty, do not vary much. Success or failure can also be seen as controllable by the individual, such as through increased effort, or uncontrollable, such as tasks with high perceived difficulty (see table 6.1).

Success is commonly attributed to four main factors: ability, effort, task difficulty, and luck. *Ability* is generally considered internal, stable, and uncontrollable. *Effort* is generally considered internal, unstable, and controllable. *Task*

difficulty is generally considered external, stable, and uncontrollable. *Luck* is generally considered external, unstable, and uncontrollable.

In OAE, attribution theory is largely linked to the provision and attribution of feedback. In general, people want to attribute cause to preserve their self-images. If they see themselves as successful, they are more prone to attribute success to their own attributes (e.g., ability or effort). If they see themselves as failure prone, they are more likely to attribute success to external factures such as luck or help from others. Conversely, people who view themselves as failures are more prone to attribute failure to internal mechanisms, whereas people who view themselves as successful are more prone to attribute failure to external mechanisms. All of this of course has significant implications for OAE professionals in how they provide feedback to participants. They should always consider how feedback might be interpreted and strive for feedback that assists participants in learning valuable lessons, promotes feelings of self-efficacy, and contributes to positive development.

Theory of Planned Behavior

Icek Ajzen (1988) built on work involving expectancy value theory, social cognitive theory, and attribution theory in his work on the theory of planned behavior (TPB). The premise of the TPB is that behaviors follow from the combined influence of a person's intention to perform a behavior and the actual behavioral control (actual ability to perform the behavior) (figure 6.4). If a person intends to go mountain climbing but lives in Florida and lacks money to travel, his or her actual ability to climb a mountain is low, and mountain climbing will not occur. Likewise, if a person lives in Alaska with excellent access to mountain terrain, but has no intention of climbing a mountain, the behavior is unlikely to occur.

Table 6.1 Components of Attribution Theory

	INTERNAL		EXTERNAL	
	Stable	Unstable	Stable	Unstable
Controllable	I can do it with average effort.	I can do it with extra effort.	I can do it because my teacher is good at explaining things.	I can do it if I ask for help.
Uncontrollable	I have the ability to do it.	I can do it if I'm in the right mood.	I can do it because the task is easy.	I can do it with luck.

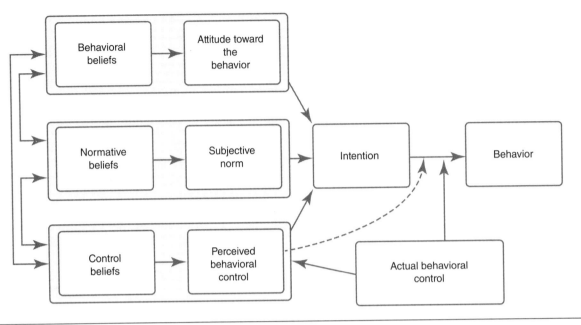

Figure 6.4 Theory of planned behavior.

Reprinted, by permission, from Icek Ajzen.

Whereas *actual* behavioral control mediates the relationship between intention and behavior, *perceived* behavioral control (the self-perceptions of behavioral control) influences behavioral intentions. Conceptually, perceived behavioral control is similar to self-efficacy, although they are often treated differently in research. Perceived behavioral control is the person's perceived ability to perform the behavior. Low perceived behavioral control can result from a number of barriers or constraints, including lack of skill, task difficulty, and lack of resources (e.g., equipment, money, access).

Behavioral intentions are influenced by perceived behavioral control, but also by an individual's attitude toward the behavior and the subjective norms. Attitude is the personal valuation, positive or negative, of the behavior. Does the individual value mountain climbing? Subjective norms are the social pressures to behave in certain ways. Does the individual's immediate family and friends support his or her interests in mountain climbing?

Beliefs underpin attitudes, subjective norms, and perceived behaviors. Beliefs, of course, can be accurate or inaccurate (consider how people once believed the world was flat). The most accurate beliefs are generally based on more substantive evidence. Behavioral beliefs involve a person's beliefs in the probability of a specific behavior leading to a specific outcome. If a person believes

that humans should work to protect the natural environment, then this influences his attitude toward humans' roles in ecological systems. Normative beliefs are dependent upon the nature of the context and the relevant referent group. If a person believes that relevant others also share his beliefs about the environment, then the social norms are conducive to normative behaviors, or behaviors that are accepted within this referent group. Control beliefs involve what an individual perceives to be facilitators or inhibitors of certain behaviors. A student might believe that minimizing environmental impact is easy to accomplish in the backcountry, but it less easily applied at home. Such beliefs would lead to high perceived behavioral control in the backcountry and low perceived behavioral control at home.

The TPB has a great deal of empirical support across a variety of settings. If a person values a behavior, has a supportive social network, and perceives that she can actually perform a behavior, the behavior is more likely to occur. In OAE, this theory can help us determine why certain behaviors (e.g., cooperation with others) may or may not be happening. Likewise, if OAE professionals want lessons from a program to continue to be applied after a program is complete, they should consider how beliefs, attitudes, subjective norms, and behavioral control will change once participants leave the program. Are there ways to prepare participants to navigate through the inevitable changes they will encounter back at home? Behavioral interventions based on the TPB typically target the behavioral, normative, and control beliefs that underlie attitudes, subjective norms, and perceived behavioral control. Thus, changing beliefs is often the foundation of changing behaviors.

Attention Restoration Theory

Attention restoration theory (ART) was initially formulated from interviews from OAE program participants and posits that attentional capacity can be restored through experiences that are rich in certain properties well aligned with nature (Kaplan & Kaplan, 1989). Directed or effortful attention is necessary to consider and attend to tasks that are not inherently interesting, yet still need attention. However, people's capacity to concentrate on tasks that are not inherently interesting is limited; willpower and attentiveness become fatigued over time. To restore fatigued attentional capacity, people should switch to tasks rich in four properties: a sense of being away, extent, compatibility, and fascination (Kaplan, 1995; 2001). Tasks that are substantially different provide a sense of change or being away from the fatiguing stimuli. Restorative tasks also tend to have the scope necessary to sustain interaction without boredom; the Kaplans term this "extent." Consider a campfire, with its scope and interactive capacity, compared to a candle. Compatibility is the task's fit with the person's current goals or inclination. Fascination is the inherent interest in the new task and is further divided into hard and soft fascination. Hard fascination, which is not restorative, is an interest or attraction that does not allow mental capacity for reflective thought. Watching sports, for example, might be interesting but might not allow cognitive capacity for reflection because viewers tend to track statistics, strategies, and performance and are generally overwhelmed by stimuli. In contrast, soft fascination is considered effortless and does not require complex cognitive process; it allows space for the mind to wander. Watching clouds pass or enjoying an ocean view might be examples of experiences with potential for soft fascination.

However, it is not the fact that ART was developed from interviews with OAE participants that makes it relevant. OAE experiences are generally rich in the restorative properties proposed in ART. Most OAE participants have chosen to participate, and a certain level of compatibility is to be expected. Most participants experience a sense of being away because they do not spend most of their time outdoors. Natural settings have been consistently found rich in both extent and opportunities for soft-fascination (Kaplan, 1995, 2001). Thus OAE seems to be especially well suited to provide restorative experiences.

Self-Determination Theory

Self-determination theory (SDT) focuses on distinguishing motivations that are autonomous from those that are highly controlled. SDT posits that when behaviors originate from autonomous volition or choice they are more likely to continue. SDT is comprised of four mini-theories that individually support the fulfillment of a person's basic psychological needs but lack the overall conceptual ability to provide a comprehensive understanding of self-determination. The first mini-theory, causality orientations theory (COT), explains differences in how one's social environment can influence feelings of autonomy, behavioral control, sense of motivation (specifically, amotivation), and overall sense of self-determination. In the basic needs theory (BNT), Ryan and Deci (2000b) suggest that well-being depends on a sense of competence, autonomy, and relatedness of universal basic psychological needs. The third mini-theory, cognitive evaluation theory (CET), explains the influence and impact of social contexts on a person's intrinsic motivation (Ryan & Deci, 2000a). The fourth mini-theory, organismic integration theory (OIT), explains the development and dynamics of extrinsic motivation by means of internalization and integration of values and regulations (Deci & Ryan, 2002). Internalization is the taking in of a value or regulation; integration is a transformation of the regulation through which the behavior will originate from one's self (Ryan & Deci, 2000b). Specifically, OIT explains the role of autonomy or autonomous feelings that lead to internalization with respect to extrinsic sources of information or motivation. Extrinsic motivation, if integrated and internalized, can become self-determined and, like intrinsic motivation, can propel learning and growth opportunities (Rigby, Deci, Patrick, & Ryan, 1992).

In OAE, SDT can inform motivational processes and help with internalization of behaviors. For example, by understanding that course participants need to have a sense of competence, autonomy, and relatedness, OAE instructors can actively work to ensure that participants are not consistently deficient in one of these domains. A participant who, for example, consistently feels incompetent, powerless, or isolated will likely struggle to succeed. Likewise, by providing a rationale, expressing empathy, and providing a level of choices, instructors might be able to help participants internalize behaviors that are not inherently interesting or enjoyable for their own sake. Carrying additional responsibilities or weight can be a source of conflict on an expedition. However, by giving participants a degree of choice, expressing empathy, and providing a reason for the additional effort, participants often accept and internalize the process as necessary and begin to self-regulate the necessary behaviors.

One of the major weaknesses of many of the aforementioned theories is their cognitive approach to behaviors, which fundamentally discounts emotional components of behavior and affective domains of learning. In contrast, learning taxonomies, optimal arousal, and the idea of multiple intelligences decentralize the cognitive domain.

KEY LEARNING CONSTRUCTS

While constructs such as attitudes, behaviors, and cognitive restoration are certainly relevant to OAE, some additional key ideas and concepts warrant inclusion in this chapter. Notably, learning taxonomies, optimal arousal and flow, and the ideas of learning styles and multiple intelligences remain central in any conversation of teaching and learning.

Learning Taxonomies

Much of the contemporary research and thinking about learning has been influenced by the creation of learning taxonomies. These taxonomies are often hierarchical and are specific to domains of learning. The best known of these is Bloom's taxonomy of the cognitive domain (Bloom, Engelhart, Furst, Hill, & Krathwohl, 1956), which was subsequently updated (Anderson & Krathwohl, 2000). Krathwohl and colleagues' affective domain taxonomy (Krathwohl, Bloom, & Masia, 1964) and Harrow's (1972) psychomotor domain taxonomy have also influenced thinking about learning central to OAE.

One interesting aspect of these taxonomies for OAE professionals is the relevance of learning across the full hierarchy of the taxonomies as well as the convergence of learning across multiple domains. For example, considering figure 6.5, it is difficult to envision an OAE program that does not involve cognitive, affective, and psychomotor goals, although some might be prioritized over others. Similarly, it is difficult to envision a program that targets solely lower-order learning. The holistic nature of OAE programs tends to necessitate the learning of basics so that more complex and deeper learning can be attempted. Hazards are described and cognitively understood so that they can be analyzed, evaluated, and a plan of action can be created. Initially, as leaders discuss the importance of the group, participants listen and generally accept these ideas, but as the program progresses, participants might begin to advocate for the group and actively manage and balance group goals and needs with their own. Fundamental paddling techniques are practiced in isolation so that skilled movements are developed and skills can be seamlessly integrated into more complex sequences. Ultimately, multiple lessons from several domains converge when, for example, a rafting group paddles a class V rapid. Hazard evaluation, genuine concern and appreciation for group members, and psychomotor performance can all be tested in a single activity.

Optimal Arousal and Flow

One of the most pervasive models associated with OAE is the model of optimal arousal. Originally proposed by Yerkes and Dodson (1908), optimal arousal refers to a level of arousal or sensation that is sought by an individual. Optimal arousal depends on both the person-environment interaction and the individual experience. In other words, individuals will seek levels of arousal that are congruent with their past experience, skill level, and situation. This relationship can be represented by an inverted U shape, as shown in figure 6.6. Although this relationship is supported in some studies, other contemporary studies have failed to find the anticipated decrease in performance as level of arousal increases, especially for simple or straightforward tasks in academic settings (Seipp, 1991). Despite the lack of consistent empirical support, the model of optimal arousal has remained popular in OAE because it intuitively makes sense. Bored participants

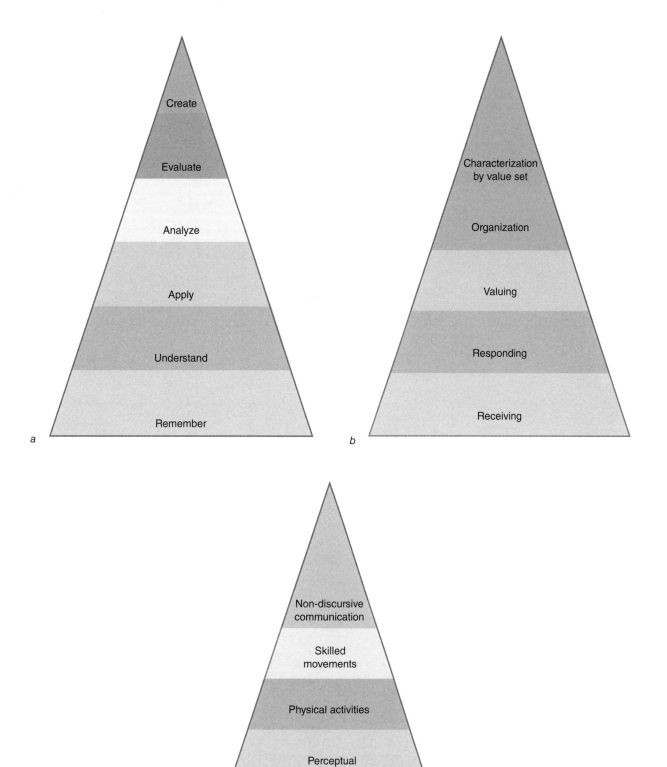

Figure 6.5 Depictions of various learning taxonomies: *(a)* cognitive; *(b)* affective; and *(c)* psychomotor.

(a) From http://www4.uwsp.edu/education/lwilson/curric/newtaxonomy.htm by Leslie Owen Wilson, Ed. D. Reprinted by permission. *(b)* and *(c)* Reprinted, by permission, from N. Dabbagh, 2013, *Instructional Design Knowledge Base* (IDKB). http://cehdclass.gmu.edu/ndabbagh/Resources/IDKB/index.htm. Figure available: http://cehdclass.gmu.edu/ndabbagh/Resources/IDKB /krathstax.htm. Retrieved 8-5-13.

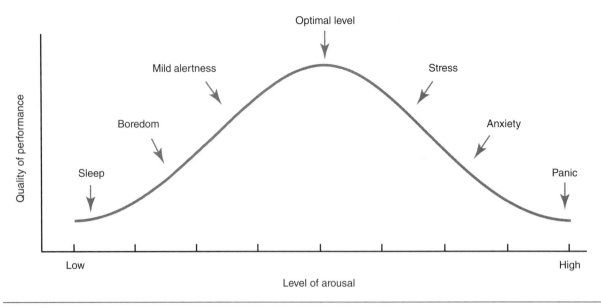

Figure 6.6 Yerkes-Dodson curve.

Reprinted from R. Yerkes and J. Dodson, 1908, "The relation of strength of stimulus to rapidity of habit-formation," *Journal of Comparative and Neurological Psychology* 18: 459-482.

will not perform well, and neither will participants who are overaroused by debilitating fear or anxiety.

Another model of optimal arousal is Csikszentmihalyi's concept of flow (Csikszentmihalyi, 1990). As we touched on in chapter 5, the concept of flow is used to explain a state of deep involvement that includes several characteristics: a merging of action and awareness, concentration on the task at hand, a sense of control, some risk and uncertainty, a loss of self-consciousness, and an altered sense of time. Flow is most likely to occur when the activity is challenging, goals are clear and feedback is immediate, and the participant has the capacity to concentrate attention. Skill and the level of challenge are central to Csikszentmihalyi's contemporary flow model (1997), which consists of eight channels or positions (figure 6.7). The general idea is that when levels of task challenge and skill are high and well matched, flow might be experienced. Matching in itself is not enough, as a match of low challenge and low skill will likely produce apathy. Thus, challenge and skill level must both be high for flow to occur. In contrast, mismatches in which skills are insufficient to navigate the challenge can produce worry, anxiety, or arousal. Similarly, if skills are more than sufficient to tackle the challenge, boredom, relaxation, or control might result.

As with the Yerkes-Dodson model, flow has generally resonated with OAE professionals. Properties of flow experiences—risk and uncertainty within challenging activities that have clear goals and immediate feedback—align well with most conceptualizations of OAE. In addition, Martin and Priest's adventure experience paradigm (1986), discussed in chapter 5, is directly built from Csikszentmihalyi's conceptualization of flow. Several studies on flow have occurred in outdoor recreation and education settings, including studies of kayaking (Jones, Hollenhorst, Perna, & Selin, 2000) and rock climbing (Csikszentmihalyi, 1975).

Learning Styles and Multiple Intelligences

OAE instructors often encounter participants who are impatient with the lecture portion of an experience or program. These participants are eager to practice a skill and to learn through trial and error. In contrast, other participants will ask instructors for further explanation of a skill. They want further description with more depth. They want to observe the skill being performed. These participants will often be the last to try to perform the skill. When they don't immediately succeed, they want to discuss each step to ensure they "get it." Such participants might easily become frustrated, and practice might not be effective for them, whereas other participants will enthusiastically embrace practice, even when their skills are imperfect.

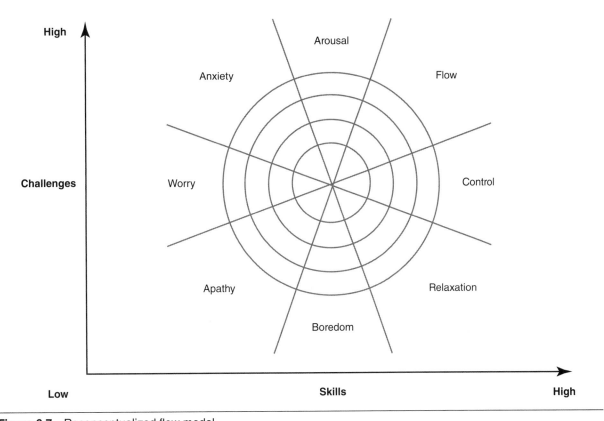

Figure 6.7 Reconceptualized flow model.

Adapted, by permission, from M. Csikszentmihalyi, 1997, *Finding flow: The psychology of engagement with everyday life* (New York, NY: Basic Books).

What the instructor is witnessing are differing modes of learning, often referred to as learning styles, or learning preferences. Most people tend to prefer a certain approach (or a combination of approaches) to learning over others. For example, *active* learners prefer to be actively involved in the educational process, whereas reflective learners prefer time alone to think about the content. *Visual* learners prefer graphics and to see what they are learning about, whereas *verbal* learners benefit from words. *Sequential* learners prefer learning to unfold in a series of logical steps (see Felder & Silverman, 1988).

Although the dimensions of learning styles and empirical evidence supporting each conceptualization of learning styles is lacking, they are intuitively compelling and remain useful in educational design. Likewise, OAE instructors should consider how participants prefer to learn, how they are used to learning, and the variances among participants and between the instructor and participants. An optimal approach to learning for some is, of course, less than ideal for others. Thus it is often best for instruction to cut across learning styles, combining active learning with reflection, for example, or employing both logical steps and a written resource.

Learning styles are often conflated with multiple intelligences, but they are different. Whereas learning styles represent how participants prefer to learn or how they are accustomed to learn, they have little relation to actual capacity in a cognitive, affective, or physical domain. Participants who prefer to learn by active or verbal means might not be better learners in these areas.

In 1983, Howard Gardner, a professor of education at Harvard, developed the theory of multiple intelligences. He contended that although people learn in a variety of ways, most people prefer some styles of learning over others and are more capable in some domains than others (Gardner, 1993). Whereas learning styles are *preferences*, multiple intelligences are more *capacities* for learning. Gardner proposed eight types of intelligence:

- Linguistic intelligence ("word smart")
- Logical-mathematical intelligence ("number smart")
- Spatial intelligence ("picture smart")

- Bodily-kinesthetic intelligence ("body smart")
- Musical intelligence ("music smart")
- Interpersonal intelligence ("people smart")
- Intrapersonal intelligence ("self smart")
- Naturalist intelligence ("nature smart")

The categories are fairly intuitive in their meaning and application. A person with an aptitude toward linguistic intelligence is one who remembers language well. This person can learn new languages more quickly than others. Logical-mathematical learners tend to learn more cognitively; they often strive to understand a skill or experience before it has happened and want to understand actions and movements before attempting them themselves. Logical-mathematical learners also prefer sequencing of thought and actions.

A spatially oriented person is adept at applying physical space into actions, such as occurs in arts and crafts. These learners are very good at putting things together or making equipment repairs.

Bodily-kinesthetic learners include many athletes. They can watch a demonstration and then conduct the skill with little effort or refinement. These are likely the participants who are impatient to get started with an activity.

Have you ever known someone who can hear a song once and immediately recall the lyrics, or someone who is extremely comfortable communicating thoughts and feelings to a group through music? This person likely has high musical intelligence.

Of course, there is a highly social person in most groups. This person is adept at communicating with others and tends to have a wide circle of friends. Many politicians and salespersons have high interpersonal intelligence.

Self-smart people are constantly drawn toward self-awareness and self-improvement. They might be either extroverted or introverted. They want to improve their skills and learn the best ways to face challenges in their lives.

Finally, nature-smart people include those who are drawn to nature and feel most comfortable in the outdoors. Unlike those who are bored by or fearful of some animals or natural occurrences in the outdoors, these learners embrace nature and feel an affinity with fauna and flora.

Some have argued for a ninth intelligence neglected by Gardner—that is, a spiritual or existential intelligence involving the ability to deal with larger and deeper issues such as the meaning of life. Gardner and others have yet to fully endorse spiritual intelligence as a ninth kind of intelligence.

According to Gardner (1993), a few caveats must be taken into account:

- Having a higher intelligence in an area does not guarantee proficiency in that area. It only means an individual will be more inclined to learn faster in that area.
- A person is not intelligent in simply one area. Most people have combinations of intelligences.
- A person who is logical-mathematical can still enjoy physical activity. It is *how* they learn, not *what* they learn that is of most use to the OAE professional.

It is a mistake to focus solely on either how participants prefer to learn or their aptitude for intelligence in a given domain. It is more important to match educational content and objectives to an educational approach. OAE instructors might easily assume that if a participant wishes to learn how to ski, he or she is likely kinesthetically attuned (body smart), but such assumptions are often mistaken. Rather than trying to determine preferred learning styles and intelligence modes for all participants, OAE instructors should strive to use a combination of teaching approaches to reach everyone. This will lead to variations in the educational objectives and content of programs. Using description, followed by demonstration, and then practice is a common approach to teaching OAE skills and cuts across most learning styles. With experience, instructors will learn to recognize when this approach is failing for one or more participants and be able to adjust instruction to allow for learning to occur for everyone.

SUMMARY

As we have discussed throughout this text, OAE is complex and multifaceted. There is no one universal construct or theory of OAE; rather, multiple theories and constructs might be in motion at any given time. Astute outdoor adventure educators are familiar with the theories most relevant to their scope of practice. Familiarity allows them to merge what is known about human behavior with the context, the social and physical setting, and their own personal experience to best facilitate rich learning opportunities for participants.

In this chapter we have identified three promising frameworks that fit well with the OAE experience: constructivism, social cognitive theory, and systems theories of development. These approaches to human development and learning align well with the philosophical and historical underpinnings of OAE. Constructivism centralizes the role of the learner and the social environment in development and growth. Social cognitive theory centralizes the importance of self-efficacy beliefs in actual performance and explains how these beliefs are developed through a combination of direct experience, observation, verbal feedback, and physiological and emotional responses. Systems theories approach development as a bidirectional network of proximal and distal influences, whereby learners are affected by and affect their environment. Each of these frameworks offers a different yet highly compatible lens through which to view an OAE experience.

Despite the potential for a holistic interpretation of OAE, numerous theories remain relevant to specific aspects of the OAE experience and have proven useful to educators. Theories such as expectancy value theory, attribution theory, and the theory of planned behavior are especially useful to educators trying to understand participant attributions and behaviors. Attention

restoration theory speaks to the potential restorative power of natural environments. Learning taxonomies provide language and a framework for different types of learning and educational objectives. The concepts of optimal arousal and flow have long resonated with OAE professionals who believe in the power of effectively engaging participants in the learning process without overloading them to the point that learning diminishes. Learning styles provide language on how our participants prefer to learn. Likewise, the theory of multiple intelligences allows educators to discuss learning potential in terms of domain-specific capacities, where some participants will inevitably be more adept than others.

The frameworks and ideas provided in this chapter are commonly accepted and potentially useful. However, OAE professionals should stay current with both thought and practice related to OAE and be open to other explanations of why and how programs and practices work. Although certainly useful, many theories have been developed with a focus on a context or population that is dissimilar to OAE or for a purpose irrelevant to a specific situation or group. Understanding and relevance of each framework should be judiciously applied by outdoor adventure educators to improve participants' experiences and learning potentials. This has always been the role and intent of theory—to help us improve our practice.

⚜ Issues for Further Discussion

1. What examples from your own experiences fit with contemporary theory in OAE?

2. What are some research questions that could be investigated given our current understanding of theory?

3. Which of the theories discussed in this chapter might be useful for you to consider in your own professional OAE practice? How so?

4. What theory or construct from the parent disciplines in social and behavioral sciences is absent in this chapter?

5. Are any constructs or theories truly unique to OAE?

Development Across the Life Span

Why This Chapter Is Important

In this chapter we help you prepare for some of the predictable differences in the many groups of people that attend OAE programs. As with most predictions, there always will be exceptions. In fact, for teen OAE experiences including excursions, exceptions might be the rule. Teens seem to think that tents are soundproof and that no one else can hear the intimate details they share with their tentmates. Although they occasionally hush their voices to low tones, they soon succumb to their inherent excitement, passion, and energy, and those nearby can hear clearly the stories about their daring, unsupervised escapades, which we can only hope are exaggerated.

College students are more savvy. They know how to conceal what they do not want you to know. They are also less compliant—you can't just tell them what to do. Older students will not passively allow an instructor to dictate discussion topics or lessons.

As you might expect, adult trips are generally more subdued. With minimal structure, the participants take charge. They teach each other. They no longer look to instructors as the main, or only, source of information. If they do not want to do something, they decline politely but forcefully. You can't say "just do it" and expect them to respond.

Older adults don't charge up the slope in a race to the summit. They need their reading glasses. They like layover days and will not plan and provision to eat solely oatmeal for seven straight days.

As we have said, for every rule there are exceptions. You will inevitably encounter the older adult who has perfect eyesight and unbounded energy. You will be happy to meet the self-directed, responsible, and socially mature young teenager. Still, it is helpful to know what you might generally expect.

Learning Outcomes

After completing this chapter, you should be able to

* compare the historical practices of OAE to the current evidence on high-quality youth programming;
* differentiate the developmental needs of young people and emerging adults;
* summarize the characteristics of adult learners; and
* explain why older adults are increasingly important to OAE and why OAE is increasingly important to older adults.

OAE serves diverse groups of clients and populations who differ developmentally as well as in purpose, motives, and intent. Knowing some developmental differences of your clients should help you improve your program design and implementation. Though we can't cover all the potential populations you might encounter—even subsets of OAE, such as wilderness therapy programs or ropes courses, serve an incredible diversity of clients—in this chapter we track common developmental differences across the life span and discuss how these interface with OAE.

Development, in a broad sense, is a combination of learning and maturation. Although not strictly age-based, development tends to progress over the life span. If students are not cognitively, physically, or emotionally prepared for a lesson, less learning will occur. On the other hand, sometimes developmentally appropriate lessons are not offered to students who are mature enough to benefit from them. Astute OAE instructors understand they must design programs for a target population yet be flexible enough to accommodate individual differences. In this chapter we discuss some of the main developmental features across the life span and provide age-based characteristics of typical youth, emerging adult, adult, and older adult populations.

Scholars continue to debate the relative importance and respective roles of nature versus nurture in human development. Although genetics, biology, and time certainly determine predisposition and some aspects of development, it is also clear that experiences and context play vital roles in how development occurs. The nature–nurture dialectic continues, yet most agree that both play roles in development across the life span (Sameroff, 2010). Just as a seed given adequate sunlight, water, and nutrients grows larger and is more resilient, people provided with high-quality experiences tend to thrive. Likewise, an environment cannot change certain genetic and biological realities.

Despite the historical attention to life-span and life-stage models of development, most scholars now acknowledge the critical role of context (see Systems Theories of Development in chapter 6). In some models of development, the more proximal connections and settings in people's lives exert greater influence on their development than the more distal connections. Family, friends, and schooling, for instance, have more direct influence than government or culture. Age alone or life stage (e.g., marriage, retirement) have less influence on development than contextual influences that can either directly support or thwart individual development across the life span.

Even with the acknowledged influence of contextual models, adults still tend to view themselves in specific life stages, such as middle-aged or retired. Thus while certain contexts certainly drive development, speaking of needs and wants in a life-stage model remains useful (Hoare, 2009), and many theorists view development as occurring through a set of age-related stages. Though most acknowledge these stages are neither linear nor entirely predictable, the stages do provide a framework for approaching development across the life span. Piaget, Erickson, and Kohlberg are notable theorists who advocate developmental stage models.

Although these stage theories are both generally accepted and widely criticized, perhaps most relevant for OAE is that they illustrate probable changes across the life span. Children tend to think in more concrete, egocentric, and unidimensional ways. At some point, most adults come to understand that most decisions involve shades of gray and that right or wrong can depend on context, values, and perspective. Commonly, this transition from concrete thinking to more postformal thinking begins during adolescence and continues into emerging adulthood.

One conceptualization of how some of these frameworks can be applied to OAE populations is presented in figure 7.1. Adolescents tend to view reality as static, knowledge as concrete, and sources of knowledge as well defined (e.g., an instructor has the knowledge). As people age, they tend to embrace the relativism of knowledge and realize there can be multiple correct answers, that knowledge is often open for interpretation, and that while sources of knowledge can differ, they can also be more or less "right" depending on the source's credibility and experience. This trend of development has been generally supported in OAE (Collins et al., 2012).

Another implication of these stage theories supports the premise that as thinking processes and approaches evolve, the circle of environmental influence also widens. In early years, circles of influence involve primarily peers, caregivers, teachers, and home and school environments. As life transitions occur and identity formation begins to stabilize, adults tend to realize their own agency in co-creating their environments.

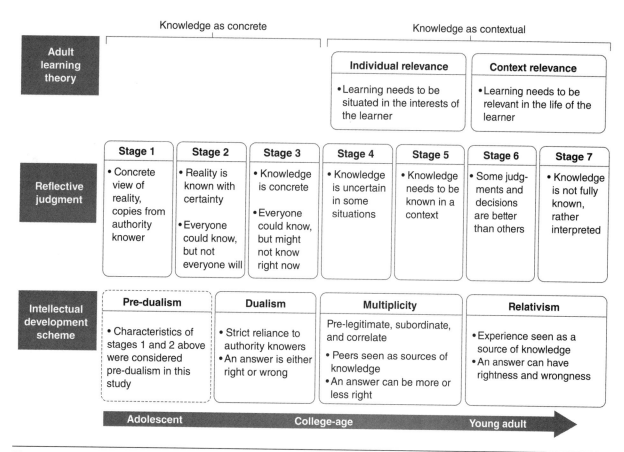

Figure 7.1 Stage theories framework as applied in OAE populations.

Reprinted, by permission, from R. Collins, K. Paisley, J. Sibthorp, and J. Gookin, 2012, "'Black and white thinkers' and 'colorful problems': Understanding student thinking in outdoor education," *Journal of Outdoor Recreation, Education, and Leadership* 4(2): 11-24.

Thus as people progress through their life span, they might work to more actively position themselves in social and environmental contexts that are more supportive of their individual needs.

For purposes of discussing developmental approaches across the life span, this chapter is divided into sections on youth, emerging adults, adults, and older adults. Definitions vary, but youth typically includes children and adolescents through their primary and secondary schooling. Emerging adulthood represents a time between supervision by a parent or legal guardian and true personal responsibility and financial independence. Although legally this time is typically viewed to be age 21, in reality a wide variance exists among individuals. Once these criteria are met, however, adulthood commences. On the other hand, older adults are a diverse group, but even in this group there are normal and predictable changes as people age; typically, somewhere in the 60s is considered to be the demarcation time from adult to older adult.

YOUTH AND ADOLESCENTS

As with most recreational and educational program offerings for youth, outdoor and adventure programs have embraced the need and desire for more holistic and balanced approaches to youth development. The phrase *positive youth development* connotes an approach to youth that involves creating opportunities for youth to explore, engage, and develop in a holistic manner that will help them prepare for successful and productive lives.

Early advocates of positive youth development spent time differentiating this approach from the historic deficit-based models of youth development that had traditionally been funded and supported. Deficit-based models focused on what was "wrong" with youth. Problems with drugs, alcohol, or violence illustrated problems that needed to be fixed in populations of young people. However, the more holistic approach

Norway's *Friluftsliv*

Carsten Roland—Finnmark University College, Alta, Norway
Sigmund Andersen—Finnmark University College, Alta, Norway

Friluftsliv might loosely be translated as an experience-oriented, noncommercial activity in a natural environment. A common definition is "open air living." Friluftsliv also connotes a continuation of an older harvesting tradition involving activities such as hunting, fishing, and berry collecting (Faarlund, 1974). The authors Vingdal and Hollekim (2001) note that sensual impressions are critical to meaningful experiences, and in a natural environment sensual impressions are often stronger and more meaningful than they can be in a classroom. Thus in friluftsliv the nature experience itself is the central goal. This goal has remained prominent in Norwegian and Scandinavian culture, and can be contrasted to outdoor activities or adventure education in many other Western countries where adventure activities themselves are the focus.

Friluftsliv outdoor educators, or conwayors, use the opportunities in nature for various learning processes based on experience. Friluftsliv conwayors must be flexible and open to using whatever experience the time in nature provides. They try to position participants as explorers. In addition, conwayors are integral to formal education in Norway. In elementary schools, one important aim of friluftsliv is to develop a nature-friendly lifestyle. In higher education, friluftsliv has existed as an independent subject since around 1970. In Norwegian texts friluftsliv is referred to as a separate subject, an activity, a teaching and learning method, and a pedagogical tool (Haslestad, 2000).

Friluftsliv curricula looks different across the life span. For younger participants, the focus is to develop an affective connection with nature and to cultivate innate curiosity. For example, upon seeing tracks from a polar fox, young participants might spontaneously generate questions about the fox's diet, travel patterns, and habitat.

With older subjects, who might have established beliefs about nature, nature experience may be used by the friluftsliv conwayor to influence life transitions. In this aspect, friluftsliv is put into an ecopedagogical context, as a deliberate pedagogical means of achieving a life in harmony with nature (Haslestad, 2000). For example, on a multiday excursion a friluftsliv conwayor might create a contrast to the subjects' daily lives by slowing down and not rushing from activity to activity. He or she might encourage using some extra time in a scenic camp during the morning and evening to allow participants to more fully experience nature, giving them space to embrace the power of nature and the feelings of integration with natural surroundings. From an ecophilosophical perspective, the human soul might be slowly integrated with the soul of the natural surroundings (Ness, 1991). The nature experience is a highly personal interaction, and participants might view themselves as more a part of nature and not separate from it. A conscientious friluftsliv conwayor uses nature experiences as tools to afford unique feelings of involvement and unity with nature. This inte-

Simply living and being in nature is a central component of friluftsliv.
Courtesy of Arctic Nature Guide study program.

gration might be the most important aspect of friluftsliv, and aptly applies to all aspects of human development across the life span as we continue to wrestle with human roles and influences in the world.

References

Faarlund, N. (1974): *Friluftsliv. Hva–hvorfor–hvordan.* HNA-trykk, Hemsedal.

Haslestad, K. (2000). *På leting etter hva friluftsliv egentlig er–med utgangspunkt i ulike perspekti-* ver–og med et spesielt fokus på friluftsliv i grunns-kolens læreplaner de siste nesten seksti årene. (Masters thesis pedagogy). University of Oslo.

Ness, A. (1991). *Økologi, samfunn og livsstil.* 5.utgave, 2. opplag. Oslo: Universitetsforlaget.

Stoknes, P. (1999). *Naturopplevelsen og det økologiske selv.* Mestre Fjellet, nr 44.

Vingdal, I., & Hollekim, I. (2001). Barn i naturen. Oslo.

to positive youth development has always been evident as an underlying philosophical approach imbedded in outdoor and adventure education.

Historical Approaches to OAE for Youth

Most of the earliest adventure education programs were aimed squarely at youth. Early movements such as scouting and organized camping offered some of the first formal adventure programming. When Outward Bound began in 1941, its primary participants were young men. However, it was Kurt Hahn's educational philosophy and approaches that came from years of running private boarding schools first in Germany and later in England that fully solidified adventure education's foundation with holistic education and youth development. By the time Hahn began Gordonstoun School in 1934, his philosophy and approach to education had coalesced. Hahn believed in educating adolescents in a way that would allow them to become meaningful members of society. At Salem, Gordonstoun, and then with the founding of Outward Bound in Aberdovey, Hahn designed educational components to teach self-regulation, social competence, leadership, and social responsibility (Miner & Boldt, 1981; Skidelsky, 1969).

At Gordonstoun, students held a great deal of responsibility for the operation of the school and were required to complete daily check sheets in an effort to cultivate self-supervision (Skidelsky, 1969). Hahn's goal was to "produce young people able to effect what they see to be right, despite hardships, despite dangers, despite inner skepticism, despite boredom, despite mockery from the world, despite emotion of the moment" (Miner & Boldt, 1981, p. 42). To this end, Hahn relied on a group leadership model in which the older boys helped the younger ones to become more responsible for their own actions.

Today's OAE programs, often based on Hahn's beliefs, maintain a student-driven leadership and promote self-regulation. Student ownership and the self-regulation of learning remain fundamental goals of OAE programs. Similar approaches remain at the core of most high-quality youth programs.

High-Quality OAE Youth Programming

Although values vary slightly, most OAE professionals agree that some core factors are essential for high-quality youth programs. The National Research Council recognizes such essential elements as developmental frameworks; commitment to accountability and assessment of outcomes; trained staff; safety; structure; supportive relationships; opportunities for belonging; positive social norms; opportunities to make a difference and build skills; and integration with family, school, and community efforts (2002). In 2007, Durlak and Weissberg conducted a meta-analysis of youth programs targeting personal and social skill development and posited that the most successful approaches are "sequential, active, focused, and explicit." *Sequential* refers to an intentional program arc and curricular design that builds and fits together. *Active* implies experiential and hands-on activities, which seem to be critical to internalization of learning for youth. *Focused* essentially means that the program should be goal oriented and have targeted outcomes for participants. *Explicit* refers to ways in which the articulated goals are subdivided and intentionally targeted within the program. For example, if the goal is to increase social skills, then an explicit objective targeting, say, team-work, might be addressed through the use and debriefing of team-focused initiatives and activities on day 2 of a program. As the best of these programs were evidence based, this meta-analysis provides additional confirmation that intentional program design and implementation matters significantly in youth programming. Gambone, Klem, and Connell (2002) condensed a number of study findings and frameworks into their Community Action Framework, which focuses on supports and opportunities necessary for the achievement of developmental outcomes for

youth. These supports and opportunities include multiple supportive relationships with adults and peers, challenging and engaging activities and learning experiences, meaningful opportunities for involvement and membership, and safety.

Consider a prototypical adventure program involving a dozen young people and three instructors on a multiday expedition. It is difficult to imagine a program *not* inherently including most of the factors just listed. What would such an expedition look like if it were not sequential or did not use trained staff and offer skill-building opportunities? What program leader does not aspire to foster supportive relationships, oppor-

Authentic decision-making experiences allow adolescents to develop higher-order thinking.
Courtesy of Jim Sibthorp.

tunities for belonging, and positive social norms? What type of an expedition is void of challenge, active learning, and meaningful involvement?

Contemporary Youth and Outdoor Adventure Education

Adolescents are going through a variety of biological and emotional changes. Growth spurts, sexual maturity, hormones, and identity formation all characterize this time period. A need for independence is often accompanied by a need for structure, and the experience that precedes good judgment and decision making is often lacking. It is these very characteristics that make OAE an ideal medium for adolescent growth and development.

Although young people often make poor decisions, their neural connections in the prefrontal cortex grow rapidly during adolescence and continue to develop through emerging adulthood. This portion of the brain is most commonly associated with higher-order thinking and problem-solving and cognitive skills, both valued and often required in OAE. Strengthening these skills with authentic decision-making situations make for a fertile context for improving decision-making processes.

Though young people can often accurately assess risk, they tend to make riskier decisions even so. Some literature suggests that adolescents are simply more risk tolerant because they are seeking to find their fit in the world; other research suggests that the presence of peers and social situations perceived as demanding can dramatically increase adolescents' propensities to take risks (cf. Albert, Chein, & Steinberg, 2013). This increase disappears as people age and become less concerned about what their peers think. Clearly, adolescent emotions are more directly tied to social appraisals (Somerville, 2013) than adult emotions are.

The centrality of peer relations in OAE programs resonates well with young people, who consistently report that social and peer relationships are very important and influential in their lives (Brown & Larson, 2009). The inherent and necessary peer interdependence of an expedition serves to intensify these relationships in OAE. This trend remains evident in current research on adventure programming, where adolescents continue to acknowledge the critical role of the social environment and social relationships during adventure and outdoor

programs (e.g., Sammet, 2010; Smith, Steele, & Gidlow, 2010).

The little research that has been done on the differences between youth- and adult-focused OAE courses largely supports the general literature on pedagogy and andragogy. For example, young people tend to think more linearly and see learning opportunities as more concrete, whereas adults tend to learn important lessons from a variety of means (Collins et al., 2012). Young people also report greater learning in interpersonal realms, such as leadership, communication, and teamwork (e.g., Sibthorp, Paisley, & Gookin, 2007). Given their relative lack of experience in these areas compared to older participants, this finding suggests that participants are more likely to experience growth and development in less well-developed areas.

EMERGING ADULTS

The line between adolescence and adulthood has been blurred in the scientific community as scholars have come to recognize and accept that youth mature and develop differently and at different ages. Physical maturity may or may not coincide with emotional, cognitive, or spiritual development. According to Tanner, Arnett, and Leis, the change to adulthood occurs when individuals become responsible for themselves, independently make decisions, and are financially independent (2009). For the purpose of our discussion, we are considering this cohort to include adults aged from 18 to 29.

Before age 18, education is largely required by society. After primary and secondary schooling, education scope, medium, and direction all involve far greater choice and autonomy. Although social and familial pressures continue, volition in selecting an OAE program is more typical as age increases. More adolescents than emerging adults are "sent" on programs. This increase in choice—in schooling, jobs, friends, leisure, and romantic relationships—makes the life experiences during this stage central to identity formation. For many, this time tends to be a self-focused age between dependence on adult caretakers and formation of a partnership or family that requires greater attention to others.

Changes in identity over this time tend to make people "less emotionally labile, more responsible, and more cautious" (Caspi, 1998, p. 347). These types of changes indicate that personality is evolving over the period of emerging adulthood, as people seek to experiment and integrate core elements of their identities. Adventure programs need to recognize that an opportunity to try new roles, activities, and behaviors is an important aspect of this time for many people.

As is true during adolescence, friendships play a critical role during emerging adulthood. In the absence of a parental or caretaker presence and without yet establishing a long-term romantic relationship, many emerging adults place friends as their most critical confidants and sources of social support (Tanner et al., 2009). Leisure time is also critical to emerging adults, as they have more discretionary time than any adults except Americans older than 55 (Bureau of Labor Statistics, 2010). As we would expect given the life-span and life-stage models, the emerging adult's brain generally becomes better at problem solving and reasoning (Giedd et al., 1999). Learning evolves from dualistic (right and wrong) to relativism and the understanding that opinions vary and that not all opinions are equally credible (cf. Perry, 1999).

OAE is well situated to provide for the needs of emerging adults. Through programs involving challenging and novel activities, emerging adults are able to explore their own identities, wrestle with complex and contextual problems, and increase their expanding leisure repertoires. The small-group aspects of most adventure programs plays well to the continued interest in peer relations, social connections, and role models. An increasing number of young adults are actively seeking "gap-year" programs that allow inter- and intrapersonal exploration before they transition to more traditional and goal-oriented career focuses. Though countries such as England, Sweden, Germany, and Australia have long encouraged young people to take time to travel and explore before taking on adult responsibilities, this is not as common in the United States.

One way OAE has come to address the need for personal exploration is through semester programs that offer college credit during expeditionary learning. Often for a price comparable to a semester at college, college-aged students can enroll in a semester program that includes college credit in environmental studies, biology, and recreation courses. Semester courses now represent a substantial portion of all field days for a number of OAE programs, such as the National Outdoor Leadership School, Outward Bound, and Summit Adventures.

ADULTS

Although history and research offer much advice on how to work with young people on adventure courses, adults and adult learning are largely ignored. Still, adults remain an important market segment for many OAE programs, and most who come are choosing to do so for a specific purpose and with intent, as opposed to younger students who might be pressured to attend or are unsure why they are there.

Most of the research on adult learners indicates they are different from young people in important ways. For example, physical and cognitive performance can and do change over the life span. Adults are not as conditioned to schooling as a way of learning and tend to view life experience as a primary source of education. Adults have a great deal of life experience that can and should be used by educators, and they value immediate relevance. Individual differences and learning preferences tend to increase with age (Lindeman, 1961). For these reasons, adults need to be significantly involved in their educational decisions, and they respond well to internal motivators (Knowles, Holton, & Swanson, 1998).

Knowles and other learning theorists (e.g., Tennant, 2006) contend that adult learners are often more self-directed than young learners are. Self-regulation and emotion-regulation strategies generally improve with age (Blanchard-Fields & Kalinauskas, 2009), which leads to more self-direction in learning. That is, adults take initiative, formulate learning needs and goals, instigate necessary learning strategies, and evaluate their learning outcomes more independently than young learners do.

Adults are also better at complex logical thinking that involves both logic and subjectivity (also known as postformal thinking) (Sinnott, 2009). They understand that a person interacts with the context to create understanding, which could be different had they interacted differently. They know they have influence within their environments. Whereas young people might feel constrained by their environment, adults typically know they have influence and can actively work to improve their situations. It might be that the postformal thinking more common in adults predisposes them to greater potential for transformational learning.

Jack Mezirow's transformation theory of adult learning aligns well with OAE. According to Mezirow (1995), learning can take place in four

Adult learners are often more self-directed than young learners.
Courtesy of Kirk Nichols.

primary ways: (1) It can occur as new content is placed within an existing meaning scheme, (2) the learning can result in the formation of a new meaning scheme, (3) the learning can transform a meaning scheme, or (4) the learning can transform a meaning perspective.

The first three types of learning are largely compatible with most current understanding of how people learn (e.g., Piaget; Schunk). However, transforming a meaning perspective is a distinct aspect of Mezirow's theory. Mezirow contends that more perspective-changing transformations occur through a process that might involve these 11 steps (not always in this order): encountering a disorienting dilemma, performing self-examination, assessing assumptions, recognizing that discontent is shared and has been negotiated by others, exploring options, planning for action, gaining the necessary knowledge or skill, trying

new roles, negotiating and renegotiating relationships, building confidence and competence in new roles, and reintegrating new perspective into one's life (Mezirow, 1995 p. 50).

Not surprisingly, this process aligns with what an OAE experience can offer. The novelty of the OAE experience is often disorienting and serves as a catalyst for self-examination and assumption testing. The extended duration of many OAE experiences allows time for contemplation, reflection, and planning. The social environment allows new roles to be adopted and relationships to be formed. Successful transformation then requires reintegration with everyday life. Consider a typical OAE course in which a participant is immersed in a new and unfamiliar context and must determine how her current assumptions mesh with her current experiences. Perhaps she assumes that leaders are always in front of a group of followers. As the course unfolds, her experience contradicts this assumption, which is initially disorienting. However, through contemplation and dialog with course mates, she begins to reconceptualize her understanding of leadership. She plans to try a new leadership approach, explore some options, and practice this new approach. After continued feedback and negotiation, she becomes more comfortable with her new idea of leadership and integrates it within her psyche. (Refer to the Outward Bound process model described in chapter 5.)

Evidence suggests that transformational learning does occur in OAE programs. Outcomes from adventure education such as a change in life perspective, appreciation for simpler life, appreciation for nature (Sibthorp, Paisley, Furman, & Gookin, 2008), challenging assumptions of self and others, profound impacts on life (Gass, Garvey, & Sugerman, 2003), and increased connection with the outdoors (Mazze, 2006) all appear to fit within the transformative learning context. An extended time in nature, the separation in time and space from normal life, the distinct nature of the social community, and the challenge and intensity of OAE experiences have been clearly linked to transformational learning (D'Amato & Krasny, 2011).

OLDER ADULTS

There is not a widely accepted definition of older adults, but most people associate older adulthood with retirement age—between 60 and 65 years of age. Predictable physiological and psychological changes occur as people age into their 50s and beyond. Bones become more brittle, the circulatory system is less efficient, muscle flexibility and strength decrease, memory is less proficient, and hearing and eyesight tend to deteriorate. Psychologically, older adults tend to refocus on making the most of their time remaining, and the invulnerable feelings of youth are less prevalent. However, the concept of successful aging has attracted a great deal of attention, and biological age is often not a good indicator of what to expect from older adults. By the time adults reach old age, how they have lived, taken care of themselves, and their health status often have more to do with their physiological and psychological status than age does.

Today's older adults are an active, engaged, and heterogeneous group, making generalizations difficult. However, most of what educators know about adult learning theory likely remains relevant to older adults. As people age, they typically need less structure, have more ownership or voice, and have greater life experience that influences how and what they learn. In addition, a large segment of this current cohort of older adults were involved in outdoor recreational pursuits when they were younger, and now more appreciate the planning, support structure, and security of a formal OAE program.

For a subset of older adults, OAE remains a popular and valued pursuit. In a study by Road Scholar (formerly Elderhostel, see roadscholar. org), about 47 percent of the adult population over 55 is well suited to active educational travel (2007). This population is often seeking mental stimulation, social engagement, physical activity, and outlets for creative expression (Elderhostel). As mental and cognitive deterioration have been linked both with aging and a lack of regular use, some older adults are enthusiastically seeking opportunities to travel with friends, explore, and learn. In addition, regular physical activity is viewed almost universally as beneficial. This combination of mental engagement, social connection, and physical activity fits well with what OAE can offer.

Though little research has been done specifically on older adults and OAE, Bobilya and colleagues (2010) do propose that this is a growth market for OAE. In the travel industry, the older adult population is highly desired because of their discretionary income, available leisure time, and segment growth as the Baby Boomer population ages and life expectancy continues to increase. One study on older adult motivations regarding outdoor adventure programs concluded that this segment is especially attracted to connecting with nature, being physically active, learning, and being among a supportive group (Sugerman, 2001).

ADDITIONAL VIEWS OF HUMAN DEVELOPMENT

Another way to look at development across the life span is to understand the role of regulation (cf. Sameroff, 2010). Small children are often regulated by others. If they are cold, their caregivers might tell them to put on a coat. At some point they understand that they can regulate their own temperature by adding or subtracting layers of clothing. As children age, they begin to be more active regulators of a variety of basic functions, including emotional responses and social behaviors. However, an external regulatory capacity always emanates from context. Although sleep is a biological necessity, most people adjust their wake and sleep patterns to meet requirements determined primarily by external forces, such as school or work schedules. Though the concept of flow (see chapter 6) is intriguing and certainly aligns with OAE, the reality is that skill and challenge are not always aligned, and people need to know how to regulate emotions when a challenge seems insurmountable or to persevere through boring tasks that, nonetheless, remain important to long-range goals. Thus one approach to human development through OAE is to increase self-regulatory capacity in participants and to help people become more self-regulatory as they increase in independence, which is typically related to maturation through adulthood. Some of the more common techniques thought to enhance self-regulation such as goal setting, planning, individual coaching, opportunities for reflection, and practicing persistence are common in OAE.

Another consideration of human development across the life span is to explore how learning interfaces with developmental needs. The promise of a high-quality educational experience manifests through an interaction with the context and the developmental readiness of the individual. For example, preschoolers and middle-schoolers might both visit a climbing wall. The preschoolers understand that falling hurts, but not the physics behind the belay system. However, the developmental capacity for abstract thought is greater in the middle-school students, who thus might take different lessons from the climbing

wall, such as connecting belay systems to science lessons involving friction or potential and kinetic energy. A similar climbing experience might be a catalyst for a shift in identity during college, as a participant begins to see him- or herself as a "climber." The experience, the reflection, and the learning all shift as the developmental needs of the individual change over the life span.

As you work to design and implement your OAE programs, always consider how your content aligns with your participants and their developmental needs. Generalizations do not pertain to all students, but there are some predictable developmental needs and transitions across the life span (table 7.1). Whether focusing on age-based transitions, life stage, or development need, matching your educational approach and intent to both your content and your population is critical to successful OAE programming.

SUMMARY

Young people remain a historically relevant and currently sizable segment of OAE participants. Thus we must strive to understand the alignment between the historical and philosophical roots of OAE and the contemporary research and literature on high-quality youth programs. Hahn's focus on ameliorating the contemporary social ills for the young people of his time led him to practices such as peer mentoring, small-group leadership, service, and physical activity that instilled responsibility, self-regulation, initiative, and leadership outcomes that remain relevant today. Programmatic elements such as staff training, sequenced experiences, skill-building

Table 7.1 Developmental Consideration Across the Life Span

	Approximate ages	Developmental considerations
Youth and adolescents	<18	• Importance of peers and social influences. • Emerging complex thinking and decision-making skills. • Risk taking is socially influenced. • More concrete thinkers.
Emerging adults	18-29	• Forming distinct identity. • Developing complex problem-solving skills. • Peers important and influential.
Adults	30-65	• Self-directed learners. • Diverse personal experiences.
Older adults	65+	• Physiological and psychological changes of aging. • Retirement brings discretionary time.

opportunities, supportive environments, and active learning are considered critical by both academics and practitioners.

Though all young people are different, are influenced by their contexts, and are constantly evolving within society, several characteristics are typical. Young people are often accustomed to structure and tend not to think in the complex ways that older participants do. The social environment and role of social interactions are likely to be more important aspects of courses for young people.

After turning 18, youths have a great deal more freedom to choose their activities, peers, and situations. However, they are often still not completely independent, and their identities are still solidifying. For these emerging adults, the complex, challenging, and novel problems common in OAE, as well as the supportive social relationships, present opportunities to try new things and discover themselves. Emerging adulthood commonly involves a transitional period, which includes active experimentation and identity formation. Emerging adults are typically capable of more reflective postformal thinking, but they are usually not as self-directed as adults.

Adults are typically self-directed learners who know what they want to get out of a course or program and believe they are active agents who can influence their environments. They are comfortable with less structure. They also bring a wealth of personal experience and seek to connect their current learning with their own experience. Older adults are a diverse and growing segment of the population. They continue to value learning, physical activity, social connections, and nature experiences, all of which are well suited to OAE.

OAE can provide critical and pivotal experiences across the life span. However, as people evolve and grow throughout their lives, they will likely come to OAE with different expectations and needs. As we have stressed, OAE is a medium that can be used for a variety of purposes. Many programs run mixed-aged groups such as parents and children. Other programs are highly focused on a specific clientele such as adolescents with substance abuse problems, veterans adjusting to postservice life, or corporate clients looking to bolster cooperation and teamwork. In such cases, it is likely that programming goals should have greater influence on the OAE program than developmental or age-based characteristics of the population will have. Though it is certainly appropriate to recognize and try to understand differences in young people, emerging adults, adults, and older adults, there are often some commonalities among these groups. Educators and programmers involved in OAE should be aware of the differences but should not forget the individual needs of students regardless of their age or life stage.

Issues for Further Discussion

1. How might young people from different backgrounds and geographic regions differently view and value OAE experiences? For example, some OAE programs now seek to bring youths from many locations, including the Middle East, North America, Europe, and Australia, together for OAE experiences. How would these OAE experiences contribute to an enhanced intercultural understanding among group members?

2. How should programmers strike a balance between the predictable development needs across the life span and the specific needs of an individual?

3. How can OAE assist with life transitions?

4. Many educators involved in OAE fall into the emerging adult category. What implications does this have for OAE instruction? For example, what advice would you have for older instructors who are working with younger populations?

5. Why are young people and emerging adults still the most common OAE program participants?

III

RESEARCH

■ ■ ■ ■ ■ ■ ■ ■ ■ ■

It is not enough to do your best;
you must know what to do,
and then do your best.
—W. Edwards Deming

As you have probably realized by now, we believe in the importance of theory and research to the future of OAE. Whereas in part II we focused on key models, theories, and constructs relevant to OAE, in part III we center on the important role of research.

The focus, and title, of chapter 8 is Evaluation Research, which has an applied purpose and focus in OAE. Evaluation remains fairly informal in most OAE programs. In our field, one way to obtain research evidence is to collect our own data to inform our own design and implementation decisions. However, formalized evaluation programs can complement other sources of evidence. In this chapter we discuss how OAE might use evaluation research to improve design and implementation.

One of the primary concerns among OAE professionals is participant outcomes. It is largely through outcomes that we defend the relevance of our field. But what types of learning outcomes are most likely to occur through OAE, and why? What attributes of OAE experiences can best be manipulated to provide certain outcomes? If you are designing a program with the end in mind, chapter 9, Outcomes of Participation, presents options for end goals as well as many thoughts on methods for eliciting desired outcomes.

In chapter 10, State of OAE Research, we discuss research in more general terms and provide an overview of the role, history, and current trends in OAE research. We discuss the notion of evidence-based practices, which are being increasingly used in allied fields such as social work and education. Although OAE research has been constrained by a number of factors, innovative methods offer new ways to inform research questions.

In chapter 11, Improving Research, we propose ways to navigate the challenges inherent in OAE research and to move the field forward. Along with recommending practical ways to strengthen OAE research, we discuss particular areas in OAE that are in need of further investigation. Finally, chapter 12, Evolving Trends and Issues, summarizes the implications of previous discussions and presents evolving trends and issues important to OAE.

As you read part III, consider how you might use the research and evidence presented to inform your own professional practice. How does the content of these chapters support or contradict the evidence presented in parts I and II? How does it fit with your own beliefs regarding how and why OAE functions?

Evaluation Research

Why This Chapter Is Important

Evaluation and evidence-based research remain important both for funding and program justification in OAE. As a result, OAE practitioners must be able to collect data, use evidence, and provide a rationale for why we do what we do. In addition, for better or worse, much of the research in OAE is evaluation research. Some of it is conducted with enough rigor and theoretical conceptualization that it can be useful beyond the original program it was conducted on. Taken as a whole, evaluation research remains an important contributor to our field's overall state of knowledge. Sometimes it is applied knowledge that is timely, specific, and contextualized, informing specific practices. By definition, the scope, utility, and importance of an evaluation project is limited, but this does not negate the value of evaluation research to both programs and the broader field of OAE. In this chapter we include several tangible examples of how evaluation research is currently used and how it continues to improve professional practice.

Learning Outcomes

After completing this chapter, you should be able to

- define evaluation in OAE,
- compare the common purposes of evaluation in OAE,
- describe the common techniques of evaluation in OAE,
- understand the concepts of best practices and benchmarking in OAE, and
- describe the main limitations of evaluation designs commonly used in OAE.

Although evaluation is a type of research, it has a different focus than basic research. Evaluation is typically applied and not concerned with generalizing findings. In other words, most evaluation is conducted to inform a particular decision within a specific context or program. Whether the data collected are useful in other contexts or for different decisions is not a primary concern or purpose of the research. In contrast, basic research typically speaks to a wider audience and involves findings that can be more generally applied. Despite these differences, much of the research conducted in OAE is applied and interested in informing professional practice. That is, OAE research can be considered evaluation research despite the potential for the findings to speak to a wider audience or create a body of knowledge for OAE. In addition, many of the approaches, techniques, and strategies employed in broader or more general forms of research remain applicable for evaluation.

At the most basic level, evaluation is about collecting and using evidence to inform a decision. Henderson and Bialeschki (2010) refer to the trilogy of evaluation:

1. Criteria (the questions)
2. Evidence (the data)
3. Judgment (the interpretation)

To inform a decision, one must know what questions to ask, where and how to access the evidence or data, and how to interpret the data in a meaningful way to inform the decision and answer the questions. Many decisions are made by OAE programs, and a variety of evaluation techniques are commonly employed in practice.

A good way to begin an evaluation is to consider these four questions:

1. What do we need to know to make a better decision?
2. Where is the information?
3. How can we get the information, and what is its quality?
4. How can we use the information we gather to inform our decision?

On the surface, this looks like a fairly simple process. But to do it well and have confidence in its application to the potential decision, the best answers are often compromises between what is ideal and what is realistic. Though basic research aspires toward an ideal in scientific process and rigor, evaluation research is helpful only if it provides useful and timely evidence to improve practice or inform a decision.

COMMON PURPOSES OF EVALUATION

There are many ways to discuss evaluation research, but one of the more common frameworks divides evaluation questions into five broad categories:

1. Needs assessment and planning
2. Assessment of logic models and program theories
3. Assessment for improvement of program process
4. Documentation and accountability
5. Efficiency assessment (cf. Rossi, Freeman, & Lipsey, 2004)

Whereas all of these types of questions can be of use to OAE professionals, some are more common than others. Some represent untapped potential. Others remain, and will continue to remain, challenging to realize given the nature of OAE programs.

Needs Assessment and Planning

This type of evaluation is generally concerned with both the participant needs and the program, activity, and resource needs to run the program. The main focus is on proactive planning. For social policy or prevention-oriented programs, needs assessments identify community or societal needs and goals to address through program offerings. However, most OAE programs already in existence use needs assessment to better understand expansion and retooling of service offerings. In addition, for programs more interested in market forces and consumer desires, these "needs" might also reflect participant desires. If participants want to go sea kayaking in Alaska and are willing to pay for this experience, then the program can be funded through sales revenue. Either way, a needs assessment begins to inform the when, where, and how of OAE programming.

Many OAE organizations use alumni surveys that inquire about interest in new programs or destinations. Patient assessment plans and program applications often include evidence that informs OAE programs on how to best plan for and run programs. Many programs collect participant information that includes expectations, goals, and interests. This can be used to customize an existing program to the needs of a group, or even an individual (figure 8.1). Location scouting or site assessment is another example of evaluation used to inform planning. Compiling information on potential travel routes, evacuation options, and possible hazards, OAE professionals are better able to make proactive changes or adjustments prior to running the program.

Assessment of Logic Models and Program Theories

The use of logic models is one of the more notable techniques being adopted by programs focused on understanding their processes. Logic models are visual representations of how a program works. Although their form and function can vary immensely, logic models usually include the program's goals, outcomes, outputs, activities, and inputs. Goals are what the program aspires to be or achieve. The program goals should stem from the organization's mission. Outcomes are typically broken into long term, intermediate, and initial and represent observable changes in the program participants. In contrast, outputs illustrate the program's scope, or size. Activities are the processes that occur during the program. Inputs are the resources necessary to run the program activities. Ideally, logic models are created from program goals. A program's goals help programmers determine the outcomes they would see in participants if the goal were achieved. Outputs delimit the breadth and depth of the program that would facilitate the identified outcomes. Current knowledge from experience, practice, and social and behavioral science informs activity choices and how the activities will be run. These choices will require certain resources, which become the inputs in the logic model.

Though this goal-first approach (also known as the backward approach) works well for new programs, it is less helpful for existing programs trying to explain how their process works. Many of these programs already have certain resources in place, they run a defined set of activities in a certain manner, and they are already a certain size. They often have some idea of the outcomes their participants realize, and their mission and goals are likely aligned. Most, if not all, senior-level employees have an implicit program theory of how and why the program works. For these organizations, the purpose of the logic model is more about ensuring that the logic and assumptions of their program theory make sense. Creating a set of logical steps from an implicit program theory provides a valuable framework for evaluation and assessment. In these cases, though the program is not designed from scratch to achieve a specific goal, the logic model allows some dialogue and intentional thought about how the program works.

A well-constructed logic model should follow a set of linking propositions; if the inputs or resources are present, the activities can be run as intended. If the activities are run as intended, a specified number of participants will engage in the program for the intended amount of time. If these participants engage in the program, they will realize initial, intermediate, and long-term outcomes, which will help the organization achieve its goals. Consider the generic logic model in table 8.1, adapted from the Wonderful Outdoor World program in Salt Lake City, Utah. The program goal is to introduce urban children to the outdoors so they can contribute toward developing a better community and protect the environment.

Although logic models are often too linear or overly simplistic to accurately capture the complexity of OAE programs, they do force OAE practitioners to consider the central components and resources involved in a program. This process can be helpful in identifying the elements of a program that might warrant additional evaluation efforts. From a planning perspective, does the program have adequate resources? From a program improvement perspective, is it running the best activities in the best manner? From an accountability perspective, is the program able to achieve its stated outcomes?

The veracity or etiology of a logic model can also be compared to the current state of knowledge in both research and practice. Are the implied links supported by literature and research? Are they consistent with similar programs or more generic models or folk theories (e.g., Walsh & Golins, 1976)? Are the data from the evaluation process congruent with what the staff sees in the field (face validity)? For additional information on using logic models and program theories in OAE, see ACA 2007; Baldwin et al., 2004; and Henderson & Bialeschki, 2010.

The more we know about your group, the better equipped we will be to design a program and choose activities that address your group's purpose for participating. Please be specific when filling out this form. Feel free to use the reverse side if you need more space. Please call the office if you have any questions (555-5555).

Your name: _____ Group: _____

Number of participants: _____ Program date: _____ Scheduled time: _____

Background

Please tell us about the nature of your group: How long has the group been together? What is their mission? What dynamics exist within the group that might have an impact on its experience?

_____

_____

_____

_____

Prior Experience

Please describe any group or experiential activities this group has done prior to coming to the course.

_____

_____

_____

_____

Goals

What do you wish to accomplish with your group through a ROPES program? This information will help us plan activities that match the needs of your group. Topics of focus might include communication, team building, empowerment, problem solving, quality improvement, individual and group responsibilities, cooperation, trust, self-awareness, incorporation of specific training topics, or skill building, among others.

_____

_____

_____

_____

Special Requests

Please explain any special requests your group has. (For example, list specific activities or exercises that you would like to do, ways you would like the group split into smaller groups, etc.) Is there anyone with special needs? _____

_____

_____

_____

_____

Figure 8.1 Example of a form used for needs assessment and planning.

Reprinted, by permission, from University of Utah.

Table 8.1   Example Logic Model: Wonderful Outdoor World, Salt Lake City, Utah

Inputs	Activities	Outputs	Initial outcomes	Long-term outcomes
• Space in an urban park • Funding from WOW and REI • AmeriCorps NCCC team • Camping gear and supplies • Program coordinator • Curricular materials • Food and cooking equipment	• Fishing • Map and compass • Environmental education • Resource map • Campfire activities • LNT activities • Rock climbing • Orienteering • Environmental service activity • Tent setup • Communication and debriefing activities	• Eight overnight camps • 25-30 children per camp • Five different park sites	• Fun outdoors • Familiar with resources in the area • Confidence in basic outdoor skills • Curious about and interested in the outdoors • Respect and understand the outdoors in their communities	• Kids more interested in nature • Kids engage in healthy outdoor activities • Kids develop a connection with the outdoors and conservation ethic

Reprinted from Utah Federation for Youth.

Assessment for Improvement of Program Process

This type of evaluation is generally concerned with how to make adjustments that improve a program's process. It might address the aspects of programs that make them better or worse and identify areas for improvement. This evaluation purpose is probably the most common in OAE, as even established programs are interested in improving and tweaking their programs and developing models that better meet the needs of a rapidly changing world. Examples of this approach range from holistic and systematic approaches to highly specific evaluation efforts.

One large-scale example of evaluation efforts to improve programs can be found in the Youth Program Quality Assessment (YPQA) system developed by the David P. Weikand Center for Youth Program Quality. Specific to outdoor education, this system has been adapted for use in camps by the American Camp Association and Campfire USA. This assessment system looks at aspects of youth programs at the "point of service," or the interaction between the program and the youths. Programmatic aspects such as participant engagement, interaction, and safety are assessed through observing camper-staff interaction, touring and observing facilities, and interviewing the camp director. From these observational and interview data points, summative scores are provided that allow a program to better understand the strengths and weakness of their programs (see figure 8.2 for an example).

Although the remote nature of most OAE programs limits the utility of evaluation reliant on direct observation by independent observers, the focus on monitoring malleable program factors is a promising direction for program and process improvement. The National Outdoor Leadership School (NOLS) now asks students to complete a course quality survey instead of their previous evaluation tool, the NOLS Outcome Instrument. This switch represents more attention to the programmatic factors within the NOLS' control (e.g., provision of feedback, allowing students autonomy, opportunities for reflection, developing rapport between students and instructors) and a de-emphasis on documenting outcomes of learning, such as leadership or outdoor skills development. Although the NOLS still assumes that students achieve these outcomes, they no longer feel a need to document them.

Evaluation for program improvement can also be very specific. Recent examples include North Carolina Outward Bound's interest in

american CAMP association®

enriching lives, building tomorrows

C-PQA Staff Best Practices

Staff Friendliness and Circulation

☐ Staff mainly uses a warm tone of voice and respectful language.

☐ Staff generally smiles, uses friendly gestures, and makes eye contact.

☐ When campers approach them, staff is attentive and responsive to campers.

☐ Staff members circulate (and spread out, if enough staff) to interact with every camper (in groups or individually) at some point during every activity.

☐ Staff interacts one on one at least once with every (or almost every) camper during every activity.

☐ Staff is actively involved with campers (e.g., they provide directions, answer questions, work as partners or team members, check in with individuals or small groups).

Emotional Safety

☐ Staff shows respect for all campers and insists that campers show respect for each other (e.g., use kind words, take turns, help each other).

☐ Staff addresses any incidents in which a camper or campers are made fun of.

☐ Campers seem as if they feel free to be themselves.

☐ When there is a conflict or an incident involving strong feelings, staff asks about and acknowledges the feelings of the campers involved. Adults ask campers what happened.

☐ When strong feelings are involved, staff consistently helps campers respond appropriately (e.g., staff encourage campers to brainstorm possible solutions, take time to cool off, find an appropriate physical outlet, etc.).

Support for Belonging

Throughout their camp experience, youths take part in many activities designed to help them feel a sense of belonging. These activities may include (should have a minimum of three in every activity):

☐ Individual welcomes   ☐ Trust games

☐ Group welcomes   ☐ Get-to-know-you games

☐ Introductions   ☐ Self-awareness activities

☐ Verbal icebreakers   ☐ Name games

☐ Physical icebreakers   ☐ Reflection or planning activities

☐ Challenge games and problem-solving games   ☐ Partner activities

☐ Communication games

High Expectations and Good Challenge

☐ All campers are encouraged to try out new skills or attempt higher levels of performance.

☐ Staff provides purposeful opportunities for development of skills (as opposed to purely recreational activities or a focus on fun) for all campers in the session.

☐ Campers seem challenged (in a good way) by the activities.

☐ Activities are appropriately challenging (not too easy, not too hard) for all or nearly all of the campers; there is little or no evidence of boredom or frustration on the part of campers.

☐ There is sufficient time for all activities (e.g., campers do not appear rushed, frustrated, bored, or distracted; most campers finish activities).

☐ Staff members use questions effectively with campers.

☐ Staff frequently asks challenging questions (i.e., questions that make campers think, require more than a quick answer, etc.).

Active and Cooperative Learning

☐ Campers have opportunities for their brains to be active. This may or may not include hands-on or physical activities but should include cognitive activities, which might involve the following:

- Hands-on activities
- Problem solving
- Tangible products
- Simulations
- Games with a purpose
- Abstract ideas and concrete experiences
- Deliberate practice on a skill
- Opportunities to express creatively
- Opportunities to build with materials

☐ Campers have the experience of collaborating with others. Activities include opportunities for campers to work toward shared goals and to have interdependent tasks (i.e., campers have different tasks or roles that come together for a task or project).

Camper Voice

☐ Campers have a say in how they spend their time at camp and during activities.

☐ All campers have the opportunity to make at least one open-ended choice within activities (e.g., campers choose roles, tools, or materials; topics in a given subject area; subtopics; or aspects of a given topic).

☐ Staff actively encourages campers to take an activity in a new or unplanned direction (e.g., staff says, "Can you guys think of a better way to do this?" or "How might we change this activity to make it more interesting or challenging?"). Staff supports campers' responses and suggestions.

☐ Staff shares control of most activities with campers, providing guidance and facilitation while retaining overall responsibility (e.g., staff uses youth leaders, semiautonomous small groups, or individually guided activities).

Planning and Reflection

☐ Campers have multiple opportunities to make individual or group plans for projects and activities (e.g., written or sketched plan for a building project, verbal plans about an art project). Staff asks, "What is your plan?"

☐ There are set times for planning during the session routine.

☐ Campers have opportunities to look back on things they are doing and make learning connections.

☐ All campers are engaged in an intentional process of reflecting on what they are doing or have done (e.g., writing in journals; reviewing minutes; sharing progress, accomplishments, or feelings about the experience).

☐ Activities involve structured times in which staff ask campers debriefing questions (e.g., questions to campers about their experiences in the activity).

Nature (may be optional)

☐ Campers have multiple opportunities to experience and explore outdoor areas.

☐ Camp activities use natural and outdoor settings.

☐ Campers have fun in nature.

☐ Staff is enthusiastic when outdoors with campers.

☐ Staff informally discuss and explore natural topics with campers. Staff members encourage campers to experience nature with their senses—to touch, see, taste, smell, and hear nature.

Figure 8.2 *Camp Program Quality Assessment Short Form Checklist.*

Originally printed in the Camp Program Quality Assessment, reprinted by permission of the American Camp Association © 2009 American Camping Association, Inc. http://www.acacamps.org/

the impact of technology on course experience (Holden, 2005) and the NOLS' recent work on calorie consumption and expenditures in backcountry settings (Ocobock & Gookin, 2011). In the latter example, the NOLS found that during active units of their courses participants were burning more calories than they were consuming from their rations, thus indicating a net energy deficit and, ultimately, weight loss. Because of this evaluation effort, the NOLS is working to adjust dietary information, food preparation classes, routes, rations, and rerationing schedules to better meet the energy and nutrition needs of their participants during extremely energy-intensive course units.

Documentation and Accountability

Most notably in OAE this type of evaluation is concerned with the documentation of participant outcomes and accountability to various program stakeholders (participants, parents, companies, funders). As documentation and accountability have become more common in general education settings, OAE programs are increasingly being asked to justify education and development to various stakeholders, including funders, participants, and parents. As we will discuss further in chapter 9, efforts have been made to link OAE programs to a wide range of outcomes, ranging from academic achievement and fitness to environmental ethics and character building. The most common of these efforts include postprogram interviews, testimonials, and surveys that include rating scale questions or open-ended questions.

One example of this kind of postprogram assessment is Outward Bound's recent effort to document the effectiveness of its courses through the use of a specifically developed instrument and randomly selected exit interviews. This effort not only provides a developing research base on specific variables but also examines and provides feedback to the organization regarding how students feel about particular items, such as instructor quality, information provided before the course, and other related issues.

Efficiency Assessment

This type of evaluation research is fairly infrequent in OAE. It generally entails work on cost-benefits, or the cost effectiveness of programs.

Although some in wilderness therapy (e.g., Gass & Young, 2007) have called for efficiency assessments, to date relatively little progress has been made. Gass (2008) did conclude that Project Adventure's Behavioral Management through Adventure program was more cost effective than other programs for Georgia offenders. However, as market forces are still primary drivers of participation in most OAE programs, as long as the participants, or their parents or guardians, favorably view the benefit of participation relative to the cost (money, time, potential of injury, etc.), then the market will determine if the programs are running efficiently enough.

CASE STUDY: THE WRMC INCIDENT REPORTING DATABASE

A good example of an industry-wide evaluation effort addressing multiple types of questions was the Wilderness Risk Management Committee's (WMRC) Incident Reporting Database. In the early 1990s, the members of the WRMC were interested in several key questions: What were the actual rates of different backcountry incidents? Did these rates differ from external perceptions? How could programs improve and reduce both frequency and severity of backcountry incidents?

From the onset, several challenges emerged. A consensus definition of a reportable incident was not readily available. Those offering legal advice questioned the wisdom of collecting data on "causes" of backcountry incidents. This prompted changes in language from "causes" to "contributing factors" and initiated the removal of value laden language such as "poor position" and "inadequate supervision" to more neutral terms such as position and supervision.

In addition, the voluntary reporting structure created some inherent problems with the data and challenges in generalizing to the industry as a whole. Though some organizations were very supportive and proactively contributed data, others ranged from reluctant to disinterested. Even supportive programs sometimes struggled to fully understand the reporting requirements, for example not providing data during a season with no reportable incidents, which artificially increased the frequency of all incidents.

Despite these limitations, findings from the database were often the best empirical data available to discuss incident rates by activity and overall frequencies and to identify trends for programs offering OAE programs. From 1996 to 2009, 1,195 incident reports from 65 organizations operating backcountry trips were entered into the database (figure 8.3). Seventy percent of all reported injuries were athletic (e.g., sprain or strain) or soft tissue (e.g., wounds, infections, bruises, burns, bites, blisters) injuries, and the most common contributing factor was a slip and fall (Leemon, 2008). Despite the attention given to mountaineering and adventure books and magazines in the popular press, some of the less mundane injuries, such as snow blindness were infrequent (.1% of reports).

In addition to the internal uses of the data to improve the industry and industry practices, the data also provided a platform to change external perceptions of risk. Participants, parents, and insurance companies were better able to discern both probability and severity of injuries one might expect on a backcountry expedition. These inci-

dent rates also provided a type of benchmarking, where preliminary comparisons can be made between activity types, over years, and to other industries.

Though there is currently no industry-wide incident-tracking database, many of the organizations that participated in the Incident Reporting Database remain committed to tracking and using incident data for internal purposes. The methodology developed to make a useful backcountry incident reporting system is still used by many organizations. In July of 2011, four NOLS students were injured in Alaska by a grizzly bear attack. The NOLS conducts a thorough investigation of such incidents to learn how to improve their practices in bear country. However, through their own incident tracking, they also know that this is the only grizzly attack NOLS students have experienced in over 30 years of operating in grizzly country.

Evaluation research such as the WRMC Incident Reporting Database has both internal and

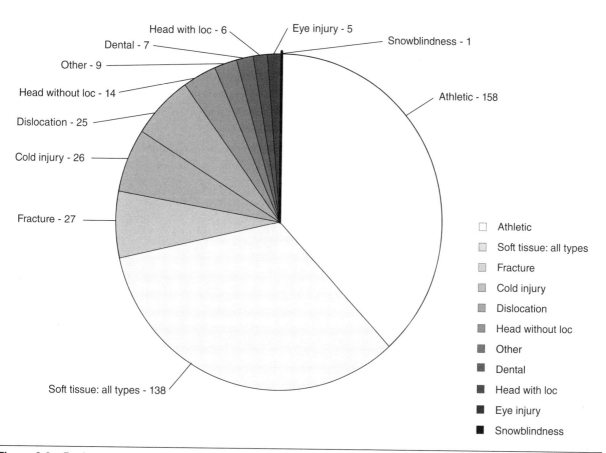

Figure 8.3 Backcountry injuries.

external purposes and can contribute to the wider body of knowledge. Incident-tracking data have allowed researchers to examine specific questions of interest to the OAE field, such as the potential role of pack weight in backpacking injuries (Hamonko, McIntosh, Schimelpfenig, & Leemon, 2010).

COMMON EVALUATION TECHNIQUES

In an industry survey conducted by AEE (Association of Experiential Education), the majority of outdoor and adventure programs reported using qualitative (37 percent) or mixed (both quantitative and qualitative) (33 percent) evaluation methods. Only 7 percent of the survey respondents reported using only quantitative means (Norling & Sibthorp, 2006). Common techniques include surveys, debriefs, and exit interviews.

Surveys, in all their forms, are the most common technique used in OAE evaluation. Survey techniques generally include giving some sort of instrument or questionnaire to individuals who can provide the data necessary to inform the evaluation questions of interest. In OAE programs, these are most typically self-report instruments, meaning respondents complete them to the best of their abilities. Survey techniques are popular because they are easy to implement, relatively inexpensive, and can be tailored to inform a variety of evaluation questions. Despite these strengths, creating a survey instrument that is easy to complete, easy to analyze, and able to inform a specific question is often a complicated task. Survey instruments can be used to collect data from a number of potential data sources, including participants, program staff, alumni, and parents or guardians. Online survey tools such as Survey Monkey or Qualtrics are increasingly making survey design, distribution, and analysis easier.

Participant surveys are one of the most common and easiest ways to access sources of data. Participants, either through the enrollment process, during the program, or upon completion, are one of the groups most willing to provide evaluation data. Such surveys might include both rating scales (e.g., 1-10) and open-ended questions and can potentially address the most common evaluation purposes in OAE programs. Despite the ease with which the data may be collected, participants do not always

have the perspective or insight necessary to provide the most useful evaluation data. These tools might also be biased to only the participant perspective.

Although participant surveys are popular given the easy access to respondents, other surveys are also used in OAE. When decisions involve staff, data from staff surveys is often necessary. Information on staff retention, satisfaction with pay and work environment, and hiring procedures are often best collected through a broad and anonymous staff survey. Program alumni can be valuable ambassadors of a program; they also have information that might be relevant to certain decisions. Alumni understand the program's strengths and may be able to recommend areas for expansion, ways to improve the program, or outcomes that they attribute to the program years afterward. For youth programs, parents or guardians are often great sources of information; survey instruments are often given to parents or guardians before or after their children participate in a program.

One of the other common sources of data used to inform the decision-making process is the group debrief. After an OAE program, participants and staff are commonly asked a series of questions by an evaluator. These responses can then be analyzed for themes or enumerated in a way that lends insight to a decision. Group interviews are fairly efficient and allow an astute evaluator to quickly get a sense of a group's opinion on a topic. However, the group process can also overemphasize the opinion of more vocal group members, and the evaluator can miss data from quieter people. Focus-group research involves a small-group discussion of a topic that is the focus of the conversation. One of the principal advantages of using focus groups is that data can be collected from a group much more quickly and cheaply than interviewing every individual (Bickman & Rog, 2009).

Exit interviews are often a good way to get detailed information from participants or staff. These allow for broad as well as targeted questions that can be closed or open ended. However, exit interviews can be very time consuming to conduct and even more time consuming to analyze in a systematic way. Most commonly, they involve an interviewer taking notes that are later synthesized into a report that focuses on the main themes and takeaway points from the interviews.

Improving OAE Through Evaluation Research

- -

M. Debora Bialeschki, PhD, Director of Research—American Camp Association

Evaluation research has grown in importance for many OAE organizations as the need to document outcomes and demonstrate accountability to funders and key stakeholders has increased over the past decade. This trend has encouraged numerous outdoor programs to move into evidence-based approaches to their programming. For the American Camp Association (ACA), the impact of the need for evidence has resulted in several evaluation research projects that have

- encouraged the creation of practical measures for youth outcomes and program quality,
- provided benchmarks and norms, and
- developed training resources that promote and translate the use of data into improved practices.

The original ACA national outcomes study documented for the first time outcomes typically achieved through the camp experience. It also demonstrated the need to identify desired outcomes and intentional opportunities with these outcomes in mind. To help camps and similar youth programs, ACA worked with the University of Utah to develop the ACA Youth Outcomes Battery (YOB), which are simple camper self-reports that allow camps and youth programs to document progress on their intentional outcomes efforts. Training materials were also created to help programs succeed in their evaluation efforts, including how to generate logic models with appropriate targets of change, create staff-training resources that connect opportunities for desired outcomes to camp jobs, and develop ways to interpret and use the findings to make evidence-based decisions, document their program's impact, and "tell their story."

Related to this effort is a focus on how to use evaluation to improve practice and thereby increase the likeliness of reaching intended outcomes. In a follow-up ACA national study focused on supports and opportunities for positive youth development, ACA translated the results of this evaluation research to begin not only to benchmark supports and opportunities offered in the camp experience, but also to develop a program-improvement process to identify steps to work toward best practices in the camp setting. The Camp Program Quality Assessment (CPQA) developed with the Weikart Center is an observation tool that helps assess best practices and provides data shared during staff discussions that result in improved practices. The CPQA has also been modified into a simple checklist of desired best practices shared with staff during staff training; this gives all staff, including the most inexperienced members, clarity on expected behaviors and interactions to use that have been proven through research to promote positive youth development.

These two examples from applied projects illustrate the importance of evaluation research to outdoor youth programs. The findings have been translated into information and benchmarks for camps to use when demonstrating the value of their experiences. The projects offered opportunities to innovate relevant tools and resources that are easy to use by OAE practitioners to generate evidence important to staff for performance and program improvement. Camps that use these two tools have a start toward systematic evaluation that begins with staff training and performance measures, that leads to feedback from youth on intentional outcomes, and that, when combined, offer data to support decision making to improve programs—all based on evidence-based approaches and resources.

ALTERNATIVE EVALUATIONS: BEST PRACTICES AND BENCHMARKING

Best practices are often based on information generated from evaluation efforts and are a field's generally accepted techniques. They are a common way for practices to improve and to learn from exemplars when an industry is working toward a standard or best way of doing things. In OAE, best practices are commonly seen as a way to use exemplary programs or practices as a standard of comparison. There are several books on best practices, and the AEE (Association of Experiential Education) and Therapeutic Adventure Professional Group (TAPG) hold a best practices conference regularly as a way to share and compare practices in therapeutic adventure. Some of the larger organizations publish or pres-

Best practices often guide how OAE is taught and practiced in the backcountry.
Courtesy of Greg Davis.

ent on their own practices, which are often seen by smaller organizations as best practices. The NOLS, for example, publishes the Wilderness Educator's Notebook, which offers a variety of practice ideas that outdoor educators and instructors have found useful.

Benchmarking, which can be used on any number of performance metrics, involves comparing one organization's performance against some standard, be it an industry average or a model company. An organization might wish to compare itself to others regarding performance metrics such as staff retention, profitability, salaries, or incidents. The ACA publishes a salary study, risk managers attend conferences and discuss injury rates, and informal and formal comparisons to industry leaders such as the NOLS, Outward Bound, and the Student Conservation Association remain common.

COMMON LIMITATIONS

There are innumerable potential pitfalls and limitations to the most common evaluation designs used by OAE programs. The problems most frequently seen are in generalizability, confounding variables, and inadequate measures.

Generalizability is a study's ability to be applied beyond its initial sampling frame. There are two main types of generalizability: conceptual generalizability and statistical generalizability. With conceptual generalizability, the findings of the study might be conceptually similar to other setting, decisions, or issues. Sometimes the findings support a theory, and this theory has application in other contexts and with other populations. Other times, the results resonate with a consumer of the evaluation data; the consumer sees an application, despite the limitations of the study, because of some conceptual similarity between the evaluation study and his or her own problem or issue.

Statistical generalizability involves being able to say, with a predetermined error rate (e.g., 5 percent) that the results from a sample can be applied to the population from which the sample was drawn. In a broad sense, OAE evaluation efforts typically do a poor job of sampling in a way that allows statistical generalizability (i.e., they infrequently use random or systematic sampling). But if the sample is from the population of interest and the statistics support generalization, the data should probably be considered evidence to inform a decision despite its potential limitations.

As we will discuss further in chapter 11, confounding variables remain problematic for OAE researchers. Confounding variables can obscure the true influences of some variable of interest (e.g., staff experience) on another variable of interest (e.g., participant learning). Aside from the inherent complexities in designing studies that can actually tease apart these influences or effects, the multidimensional and holistic nature of OAE programs makes detangling relationships extremely challenging.

As survey instruments are such common sources of evaluation data, poor measures are a recurring challenge for OAE evaluation efforts. Though some advocate for the use of existing questionnaires because they have more evidence of reliability and validity, this approach often does not fully capture the contextual nature of the evaluation data needed to inform a specific decision. Some of the items or scales might simply be irrelevant or inappropriate, and without a full understanding of the instrument's psychometrics customization can be a daunting task.

Over the years, we have tried to use a number of existing scales for evaluation and research efforts related to outdoor and adventure programs. Some of these have worked fairly well, but others have necessitated substantial adaptation or have included inappropriate items. For example, Gambone's Youth Survey was used with summer camps. One of the items from a school setting asked whether participants were exposed to knives during the day. Agreement was an indicator of an unsafe environment. At some camps, woodcraft or an expectation of campers having access to pocket knives, made this item problematic. We have also had to remove or substitute terms for references to "homework," "teachers," and "desks" from instruments intended to measure self-regulation in a school setting.

Other organizations have gone to extensive efforts to develop, customize, and validate their own evaluation measures to best answer the questions they want answered. Over the last decade both Outward Bound and the NOLS have spent years and substantial resources to develop their own measures. Though other organizations are often interested in these instruments, it is important to remember they were designed to fit the needs, targeted outcomes, and programmatic features distinct to a specific program and might not be of use to other programs. As John Gookin from the NOLS likes to say, "the NOLS Outcome Instrument will help you understand if you run a good NOLS course." Whatever route evaluators take regarding measurement, creating a good instrument is challenging and time consuming. At a minimum, most instruments require careful scrutiny, potential modification, and program-specific piloting.

In this chapter we have provided an overview of the current state of evaluation in OAE and given several examples, but we have not intended to provide the necessary details to plan and implement an evaluation project. Issues such as measurement, data analysis, and sampling can be very complex. Ill-conceived and poorly designed evaluation projects might still provide data to inform a decision, but the limits of the evaluation project must be understood. For more information or guidance on the specifics of evaluation research, see Henderson and Bialeschki (2010) or Rossi et al. (2004).

SUMMARY

Broadly, evaluation is about collecting and using evidence to make better decisions, but in OAE, it is still evolving in both form and function. Evaluation can be conducted for a variety of reasons. Several of these are relatively common in OAE, including needs assessment and planning, assessment for improvement of the program process, and documentation and accountability. Other categories of evaluation research are relatively rare in OAE, including assessment of logic models and program theories and efficiency assessment. Despite the plethora of potential evaluation techniques, some are certainly more prevalent in practice than others. Surveys, in a variety of forms, remain popular ways to evaluate programs. Debriefs and exit interviews are also relatively common. However, the challenge of deploying a comprehensive evaluation strategy has prompted some organizations to look to best practices, examining what the most well-established and highly regarded programs do. Other programs might choose to benchmark their own performance against other organizations, for example comparing their pay levels to peer organizations or industry norms. Regardless of the evaluation strategy used, OAE organizations and professionals have struggled to design studies that provide generalizable results, successfully isolate processes of interest from potential confounds, and adequately operationalize or measure their key constructs of interest.

Ultimately, for evaluation to be of value, decision makers must welcome the input of new evidence or data, even if it conflicts with their previous viewpoint. If a culture of feedback is not the norm, then evaluation and the efforts to collect data are probably not worth much effort. However, if feedback and evidence are desired for informing any type of decision, evaluation has a role. In addition, given the current state of research in OAE, evaluation research remains critical in shaping the broader state of knowledge. With technology and information management today, there is no shortage of data. However, the data available often cannot directly inform a highly specific and contextual decision. Relevant information is needed. This is the role of evaluation.

Issues for Further Discussion

1. Why are so many OAE programs resistant to using systematic evaluation programs? What might change this perspective?
2. If the empirical evidence collected through an evaluation effort contradicts the historical or philosophical evidence (experiential evidence) of a program's senior leadership, how might an organization resolve this discrepancy?
3. If OAE programs are holistic and amorphous by nature, which types of evaluation techniques might be best suited to investigate them?
4. How might the use of technology impact the collection, analysis, and use of evaluation data in the future?
5. What would an OAE industry-wide evaluation strategy look like? What would it take to make this happen?

Outcomes of Participation

Few people question the merits of public education. People tend to see the value in having a society that is literate and can do at least basic math. But what are the basic and essential skills, or outcomes, derived from OAE programs, and how are they important to society? There is no question that OAE provides participants with individual benefits, but data connecting these benefits to broader societal values are somewhat scarce. Health and wellness stand out as an area in which OAE intersects with social ideals.

Understanding the outcomes we want our programs to elicit allows us to consider the processes we employ to achieve them. Outcome-related concerns lead us to ask important questions such as these: How much do our program participants learn? How valuable is the learning? How can we make the learning more effective? What educational opportunities are the most cost effective? What do we do in OAE that is dis-

tinct from other teaching methods? What do we do that is similar? In this chapter we will discuss how a number of inherent qualities in OAE can be exploited to maximize the potential of OAE for a broader audience.

As you progress in your involvement in OAE, consider how what you do aligns with our cultural values. How do you make a difference? What do you offer that is special? Though the short-term benefits of OAE are relatively apparent, in this chapter we will explore more long-term outcomes of OAE and attributes that distinguish OAE from other processes of learning. Good education is often messy. Although we want our programs to be purposeful, we should also embrace the unpredictable nature of what we do. Sometimes things work out the way we want them to; other times they do not. Sometimes they don't work out well at all. This is the nature of OAE.

Learning Outcomes

After completing this chapter, you should be able to

* name the common outcome categories of OAE participation;
* compare intrapersonal and interpersonal outcomes;
* identify key OAE program qualities that can lead to developmental outcomes; and
* discuss the concept of affordance and how OAE can help program participants better appreciate opportunities previously unrecognized.

OAE experiences have long been valued for promoting personal growth, development, and learning. Various health and wellness benefits are attributed to outdoor and adventure experiences, most of them consistent with cultural wellness values. Rising concerns about obesity and increasingly sedentary lifestyles demand lifelong leisure pursuits as a way to engage people in enjoyable activities that result in physical, mental, emotional, and spiritual health benefits.

Despite the potential benefits, barriers to the pursuit of outdoor activities remain, including lack of exposure, lack of knowledge, and lack of outdoor skills. OAE programs can help participants navigate these barriers. Technical outdoor skill development is fundamental in almost all OAE programs. The development of outdoor skills in OAE is generally understood as a benefit on its own right as well as being a base for other opportunities. Learning to travel in the backcountry, paddle a class V river, or cook on a camp stove opens other outdoor options, including the chance to teach these skills to others.

Thus many OAE programs view technical skills as a necessary platform for learning other lessons. Backpacking and navigation skills allow participants to immerse themselves in nature for the reasons of personal or spiritual reflection. Sailing a 45-foot boat inherently involves teamwork and leadership skills. The unpredictable nature of a backcountry classroom provides an abundance of decision-making opportunities and challenges to overcome. Thus, although technical outdoor skill development remains a critical outcome of many OAE programs, this development is often a platform for a broader spectrum of interpersonal and intrapersonal outcomes.

Ultimately, OAE does not *create* outcomes for participants but rather presents opportunities to achieve such outcomes as personal growth and development. What participants take away from a program depends not only on what the program provides but also on what the participant chooses, either consciously or subconsciously, to process and learn from.

COMMON PARTICIPATION OUTCOMES

Learning generally consists of cognitive, skill-based, and affective outcomes (Kraiger, Ford, & Salas, 1993). *Cognitive* outcomes involve both quantity and type of knowledge (e.g., declarative,

procedural, or conditional). Knowledge about the meaning of latitude and longitude coordinates is an example of a cognitive outcome. *Skill-based* outcomes involve performance of a process or procedures. Although explaining how to locate your position in the backcountry would be considered cognitive knowledge, actually finding your way is a skill-based outcome. Finally, *affective* outcomes depend on the individual and include such outcomes as confidence in one's ability to travel in the backcountry or motivation to embark on an outdoor adventure. Affective outcomes vary immensely from person to person and include motives, attitudes, self-perceptions, and feelings.

Most of the important outcomes of any educational experience involve a combination of cognitive, skill-based, and affective domains. The knowledge of latitude and longitude without the ability to travel in the backcountry or the motivation to try route finding is of little practical use. Similarly, strong motivation without the requisite cognitive knowledge can invite trouble. In the end, the overlap of outcomes targeted and learned during OAE programs is a strength of the industry. OAE programs are commonly holistic in nature and range across domains.

One of the most comprehensive examinations of OAE outcomes to date was conducted by Hattie, Marsh, Neill, and Richards through a comprehensive meta-analysis (1997). In an analysis of 96 reports, papers, and studies involving 151 samples, they found 40 outcomes that they classified into six broad categories: academic, leadership, self-concept, personality, interpersonal, and adventuresome (table 9.1).

Other research on outcomes has shown similar results. In 1998 a study of 450 participants in three national wilderness education programs found that commonly reported outcomes were personal, intellectual, and behavioral in nature (Kellert, 1998). The more common outcomes included interest and participation in outdoor activities, affective and spiritual connection with nature, self-confidence and self-esteem, problem-solving skills, autonomy and independence, initiative, interpersonal relationships, and career choices (Kellert). In 2002 the Association of Experiential Education (AEE) conducted a membership survey regarding targeted program outcomes. These 39 outcomes generally split into four major categories: professional development, therapeutic, cognitive, and personal development (Norling & Sibthorp, 2006). Members who represented OAE programs reported most commonly

Table 9.1 Outcomes of Adventure Education

Category or subdomain	Examples or other names
ACADEMIC	
Academic, direct	Mathematics, reading
Academic, general	GPA, problem solving
LEADERSHIP	
Conscientiousness	Attention to detail
Decision making	Reasoned decision making
Leadership, general	Task leadership
Leadership, teamwork	Seek and use advice, consultative leadership
Organizational ability	Organizational competence, active initiative
Time management	Time efficiency
Values	Values orientation
Goals	Setting goals
SELF-CONCEPT	
Physical ability	
Peer relations	Self-peers, self-same sex, opposite sex self-concept
General self	Self-values, self-general, self-esteem, self-concept
Physical appearance	
Academic	Self-problem solving
Confidence	Potency, emotional self
Self-efficacy	Self-control, self-sufficient, self-reliance
Family	Self-parents, self-home
Self-understanding	Self-honesty, self-disclosure, self-criticism, self-awareness
Well-being	Life success, satisfaction, positive endeavor
Independence	Autonomy
PERSONALITY	
Femininity	
Masculinity	
Achievement motivation	
Emotional stability	Emotional control, emotional understanding
Aggression	Reduce aggression
Assertiveness	Forthrightness
Locus of control	Internal locus of control
Maturity	
Neurosis reduction	Nonrepression, defensive, reduction in malaise

(continued)

Table 9.1 *(continued)*

Category or subdomain	Examples or other names
INTERPERSONAL	
Cooperation	Productive teamwork, group cooperation
Interpersonal communication	Likeability, trusting, listening
Social competence	Social aptitude, sociability, friendliness
Behavior	Positive behavior, reducing behavior problems
Relating skills	Evaluation from others, sensitivity to others
Recidivism	Reduction in recidivism
ADVENTURESOME	
Challenge	Venturesome, challenge seeking, adventurousness
Flexibility	Openness to new ideas, adaptability, resourceful, imaginative
Physical fitness	Sit-ups, physical ability, resting pulse, physical strength
Environmental awareness	Wilderness appreciation, in tune with nature

Reprinted, by permission, from J. Hattie et al., 1997, "Adventure education and Outward Bound: Out-of-class experiences that make a lasting difference," *Review of Educational Research* 67(1): 43-87.

targeting cognitive and personal development outcomes. The cognitive category included outcomes such as skill building, environmental education, and academic development. The personal development category included outcomes such as self-esteem, self-determination, and self-awareness. In 2007, Sibthorp and colleagues surveyed a random sample of alumni from the National Outdoor Leadership School (NOLS) to determine which lessons from their courses were most useful in their everyday lives (Sibthorp, Paisley, Furman, & Gookin, 2008; Sibthorp et al., 2011). These transferable outcomes included outdoor skills, changes in life perspective, appreciation for nature, self-confidence, ability to serve in a leadership role, self-awareness, ability to function under difficult circumstances, and ability to work as a team member (2011, p. 118). In other recent research, a team tracked a sample of NOLS and Outward Bound participants for several years. These participants consistently reported values of their OAE experiences to include outcomes such as relationships with others, self-awareness, enjoyment of life, sense of accomplishment, self-esteem and self-confidence, and self-fulfillment (Goldenberg et al., 2010). Although some studies have provided overviews of outcomes, more targeted studies have posited that OAE is especially well suited to foster resilience (Ewert & Yoshino,

2011; Shellman, 2011) and spirituality (Stringer & McAvoy, 1992; Hitzhusen, 2005).

In addition to the work done on more traditional OAE programs, the American Camp Association (ACA) has done significant research on the outcomes of organized camping for youth (Bialeschki & Sibthorp, 2011). Common reported outcomes included self-confidence, self-esteem, independence, leadership, adventurousness, social skills, and spirituality (ACA, 2005). ACA has also worked to develop a battery of measures for outcome assessment in organized camping. The current battery includes 11 self-report outcome measures: family citizenship, friendship skills, independence, interest in exploration, perceived competence, responsibility, teamwork, affinity for nature, problem-solving confidence, camp connectedness, and spiritual well-being (ACA, 2011).

There is no universal classification for the outcomes of OAE programs, and many of the existing classification schemes (e.g., Rickinson et al., 2004) readily acknowledge the overlap of domains. In addition to the potential divisions already mentioned, commonly identified classes of outcomes include psychological, sociological, education, and physical (Ewert, 1989) as well as cognitive, affective, social-interpersonal, and physical-behavioral (Rickinson et al., 2004).

However, within these frameworks are substantially different levels of support for the types of outcomes that OAE programs provide. For ease of discussion we have divided common outcomes into those with an interpersonal focus and those with an intrapersonal focus and concentrated on the outcomes that exhibit the best empirical and theoretical support.

Interpersonal Development

Interpersonal development involves changes in how a person interacts with others. OAE programs have proven fertile for interpersonal development because of some of their inherent properties. The remoteness, the other students, the presence of instructors, the shared goals, and the small-group expeditionary program design combine to create a powerful medium for interpersonal development. The remoteness of the group forces participants to use each other and their instructors as resources and counsel rather than more external sources such as the Internet. Almost all OAE programs involve groups with a shared goal in common. Although group goals, sizes, and composition vary immensely, the fundamental nature of a group working toward a shared goal in an outdoor setting commonly yields certain outcomes. Leaders and followers toward the goal commonly emerge. In the active quest to achieve the goal, the group tends to function as a team.

In many OAE models, the group needs to stay intact for practical reasons. Although this requirement is sometimes logistical or a result of risk management (e.g., each group needs to have an instructor and appropriate equipment), it necessitates that the group collectively maintain a minimum level of functionality. Unpopular students cannot be removed from the group without cause, and it is often difficult to truly avoid interacting with other group members when conflict arises. Necessary teamwork also creates an authentic need for patience and communication skills, outcomes frequently reported in OAE.

Such an environment affects both the individual members and the group collective. This relationship between the individual and the group is bidirectional because what occurs at the group level affects the individual, and what occurs at the individual level affects the group. Although interpersonal development occurs at both the group and individual levels, neither occurs in isolation. These interdependent outcomes can be considered group outcomes and group-dependent outcomes. Group outcomes are related to the group's performance or functionality.

Group Outcomes

OAE has a long history of targeting and fostering group outcomes such as group cohesion, sense of community, and collective efficacy (Breunig et al., 2008; Glass & Benshoff, 2002). These constructs describe the group (e.g., the group is cohesive; the group is collectively successful).

Group cohesion is generally related to factors that keep a group together, which might be either task related (e.g., motives to stay together to complete the expedition) or socially related (e.g., motives to stay together because of enjoyment or personal and intrinsic reasons). Group cohesion is generally advantageous in groups and links to performance, intragroup communication, and group goal achievement. The time together as well as the remote nature of OAE experiences tends to make them conducive to developing group cohesion.

Sense of community is often related to a sense of belonging in a group, mattering to other members, and a sense of mutual commitment among members (McMillian & Chavis, 1986). Like group cohesion, a sense of community commonly develops as an OAE program unfolds (cf. Breunig et al., 2008). Although terms and definitions vary, evidence supports the premise that participation in OAE programs affords opportunities for individuals to bond together, develop an increased sense of mutual understanding, and form a cohesive group or team.

Collective efficacy is an aggregate of group members' individual beliefs in the group's ability to perform a task or in a given domain. If a group of individuals believes that their group can summit a peak, the group would have a high level of collective efficacy regarding that task. Likewise, a group of people might believe their expedition group will be unable to hike 10 miles in a day—another example of collective efficacy. OAE has been shown to improve collective efficacy in families (Wells, Widmer, & McCoy, 2004).

Group-Dependent Outcomes

In contrast to group outcomes, group-dependent outcomes are tied to an individual yet require a group for performance. Leadership and social competence are common outcomes reported by students in OAE (Paisley, Furman, Sibthorp, & Gookin, 2008). Although these outcomes pertain

A sense of community commonly develops as an OAE program unfolds.
Courtesy of Nate Bricker.

to individuals, they are typically learned and performed in the presence, or for the benefits, of others.

Leadership is one of the more commonly reported outcomes of OAE programs, yet it remains elusive and ill defined in the broader body of literature. For measurement and research, leadership is often subdivided into skills considered valuable to leaders, such as communication skills, social competence, and charisma. Given the expeditionary nature of OAE programs, opportunities to practice leadership tend to be inherent. So, although the term "leadership" remains problematic, evidence suggests that leadership can be and is developed through OAE experiences (Paisley et al., 2008; Sibthorp et al., 2011).

Leadership is often inherent in OAE program design. Some programs use formal leadership curricula and have designated leaders for portions of the program (e.g., leader of the day). Others have a looser leadership structure. Either way, leaders generally emerge to help focus the team on achieving their goal(s). As group leaders learn how to lead by actually leading, other group members learn how to support and work with the leader through being active and productive followers.

Social skills, social competence, and social self-efficacy are all related to competence and effectance (the ability to make something happen) in social situations. Fostering these outcomes relies on a program's ability to provide practice in social settings. Likewise, developing teamwork skills, or skills to work and function productively as part of a small, goal-oriented group, are also commonly reported benefits of OAE participation. Teamwork remains especially interesting to corporate groups in which intact groups of workers are sent to OAE programs with the explicit goal of becoming more effective in working together as a team.

Intact Groups

Some OAE programs cater specifically to intact groups that are seeking interpersonal growth, such as a group of astronauts preparing for a space mission, a group of corporate executives looking for increased cohesion and communication, or families seeking to reconnect through a shared experience. Intact groups have the benefit and disadvantage of preexisting relationships and dynamics that they bring with them into the adventure program. These preexisting relations can be a strength for the group to build on or a constraint to overcome as they work toward improved group functioning.

Another clear advantage of interpersonal development for intact groups is the increased potential for postprogram retention and application of learning. Group cohesion, improved communication, teamwork, or leadership can be directly applied by the group in their postcourse settings. The adventure program serves as a point of reference as the group continues to evolve postprogram.

Despite the wide potential of interpersonal growth, groups often do not remain intact in a meaningful way after an adventure program. Thus for lessons to be useful, they must be able to be applied in different contexts. Just as with technical skills, some programs view interpersonal aspects of the course as potentially influential bases for intrapersonal development.

Intrapersonal Development

Developmental outcomes of an individual nature have been stalwarts of OAE programs since their inception. Outcomes such as self-confidence, self-awareness, and spirituality are considered intrapersonal. Intrapersonal development is further divided into self-constructs, skill-building (cognitive and physical), values, and mental or emotional states.

Early OAE programs were said to instill "character" in young people. Although character education often targets moral and ethical development, in its broadest sense, a person's character is the distinct combination of individual characteristics that make a person who he or she is. Unlike interpersonal development, intrapersonal development occurs primarily through unobservable mental changes in participants' psyches.

Self-Constructs

Sense of self is often used as an umbrella term to discuss interrelated self-perceptions such as self-esteem, self-confidence, and self-concept. Ultimately, these outcomes are about how a person views him- or herself. Early research on OAE programs assessed changes in self-perception with some success (see Ewert, 1983). Despite some general discomfort in the scientific community regarding the broadness of some of these constructs, and thus their inability to accurately predict behavior, it remains common for participants to note personal changes in self-confidence after course completion (Goldenberg et al., 2010; Sibthorp et al., 2011). More recent research has focused in on targeted changes in variables such as self-efficacy and self-awareness.

Widely examined in OAE (e.g., Probst & Koesler, 1998; Paxton & McAvoy, 1998; Sibthorp, 2003a), self-efficacy is generally viewed as task specific and as encompassing level, strength, and generality. Self-efficacy has been shown to be predictive of both motivation to attempt a behavior and the performance of the behavior; its four sources are well aligned with the types of experiences offered in OAE programs. Despite links to increases in self-efficacy through OAE programs and its widespread use and examination, programs might be better serving participants by increasing the accuracy of the self-assessment rather than simply increasing the perception in ability to perform a certain task. Recent research on self-efficacy has found that inaccurately high self-efficacy can motivate participants to attempt

Research on Interpersonal Outcomes

Timothy S. O'Connell, PhD—Brock University, St. Catharines, Ontario, Canada

Interpersonal outcomes such as sense of community, group cohesion, and inclusion are common goals of most OAE providers. Depending on the organization, these outcomes might be an explicit part of a program's design or be a byproduct of engaging in OAE activities that place small groups of people in remote and unfamiliar environments to work toward common goals. Regardless of how these outcomes emerge, they have been recognized as some of the most important impacts of participating in OAE programs.

The nature of OAE activities is well suited in supporting the development of these outcomes. For example, sense of community or the "feeling an individual has about belonging to a group and involves the strength of the attachment people feel for their communities or group" (Halamova, 2001, p. 137) is comprised of four core factors. These include *membership* (bonds, level of members' attraction to one another, and group unity), *influence* (a bidirectional concept in which an individual member can affect the group while being open to the authority of the group), *integration and fulfillment of needs* (individual's needs are met in conjunction with the group's needs being met), and *shared emotional connection* (the affective "groupness," or camaraderie, developed through sharing common experiences) (McMillan & Chavis, 1986).

These four factors are inherent in most (but not all) groups of people participating in OAE pursuits and develop through program activities as well as group interactions with the natural environment. OAE activities (especially those involving extended wilderness travel) often promote feelings of community as group members are removed from the routines and their personas of everyday life and must focus on basic needs such as getting from place to place, eating, and being self-reliant for shelter. Lounsbury and DeNeui (1995) noted a positive relationship between basic living needs and heightened feelings of community. When coupled with the fact that OAE groups generally have shared goals (e.g., to climb a certain route, to complete a portage) and that members expend energy on reaching these goals together, sense of community, group cohesion, and inclusion can flourish. As groups encounter continued success, stronger social attachments develop and sense of community is enhanced (Hogg & Abrams, 2001).

In terms of programmatic factors that promote interpersonal outcomes, research suggests several items that outdoor adventure educators can manipulate (Breunig, O'Connell, Todd, Anderson, & Young, 2010). First, pretrip and posttrip activities intentionally designed to foster community help set the stage for continued development of interpersonal outcomes. Second, OAE leaders can establish routine behaviors and procedures that promote interpersonal outcomes such as daily debriefing sessions during programs (Lyons, 2003). Third, a deliberate focus on developing structures that encourage perceptions of influence can enhance interpersonal outcomes.

Research suggests that OAE leaders can promote interpersonal outcomes by intentionally designing activities that promote community.
Courtesy of Tim O'Connell.

These might include activities showcasing group effectiveness while allowing for individual inputs such as rotating cooking chores. Finally, OAE leaders can attempt to balance the level of challenge with the group's skill level to provide just the right dose of confrontation. This allows the group to come together through a difficult situation by providing direct and immediate feedback. Choosing an appropriate route for the group's ability or modifying activities based on environmental factors and individuals' physical and mental capacities helps in this process. OAE leaders should also be aware of other factors that can influence interpersonal outcomes. For example, poor weather conditions often push group members into "self-care mode" or prompt people to seek shelter in tents that segments the group and detracts from interpersonal outcomes being reached. By implementing the appropriate leadership or facilitation style required for the situation at hand, OAE leaders can take steps to confront destructive individual behaviors and not allow cliques to affect interpersonal outcomes.

OAE activities generally promote positive interpersonal outcomes through their inherent characteristics. However, research supports the notion that intentionality of program design and prompt attention to behaviors or conditions that detract from positive group interactions are important in maximizing the achievement of interpersonal outcomes. Positive interpersonal outcomes can, in turn, enhance other program outcomes as well.

References

Breunig, M., O'Connell, T., Todd, S., Anderson, L., & Young, A. (2010). The impact of outdoor pursuits on college students' perceived sense of community. *Journal of Leisure Research, 42*(4): 551-572.

Hogg, M., & Abrams, D. (2001). *Intergroup relations: Essential readings*. London: Taylor & Francis.

Lounsbury, J., & DeNeui, D. (1995). Psychological sense of community on campus. *College Student Journal, 29*, 270-277.

Lyons, K. (2003). Exploring meanings of community among summer camp staff. *World Leisure, 4*, 55-61.

McMillan, D., & Chavis, D. (1986). Sense of community: A definition and theory. *Journal of Community Psychology, 14*, 6-23.

tasks they are not able to perform and to underprepare for difficult tasks they could have accomplished if they had planned better (e.g., Vancouver & Kendall, 2006; Vancouver, Thompson, Tischner, & Putka, 2002). Inaccurately low self-efficacy can result in task avoidance, denying participants experiences they were ready to engage in.

Self-awareness is another outcome commonly reported by OAE participants. Increases in self-awareness involve an accurate understanding and mindful observation of one's self and can assist performance in many ways. Self-understanding and recognition of strengths and weaknesses are facets of self-awareness. OAE participants commonly report learning about themselves through self-reflection as well as through feedback from both instructors and coparticipants (e.g., Sibthorp et al., 2011).

Skill Building

A skill is a combination of knowledge and ability that allows an individual to successfully complete a task. As we have noted, although technical outdoor skills and interpersonal skills such as communication and teamwork are common outcomes of OAE programs, many of the skills derived from OAE are more intrapersonal in nature.

Increases in problem-solving and decision-making skills are often cited by participants as benefits of OAE programs (Hattie et al., 1997). Collins and colleagues contend that one reason OAE programs are well suited to improve decision making and problem solving is the plethora of ill-structured problems inherent in OAE programs (Collins et al., 2012). Ill-structured problems are those that do not have only one way of solving them and don't have a single correct answer. Solving such problems demands a more abstract thought process and requires students to weigh different sources of evidence and ways of knowing. Tackling such complex problems in OAE programs is believed to prepare students for coping with complex decisions in the future.

Self-regulation is related to self-awareness but has more to do with a person's ability to modify and adjust his or her own motivational, affective, cognitive, and behavioral strategies while working toward a goal. These types of adjustments flow directly from self-awareness but result directly in changes that better allow for goal achievement.

Outcomes such as the abilities to organize and plan, control emotions, and manage time (Hattie et al., 1997) are examples of an individual's ability to self-regulate. Self-regulatory skills are often inherent in OAE programs in which goals and planning are necessary to successfully travel and live in the backcountry.

Another area that remains of interest to OAE is resilience and related outcomes such as coping skills or tolerance for adversity. These outcomes involve an individual's capacity to rebound from and excel when facing a challenge or setback. Although definitions vary, the central premise of resilience is that individuals are differentially equipped to recover from and overcome adversity. Some authors claim that resilience is the central goal of the Outward Bound program model, a model on which many OAE programs are based (Shellman, 2011), and most authors in the field agree that the process of overcoming the challenges inherent in OAE programs is the driver behind improved resilience in this setting (Ewert & Yoshino, 2011; Gookin, 2011; Neill & Dias, 2001).

Values

Personal values can be defined as enduring beliefs about what is good or desirable and what is not. Personal values include moral beliefs about right and wrong, wilderness ethics, and tolerance and appreciation for diversity.

Spiritual development is an outcome commonly reported by OAE participants, especially those immersed in nature (Heintzman, 2010; Stringer & McAvoy, 1992). Spirituality is typically differentiated from religion and can be defined as a way of being and experiencing that comes about through awareness of a transcendent dimension and is often characterized by certain identifiable values in regard to self, others, nature, life, and whatever one considers to be Ultimate (Elkins, Hedstrom, Hughes, Leaf, & Saunders, 1988, p. 10). However, much of the research on spirituality in OAE has left the definition to the study participants (Heintzman, 2010). Feelings of transcendence, or being a part of something greater, appear to be especially important during OAE experiences (Marsh, 2008). Spiritual outcomes might be particularly linked to wilderness or nature-based experiences, solitude, relationships with others, and challenge (Griffin & LeDuc, 2009).

Change in perspective is another outcome that OAE participants report. Sometimes this change is in the way participants appreciate wilderness or connect with nature. Other times it is simply about how they perceive the world around them. Although this might be related to the transforma-

Overcoming the challenges inherent in OAE programs helps participants to become more resilient.
Courtesy of Scott Schumann.

tional nature of the OAE experience, it might also be attributed to a powerful and distinctly individual learning event. Many of these changes are idiosyncratic and difficult to predict. Changes in perspectives that are tied to wilderness or nature are commonly driven by the power of immersion in the natural environment or a peak experience in nature.

Mental States

States are transitory variables that vary over days or even over hours within an individual. They are typically of short duration, observable in the moment, reactive to external stimuli, and situational in nature (Fridhandler, 1986). Although outcomes such as leadership skills and resilience can and do shift, they do not change as dramatically as state variables such as moods or energy levels. Most people can be in a bad mood or fatigued at one point in a day and then in a better mood or recharged later the same day. Such changes are typical of state variables.

The restoration of cognitive fatigue is an important outcome often linked to experiences in natural environments (Hartig, Mang, & Evans, 1991; Kaplan & Kaplan, 1989). However, whereas the Kaplans' original research was based on interviews with backpackers participating in two weeklong Outdoor Challenge Program trips in Michigan (Talbot & Kaplan, 1986), most of the recent research in this area has not involved OAE program participants. One notable exception is some of the recent work David Strayer and colleagues are doing on cognition in the wild (e.g., Atchley, Strayer, & Atchley, 2012).

Other situational or state variables have also been studied in OAE programs. Wilderness and adventure programs have demonstrated ability to reduce negative moods (e.g., Fry & Heubeck, 1998), increase incidents of flow or optimal arousal (e.g., Jones, Hollenhorst, Perna, & Selin, 2000), and produce increased frequency of optimal engagement (Sibthorp et al., 2010).

PROGRAM QUALITIES

OAE programs involve a wide range of purposes, contexts, and designs, and thus the outcomes they target, populations they attract, and experiences they provide vary significantly. Outcomes from a weeklong corporate team-building sea kayaking program in Alaska should look very different from outcomes realized by a group of young people on an environmentally focused backpacking trip to the Adirondacks. Therapeutic programs for substance abusers have very different goals compared to programs that serve people with disabilities or programs that work alongside schools to support the science curriculum and academic mission.

These differences can have dramatic impacts on program design and implementation as well as on the outcomes gained by participants. For example, several studies looking at inclusive OAE programs have generally found changes in attitudes and perspectives related to people with disabilities (e.g., Anderson, Schleien, McAvoy, & Lais, 1997; Holman & McAvoy, 2005) in addition to more typical OAE outcomes. Likewise, programs targeting therapeutic goals have led to therapeutic outcomes such as reduced substance use and lower frequency of depression (Russell, 2006) in addition to more common OAE outcomes. Programs with an academic focus have found more academic outcomes (e.g., Lieberman & Hoody, 2002; Rickinson et al., 2004).

Ultimately, OAE programs are bases that can be designed and implemented in many ways to provide desired experiences that can, at the discretion of participants, pay off in a number of lessons. Sometimes these lessons are predictable in a general sense; sometimes they are idiosyncratic or unique to the individual learner. It is difficult to determine the outcomes of OAE programs precisely because OAE programs are still primarily considered educational venues in which any number of lessons might be learned. It would be nonsensical to try to determine outcomes of formal schooling without a close look at the school's curriculum. It makes as little sense to say "OAE programs are good at teaching teamwork" as to say "school is good for teaching math." However, certain inherent qualities in most OAE programs do make them well suited to learning certain lessons.

Common Qualities and Outcomes

A lot goes on in an OAE program, and it is difficult to isolate certain qualities of a program that make it developmental. Discrete aspects of OAE programs, such as small groups or challenge, can be important catalysts for developmental experiences, but they can also be inconveniences, constraints, or simply nonfactors in development. It is best to consider OAE programs as compact and responsive systems.

Systems theory has been widely applied to learning and development and offers a viable explanation of why OAE programs are especially well suited to foster both interpersonal and intrapersonal growth. By their very nature, the remoteness of many OAE programs separates participants from their lives at home and their existing relationships. This can sometimes limit the connection made between what is learning during the OAE experience and what is remembered or practiced when back to "normal life." The short-term nature of the OAE experience, however, can often be thought of as a microcosm for everyday life. In the more compact OAE system, it is often easier to see connections among learning, attitudes, and individual behaviors. Thus participants receive more specific and timely feedback because the impacts of their behaviors, both positive and negative, are directly observable and captured within the microcosm of the small group.

OAE is also a system in which many of the lessons are authentic and immediately relevant to participants. The outdoor environment and small-group format requires attention to certain technical and group skills. The presence of adult leaders and curriculum provides structure but flexibility. Challenge, novelty, and risk activate innate human needs to explore and learn. Despite the holistic focus and abundance of potential outcomes, the importance of the individual and his or her motivation, experiences, and disposition ultimately determine which, if any, outcomes result from participation in an OAE program.

The common outcomes of OAE programs include initial, intermediate, and long-term outcomes. Improved mood immediately after a peak ascent is an initial outcome that is temporally and contextually tied to the experience. Changes in self-efficacy after a successful climb or improved teamwork after a small-group expedition are intermediate outcomes that are slower to evolve but also more stable. The intermediate outcomes listed in table 9.2 are generally supported in OAE research. In contrast, longer-term outcomes often logically follow from intermediate outcomes and are tied to general health and wellness.

Long-term (distal) outcomes are difficult to directly link to OAE experiences. However, many intermediate outcomes are directly linked to long-term outcomes in the research literature. Teamwork, communication skills, and leadership are intermediate outcomes that, when extended and applied in later life, are highly valued in the workplace. Group cohesion is linked to better group performance (Evans & Dion, 1991). Self-efficacy is associated with a variety of health outcomes ranging from illness management (e.g., Williams & Bond, 2002) to life satisfaction and psychological well-being (e.g., Hampton, 2000). Cognitive restoration has been linked to improved task performance and illness and stress recovery (e.g., Ulrich, et al., 1991). Problem-solving skills are valued in numerous life settings. Outdoor skills provide an ability to further experience the outdoors and to enjoy physically active recreation or spiritually reconnect (e.g., Heintzman, 2010).

Table 9.2   Common Qualities and Outcomes of OAE Programs

Qualities	Intermediate outcomes	Long-term outcomes
Small groups Shared goals Remoteness Technical skills requirement Novelty Challenge Outdoor environment Risk and uncertainty Curriculum and program goals Active, experiential learning Presence of adult leaders	Interpersonal • Teamwork • Leadership • Communication skills • Group cohesion	• School and work performance • Psychological well-being • Quality of life • Physically active lifestyle • Physical, spiritual, and mental health
	Intrapersonal • Self-constructs (e.g., self-confidence, self-concept) • Values (e.g., connection to nature, spirituality) • Cognitive and physical skills (e.g., problem-solving skills, technical outdoor skills) • Mental states (e.g., mood, cognitive restoration)	

Affording Opportunities for Development

Possibilities for action within an environment have been called *affordances* (Gibson, 1979). These can be either perceived by program participants or hidden from them, and they are highly dependent on participants' skills, interests, and previous experiences (Gaver, 1991; Norman, 1988). For someone unskilled in backcountry travel, a large, undeveloped wilderness area might afford opportunities to get lost, experience stress, and be bitten by a snake. For a more experienced and skilled participant, the wilderness area might still afford these undesired experiences but might also afford opportunities to relax, explore, catch fish, and reconnect with friends or family.

As mentioned, what an OAE program affords can be either hidden or evident to a participant. Much of the role of the program's designers and leaders is to help participants appreciate opportunities that they might not have previously recognized. This occurs both through the development of skills and within the socioemotional environment. Through learning technical skills, participants become more adept at successfully navigating hazards and avoiding undesirable outcomes. Reactions and feedback from instructors and peers can either encourage participants to tackle new challenges or to avoid them. Ultimately, this social-emotional context combines with participants' actual skills and interests and determines their capacity to act. Through OAE programs, participants often become aware of more opportunities than they previously perceived. Specifically, more positive and developmental affordances are perceived. Additional opportunities for growth and development thus become available to participants.

SUMMARY

There is considerable breadth and overlap among the types of outcomes to expect from OAE programs. Although some of the outcomes are primarily a function of the purpose and population of the program, others can be relatively idiosyncratic in nature. However, a core of outcomes appears to include both interpersonal and intrapersonal outcomes that span across the cognitive, affective, and physical skills domains. Interpersonal outcomes include both group outcomes, such as group cohesion and collective efficacy, and group-dependent outcomes, such as leadership, social competence, and teamwork skills. Intrapersonal outcomes reside within an individual's psyche, and although they might result in behavior change, they can also go undetected by others. Changes in self-concept, problem-solving skills, personal values, and an affective connection to nature are primarily intrapersonal in nature.

In addition to the initial and intermediate outcomes reported by participants, OAE can be an important venue for personal health and wellness. General affective outcomes such as self-efficacy and resilience have been linked to a variety of health and wellness indicators. Although this link is important, the health benefits of lifelong engagement in physically active outdoor pursuits are potentially more influential. The skills to travel in the backcountry coupled with the desire to be in nature provide a powerful catalyst for many individuals. Although nature can provide both cognitive and affective learning, there are also physical benefits from a physically active lifestyle. The challenges concerning obesity in children and adults are well known (James, Leach, Kalamara, & Shayeghi, 2001), and physically active lifestyles that include active leisure pursuits offer a healthy alternative to more sedentary lifestyles.

The very nature of OAE programs can create rich learning environments. Qualities such as small groups pursuing group goals in remote and novel outdoor settings under the stewardship of adult leaders provide opportunities for growth. However, professionals in the OAE field need to embrace the unpredictability of learning and the complex nature of human development. Although OAE practitioners can help participants recognize the possibilities available to them (affordances), what individuals ultimately take away from an experience depends on them. Although intentionally targeting outcomes has become a hallmark of successful OAE programs, accepting that participants often learn unintended lessons and develop in unexpected ways is essential. Despite these caveats, OAE programs are well positioned to provide a wide range of health and wellness benefits to participants.

Issues for Further Discussion

1. What outcomes for OAE have you personally observed? Are these consistent with those described in the broader research on OAE?

2. How would you articulate the benefits and outcomes of OAE to someone unfamiliar with the field?

3. One way for OAE to connect with larger societal issues is through health and wellness. What are other avenues for forging this connection?

4. Which outcomes are the easiest to observe or measure?

5. Considering table 9.2, which of the OAE program qualities would you directly link to intermediate outcomes?

6. What is the proper balance between intentionally targeting outcomes and designing programs to provide certain benefits and encouraging individuals to select and pursue whatever is most important to their own growth?

State of OAE Research

Why This Chapter Is Important

Reviewing research that is 20 years old can be not only tedious but misleading. One wonders how findings from a distant yesterday can be relevant for today or tomorrow. That said, it can be instructive to look back because doing so enables us to see what has been discovered and done before; it also reaffirms that today's research methods allow us to illuminate the OAE industry in a more sophisticated light than could be done in days of old. The largest volume of historical studies in OAE remains research as pedagogy, and much of the work is somewhat episodic and idiosyncratic and often conducted by graduate students. The genesis of these studies typically involve statements such as the following: "I am interested in X"; "I have access to Y population"; "This study can be conducted in nine months"; "I have always wanted to learn how to do Z research technique." We in OAE tend to do a lot of exploring and describing in our research: *Wouldn't it be fun to know about X?* We have been conducting poorly designed outcome studies for, literally, decades with largely the same results: OAE can produce some outcomes, sometimes, for some students. What we do not do is a lot of explaining: This is how it works. This is why it works.

Moreover, instead of striving to develop and test theories, much of the research in OAE is led by OAE practice. That is, practice is working on assumptions and experiential evidence that are not, and sometimes cannot be, defined, measured, or understood through formal research efforts. In addition, practice usually wants answers to nontheoretical, market-level types of questions, such as, How many and who are coming to our program? and What is the best way to advertise? Yes, this type of research might be viewed as exhibiting strength of professional practice, but from a research perspective it is a weakness for our field. Anecdotes are nice. They are easy to come by. They are compelling. And they are sometimes easy to misinterpret. We say we do wonderful things; we change lives; we create leaders. Other programs say they do these things, too. Do we have evidence that we are more wonderful than they are? More powerful? More worthy of funding?

We need to understand how and why OAE is unique. What is it that OAE does better than other educational approaches? What practices are supported by evidence? (Yes, some of this should be *research* evidence.) Although research evidence and the efforts to develop and test new or existing theories are often discounted by the field, they remain the most prized forms of evidence to a growing number of external parties, including funding agencies, policy makers, and educators. To categorize research as too difficult, irrelevant, or time consuming is a mistake that hinders the development of the OAE field.

In this chapter we introduce the main purposes of research, review the current status of OAE research, and explore current trends. We suggest that some promising innovations and developments will drive the next decade of research.

Learning Outcomes

After completing this chapter, you should be able to

❀ describe different categories and goals of research in OAE;

❀ compare early OAE research to contemporary research;

❀ explain the importance of theoretical frameworks in OAE research;

❀ articulate the role of evidence-based practice in OAE;

❀ name five practices in OAE that are supported by research evidence; and

❀ summarize three of the innovative research approaches being used in OAE.

esearch and evaluation helps us understand the influence of OAE on individuals and groups. However, the inherent field-based and constructivist nature of OAE has long challenged traditional research approaches and the application of extant theory. Despite this challenge, researchers aspire to improve professional practice, advance the credibility of OAE as a behavioral intervention, and build a contemporary state of knowledge.

THE ROLE OF RESEARCH

Key research terms are defined in table 10.1. In general, research can be divided into several categories, including process, outcome, logic, time, and purpose. Research techniques might be quantitative, qualitative, or mixed methods. The outcome of research can be either applied or basic, which implies foundational understanding. Logic can be inductive or deductive, and time can include categories such as cross-sectional, longitudinal, and retrospective. Research is sometimes considered empirical or conceptual. Whereas empirical research prioritizes data, conceptual research tends to develop theory, synthesize understanding, and question assumptions. Though each of these potential divisions is important, great variability exists across categories, with a paucity of OAE research existing in some categories and others being well represented. A recent review of OAE-related research found a relatively equitable balance between positivistic research (typically quantitative, deductive) and construc-

tivist research (typically qualitative, inductive) (Thomas, Potter, & Allison, 2009). In contrast, longitudinal research is extremely rare in OAE.

Traditionally, empirical research targets one of four main goals: exploration, description, prediction, or explanation (cf. Brown, Cozby, Kee, & Worden, 1999). *Exploratory* studies typically look to data for ideas about key concepts or constructs and pose potentially worthwhile research questions. As an example, Fry and Heubeck (1998) offered an exploratory examination of Outward Bound participants' mood state over their course. *Descriptive* studies are typically interested in explaining the current state of OAE, such as a study done by Galloway (2000) in which he surveyed wilderness orientation programs to help people better understand the size and scope of that industry. *Predictive* studies are typically interested in relationships among variables. Are higher or lower levels of a certain variable consistently related to another variable? For example, Sibthorp and colleagues have found that a participant's sense of personal empowerment is generally predictive of reported learning in both technical and interpersonal skills (e.g., Sibthorp et al., 2007). *Explanatory* studies are interested in explaining how a process occurs. For example, Shooter, Paisley, & Sibthorp (2010) manipulated the level of instructor benevolence, ability, and integrity through a series of vignettes. They found that trust in the instructor was related primarily to the instructor's ability but was also influenced by the instructor's benevolence and integrity. However, well-designed explanatory studies are not without their problems. They often control and operationalize aspects of the study in ways that maximize internal validity, but sacrifice external validity.

Research often involves trading internal validity for external validity. *Internal* validity is concerned with the ability to draw a conclusion within the given parameters of a study. In a highly controlled setting, we might be able to see the influence of a variable on another variable. In the example we just mentioned (Shooter, Paisley, & Sibthorp, 2010), the study used an effective research design, randomization, and controls that allowed the authors to conclude that trust was dependent on instructor ability. In contrast, *external* validity is concerned with how well results generalize, or can be applied in a nonresearch setting. It is unlikely that a written vignette can adequately capture the subtleties of an adventure experience in the same ways as field-based research. Thus a vignette- or case-based study might have limited external validity.

Although inconsistent with traditional categories of research (i.e., description, prediction, exploration, explanation), much of the OAE research is categorized as either outcome- or process-focused research. *Outcome research* is typically interested in demonstrating the efficacy of OAE. Like many areas of education, OAE is being asked to demonstrate its value and utility to funders and stakeholders. This has necessitated some research focus on describing what outcomes come from OAE experiences. Recent summaries of research and meta-analyses all seem to come to similar conclusions. Broadly, OAE can facilitate a number of diverse outcomes, ranging from interpersonal skills to attitudes and knowledge (cf. Hattie et al., 1997; Rickinson et al., 2004). Most of these summaries, however, also suggest a great deal of variance in the effectiveness of adventure programs and that not all programs are effective at fostering positive development. This premise is not new and has long instigated the need for more process research to better explicate the facets of OAE that make it most developmental.

Process research is typically interested in both describing and explaining mechanisms and components of OAE that lead to outcomes. Such research can be conceptual, inductive, and deductive. Some of the recent meta-analyses and syntheses support the efficacy of intentionality, program length, and type of program (Hattie et al., 1997; Rickinson et al., 2004). There is also general support for elements such as personal challenge, learning, reflection, empowerment (e.g., O'Connell, 2010; Shellman, 2008; Sibthorp & Arthur-Banning, 2004), and instructor and peer support (Sibthorp, Furman, Paisley, Schumann, & Gookin, 2011).

Table 10.1   Key Research Terms Defined

Term	Definition
Quantitative research	Research using numerical measures to quantify the level of research variables.
Qualitative research	Research that relies on understanding and meaning making in naturalistic (real) settings; focuses on qualities more than quantities.
Mixed-methods research (also called multimethod research)	Research that employs several approaches to derive a more holistic view of a phenomenon (e.g., uses both qualitative interviews and a quantitative questionnaire).
Deductive research	Researchers have a predetermined hypothesis they seek to test.
Inductive research	The research is building understanding from the data.
Longitudinal research	Research that follows the same people repeatedly over time, typically to detect changes.
Cross-sectional research	Research that examines a group of people at one specific point of time.
Retrospective research	Research that focuses on what people recall or remember about a previous time or experience.

Research and the Black Box

Pete Allison, PhD—The Institute for Sport, Physical Education and Health Sciences, The University of Edinburgh, Scotland

My research in experiential learning and adventure education is primarily concerned with exploring what Ewert refers to as the "black box." Although the majority of research in experiential learning has focused on outcomes, because doing so is pragmatically interesting and useful (for example, to help to secure funding), there is very little work exploring the black box or the change processes (Allison & Pomeroy, 2000).

In this short summary I consider some research that I undertook over a 10-year period during which I explored individuals' experiences of returning to their home environment after extended periods in the wilderness. The context of most of the research has involved wilderness and young people of ages 17 to 25. Most of my work has been on expeditions for purposes of adventure and science, with an underpinning focus on personal development. Some work has been on tall ship sailing, particularly the work of Sail Training International (STI).

In the early stages of my research I took an inductive approach to gaining perspectives and reflections on time in the wilderness. Through this process I was struck by the number of people who reported difficulties in the return to "normal life." This led me to read about posttraumatic stress disorder (PTSD), culture shock, and reverse culture shock and to become interested more generally in culture and education. In early thinking I referred to the phenomenon as postexpedition adjustment, and then later as postresidential syndrome, and finally as expedition reverse culture shock. The different names refer to different aspects of the experiences and to my own journey in trying to understand and develop a theory around the evidence that I had collected. I became uncomfortable with referring to this phenomenon as a "syndrome" because that can have negative connotations. My thinking settled on expedition reverse culture shock (ERCS) as being something to be expected when changes are occurring in the wilderness (as we believe them to be), and thus something to be acknowledged. Three main themes emerged:

- A sense of isolation
- Extending lessons from the group
- Using the group as a compass for the future (Allison, Davis-Berman, & Berman, 2011)

My work thus far described spawned further work and interest in the learning process and in how outcomes are achieved. Working with Sail Training International, Kris Von Wald and I created a self-assessment tool kit to help individuals and organizations develop a language and way of thinking about their work. This was based on my own research, a review of the literature, and on testing the tool kit on those involved in sail training. The tool kit is based on a model that identifies three main purposes of sail training (skills, curriculum, and personal and social education) and uses four key practice areas and five youth-development outcomes. The model (see figure 1) has provided a useful

People spending time in the wilderness often experience aspects of expedition reverse culture shock on return to their home environment.
Courtesy of Pete Allison.

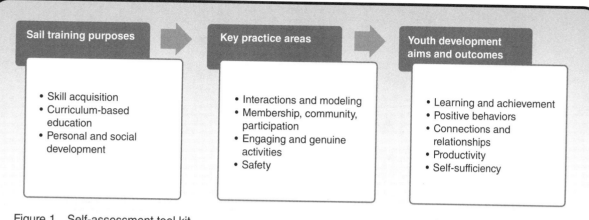

Figure 1   Self-assessment tool kit.

Reprinted, by permission, from K. Von Wald and P. Allison, 2011, *Sail training programme: Self-assessment toolkit,* 2nd ed. (Gosport, UK: Sail Training International), 7.

way for us to engage with sail-training practitioners to improve practice. To this end we have been concerned with evidence-based practice and practice-based evidence, or, as we say in the UK, research and knowledge exchange.

References

Allison, P., Davis-Berman, J., & Berman, D. (2011). Changes in latitude, changes in attitude: Analysis of the effects of reverse culture shock—a study of students returning from youth expeditions. *Leisure Studies, 31*(4), 487-503.

Allison, P., & Pomeroy, E. (2000). How shall we "know?": Epistemological concerns in research in experiential education. *Journal of Experiential Education, 23*(2): 91–97.

Von Wald, K., & Allison, P. (2011). *Sail training programme: Self-assessment toolkit* (2nd edition). Gosport, UK: Sail Training International.

EARLY RESEARCH IN OAE

Although much of the research that influences OAE originated in the social and behavioral sciences, early forms of OAE and subsequent research also appeared in the camping literature. By the 1950s, however, research on OAE began in earnest. During this time efforts were first made to identify the extent and impact of adventure-based activities on the individual. For example, Schraer (1954) attempted to identify the number of public schools using survival training programs in their curricula. Morse wrote one of the first "scientific" articles on the therapeutic values of outdoor camping (1951). His points regarding the advantages of outdoor programs included control without institutionalization, real living situations, motor outlets for catharsis, creative learning, and adventures without antisocial behavior. These early findings serve to remind subsequent researchers not to reinvent the wheel but rather to move on to more current areas of concern.

The 1960s marked the beginning of the social benefits phase of outdoor adventure recreation. The works by Kelly and Baer (1968, 1969, 1971) provided some initial and relatively conclusive evidence that adventure-based activities can produce socially desirable benefits, such as reduced recidivism rates. In addition, the work by Moses (1968) and Moses and Peterson (1970) provided additional support for the positive effects of participation in adventure-based survival courses with demonstrated improvements in GPA and eligibility for academic readmission. The first of a long line of research efforts on benefits to the individual also occurred at this time.

By the 1980s, research in OAE included a broad spectrum of outcome variables, such as motivations (Young, 1983; Mitchell, 1983; Kaplan, 1984; Ewert, 1985b), expected benefits (Lambert, 1978; Ewert, 1987a), and levels of satisfaction (Manning, 1986; LaPage, 1983). Inherent in many of these studies is the underlying dimension of participation in some form of outdoor adventure recreation (e.g., backpacking, rock climbing, or whitewater canoeing) often engaged in within a wilderness context or remote setting.

Related to the growth of research associated with OAE was the emergence of works providing a compendium of research efforts. Chief among

OAE-related research in the 1960s demonstrated many social benefits of participation.
Courtesy of Scott Schumann.

these was Shore's (1977) *Outward Bound: A Reference Volume.* Although principally organized around Outward Bound, this work provided the research community with the first structured perspective on completed research, the outcomes, the variables studied, and the overall evaluation of the rigor of the study.

Subsequent works (e.g., Ewert, 1983) investigated a number of other variables, such as the effect of OAE on self-systems (e.g., self-concept, self-esteem, self-awareness). Early OAE research also established outdoor adventure as a form of therapy, with goals such as enhanced self-concept, improved social attitudes and behavior, improved physical health, and reduced emotional problems (Barcus & Bergeson, 1972; Wright, 1982; Smith, 1982, 1985a; Robb & Ewert, 1987).

During the late 1980s a number of researchers were focusing on Outward Bound. Research on fear and anxiety (e.g., Drebing, Willis, & Genet, 1987; Ewert, 1988a; 1988b) posed the ideas that anxiety could be reduced through Outward Bound experiences, that an optimal or preferred level of anxiety exists that is more fruitful for development, and that social fears remain critical during small-group expeditions. Mitchell and Mitchell (1988) provided early evidence of learning transfer from Outward Bound courses. Marsh, Richards, and Barnes (e.g., Marsh, Richards, &

Barnes, 1987; Marsh & Richards, 1989) found that Outward Bound courses could influence aspects of self-concept as well as masculinity and femininity.

OAE RESEARCH MATURES

Published research on adventure programs has increased significantly since 1990. In addition to the *Journal of Outdoor Education, Taproot,* and the *Journal of Experiential Education,* publications such as *Research in Outdoor Education, Journal of Adventure Education and Outdoor Learning, Australian Journal of Outdoor Education, New Zealand Journal of Outdoor Education,* and the *Journal of Outdoor Recreation, Education, and Leadership* all started up during this time period. These publications significantly increased dissemination options for both applied and theoretical research.

As dissemination outlets proliferated, outcome research blossomed. Reports varied, but commonly named benefits of adventure programs included perceived competence and self-efficacy (e.g., Sibthorp, 2003a), interpersonal skills (e.g., Moote & Wodarski, 1997; Sammet, 2010), identity development (e.g., Duerden, Widmer, Taniguchi, & McCoy, 2009), and resilience (e.g., Ewert & Yoshino, 2011; Green, Kleiber, & Tarrant, 2000;

Neill & Dias, 2001). In a comprehensive meta-analysis, Hattie and colleagues categorized the major outcomes of adventure programs into academic outcomes, leadership, self-concept, personality, interpersonal outcomes, and adventuresome qualities (1997; see table 9.1). Recent research on long-term outcomes from adventure programs includes ability to function effectively under difficult circumstances, self-confidence, ability to serve in a leadership role, ability to work as a team member, and an appreciation of nature (Sibthorp, Paisley, Furman, & Gookin, 2008). This research indicated that adventure programs might be especially well suited to foster these types of outcomes compared to home, school, work, or sport environments.

Process research has also moved forward. The meta-analyses have provided good overviews. For instance, Hattie et al. (1997) found that longer duration programs and programs with specific and intentional focus were generally found to be more effective than programs lacking these traits. The number of explicitly OAE process-oriented studies has increased. McKenzie (2003) and Sibthorp (2003a) have further investigated the adventure process as originally proposed by Walsh and Golins (1976), with findings generally supporting the hypothesized influence of instructors, social groups, physical environment, and curriculum. In a recent study on the National Outdoor Leadership School (NOLS), Sibthorp, Paisley, and Gookin found that rapport with adult leaders, support groups, and personal empowerment were all related to developmental outcomes for students involved in adventure programming (2007). Looking at long-term change and growth, a cohort study 1 to 10 years after participation found that transferable and valuable course outcomes were linked to mechanisms ranging from curriculum and educational philosophy to physical environment and personal triumph (Sibthorp, Furman, Paisley, Schumann, & Gookin, 2011). That said, instructors were the most frequently reported agents of long-term change. Instructors played critical roles as supportive role models, educators, and sources of inspiration. Other students and group dynamics were also critical catalysts for growth in areas involving self-awareness and the development of capacity for successful teamwork. Many of these findings depend on the individual student, indicating the learner's centrality in the learning process and the idiosyncratic nature of development through adventure.

In addition to these broader studies, many studies have examined specific aspects of the adventure process and how process is related to specific outcomes. Work on facilitation style has generally supported the premise that more intentional framing, debriefing, and the conscious use of metaphor leads to more meaningful and lasting lessons (e.g., Gass & Priest, 2006). Studies focusing on instructors have generally supported their importance as role models, providers of content and feedback, and patient and empathetic mentors (Schumann et al., 2009). Ewert and Yoshino (2011) identified six factors that emerged as important aspects of developing a sense of resilience: perseverance, self-awareness, social support, confidence, responsibility to others, and achievement.

As a result of these and other research efforts, a growing body of knowledge now exists that characterizes and describes the OAE process and the likely outcomes of engagement in such a process. Table 10.2 summarizes some of the primary works that discuss research efforts in the OAE field.

Looking at table 10.2, you probably notice that many of the same OAE issues raised 20 years ago remain relevant today. Although progress has been made on the methodological pluralism advocated by Ewert in 1989, many of the same deficiencies exist. Ultimately, if research is to make a difference in policy and practice, it needs to evolve in both purpose and focus. Typically, reviews of OAE-related research identify several common factors, including an overreliance on exploratory and descriptive studies, a lack of theoretical conceptualization, and disparate studies that do not contribute to an identifiable body of knowledge (e.g., Rickinson et al., 2004; Thomas et al., 2009).

CURRENT TRENDS

Given the historical state of research in OAE, much of the current research is attempting to redress some of these deficiencies. Theoretical frameworks are now being used to conceptualize research and place it within a wider body of knowledge. Advocates of evidence-based practices are increasingly demanding empirical data rather than solely historical precedence for justification of professional practice. Innovative research approaches are being successfully adapted to OAE, in many cases allowing researchers to ask and answer more complex and multifaceted research questions.

Table 10.2   Summary of Select Contemporary Research in OAE

Study	Summary	Key implications for OAE research
Ewert, 1989	Chapter on research and evaluation reviews most research and larger research syntheses conducted prior to 1987.	• Lack of theoretical or conceptual grounding. • Unsophisticated designs and analyses. • Overreliance on self-report data and a need to diversify data sources. • Lack of process research and explanatory research. • Research is fragmented and does not build a cohesive body of knowledge.
Barret & Greenaway, 1995	Review of empirical adventure-related research prior to 1995. Intention and focus were on studies and implications for the United Kingdom.	• The group dimension is powerful. • Greater need for process research. • Research at the time was neither explanatory nor generalizable. • Too little research in the voice of the participant; need for more constructivist and qualitative research. • Notable gap between research and practice.
Hattie et al., 1997	Meta-analysis of 96 adventure education studies published between 1968 and 1994. Included 1,728 effect sizes and 151 unique samples.	• Benefits of programs generally supported across a wide range of outcomes. • Outcomes may even increase over time. • Improved research designs, samples, measurement, and more detailed program descriptions would all assist future research. • Instructor influences and variable interactions are notable research needs. • More theoretically grounded and process focused research is needed.
Ewert & McAvoy, 2000	Review of studies and research conducted on groups using wilderness settings.	• More process and explanatory research is needed. • General support for power and benefit of wilderness programs on participants. • The group dimension of the programs can be powerful. • Inherent isolation and authentic experiences can be powerful mechanisms of change. • More research is needed on the qualities and types of leadership during wilderness education. • Field-based research and quantifiable measure remain challenges. • Complex variable interactions warrant more sophisticated research strategies.
Neill, 2003	Overview of five adventure education related meta-analyses conducted between 1994 and 2002.	• Programs are generally beneficial. • More process-related research is needed. • More research on why specific programs seem to better afford developmental experiences. • More research on why participants are influenced differently by experiences.
Rickinson et al., 2004	Reviewed 150 studies of primary, secondary, and tertiary schools involved in outdoor education and published between 1993 and 2003. One of the three areas specifically examined was OAE.	• Wide variance in the effectiveness across programs and populations. • Better outcomes from longer programs. • Well-designed programs. • Programs with follow-up. • Programs linked to formal schooling. • Intentionality between aims and practice. • Need to improve methodological rigor. • Many studies have poor conceptualization and design. • Need for more process research—how and why programs work.
Thomas et al., 2009	Review of articles published in three adventure or outdoor oriented refereed journals between 1998 and 2007.	• A more prominent and substantive research culture is evolving in outdoor and adventure journals. • Research does not build to a substantive body of knowledge; previous writing on topics needs to be integrated with current work. • Many papers lack conceptual development. • Research is a mix of constructivist and positivist approaches.

Theoretical Frameworks

Theoretical frameworks are now the norm for OAE research. Deductive (commonly quantitative) research is largely expected to begin with an *a priori* framework including testable hypotheses, and inductive studies (commonly qualitative) are increasingly being asked to position their findings into a broader framework for the reader or, in the context of grounded theory, to create a theory based on the study data. Though most of the peer-reviewed journals that publish OAE research explicitly request a theoretical framework (e.g., *Journal of Experiential Education, Research in Outdoor Education*), a precise definition of this request remains elusive.

In chapters 5 and 6 of this book we described a number of theories and models used in OAE. These chapters offer a number of relevant theoretical frameworks in which studies may be positioned. However, there are numerous other possibilities and a consistently fluid pool of options for researchers as theories gain and lose favor. Ultimately, a theoretical framework needs to situate research findings within a wider body of knowledge.

Another approach that has gained momentum is to create a program-level theory or test a "folk theory." Walsh and Golin's model (presented in chapter 5) tested deductively by Sibthorp (2003a) and inductively supported by McKenzie (2003) is an example of this approach. The idea of using program-level theory in OAE (cf. Baldwin et al., 2004) allows for program-specific hypotheses but also maps the *how* and the *why* to the *what*.

Evidence-Based Practice

The consistent use of evidence to inform practice is gaining momentum in OAE. In general, it is difficult to disparage the notion of using evidence as a source of information to improve professional practice. However, the challenge is in defining evidence in a manner that is universally accepted. To date, much of the work involving evidence-based practices has privileged quantitative, deductive, and positivistic evidence over more subjective sources. Although this approach tends to focus on the traditional view of evidence-based practices, it tends to devalue other ways of knowing and is not entirely compatible with the constructivist approach to education commonly embraced in OAE programs. To distance the more general concepts from the traditional views of evidence-based practices, other terms are sometimes used, such as evidence-informed, evidence-influenced, or evidence-aware practices. Table 10.3 shows some of the challenges associated with evidence-based practices.

One contemporary view of evidence on which to base practice and policy decisions involves three main categories of evidence (figure 10.1) (Puddy & Wilkins, 2011). *Experiential* evidence is learned and internalized through direct history, experience, and practice. It is sometimes linked to intuition or implicit knowledge. This type of evidence is the most common in OAE, which has a long practice-based history. *Contextual* evidence is based on factors regarding practice implications in a specific context or situation or with a specific population. Do the generalizations apply in this context? Experienced outdoor adventure

Table 10.3   Challenges With Evidence-Based Practice

Traditional views of EBP	Challenges with the traditional view of EBP
• Interested in the most effective way to practice (educate, practice medicine, conduct social work, etc.) • Interested in what works • Interested in mechanisms of change • Interested in process, program theory, causation • Interested in cracking open the "black box" of adventure programming	• Focus is on what worked in some context, not what works in the new context • Focus is on generalizing to populations but at the expense of the individual • Education, unlike "medicine," depends largely on the learner • The end goal (e.g., cure) is often clear in medical practice ("effective for what?") • Research should also be used to challenge traditional education, not just to provide evidence • Evidence of what is best is not always reasonable or practical • Often err when trying to make simple the complex

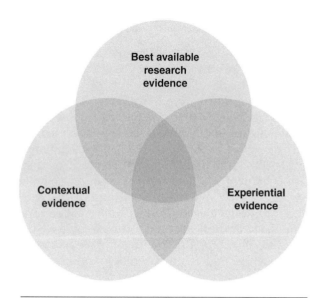

Figure 10.1 Sources of evidence.
Reprinted from Puddy and Wilkins 2011.

what they do to best meet contextual demands. In contrast, *best available research* evidence is supported by empirical data that is intentionally collected to address a research question. Although OAE relies heavily on both experiential and contextual evidence, the paucity of research evidence behind many practices and approaches substantially weakens the profession. The convergence of the three sources of evidence provides the best level of support for practices, policies, and decisions.

Despite the controversy surrounding evidence-based practices, it is likely that this term will remain a part of OAE as the field matures. Early adopters of the evidence-based approach seem to have come to terms with the need for balance. As Sackett and colleagues (1996) state, "evidence based medicine is the conscientious, explicit and judicious use of current best evidence in making decisions about the care of individual patients. This practice means integrating individual clinical experience with the best available external clinical evidence from systematic research" (p. 71). The obvious implication of

educators are typically adept at applying this evidence as well. They tend to be skeptical of universal rules and commonly modify how, why, and

Table 10.4　Example Practices in OAE and Level of Evidence

Practice	Theoretical support	Level of evidence in OAE research	Key studies in adventure contexts
Value of reflection	High	Medium	Collins et al., 2012; Gassner & Russell, 2008; Leberman & Martin, 2004
Value of feedback	High	Medium	Hattie et al., 1997; Paisley et al., 2008; Schumann et al., 2009
Processing and facilitation	High	Medium	Gass & Priest, 2006
Challenge by choice	Low	Low	Carlson & Evans, 2001; Haras, Bunting, & Witt, 2006
Framing experiences	High	Medium	Gass & Priest, 2006
Autonomy and choice	High	High	Sibthorp & Arthur-Banning, 2004; Sibthorp et al., 2007; Paisley et al., 2008
Full-value contracts	Medium	Low	Smith, Strand, & Bunting, 2002
Leader of the day	High through direct experience	Medium	Sibthorp et al., 2011
Goal setting	High	Medium	Crane, Hattie, & Houghton, 1997
Student solo experience	Medium	Medium	Bobilya et al., 2005; Kalisch et al., 2011
Autonomous student expeditions	High	Medium	Bobilya et al., 2010; Sibthorp et al., 2008
Succeeding at challenges	High	Medium	Sibthorp et al., 2011

this perspective is that generalizable research, leader expertise, and individual participant considerations all warrant attention in order to make optimal decisions in professional practice (see table 10.4).

Innovative Methods

Although many of the approaches to design and data analysis have not changed much over the last two decades, some approaches have transformed the research landscape and opened new questions to study. Common historical research methods have included case studies, interviews, enumeration of open-ended questions, and self-reported data analyzed by t-tests and ANOVA tests. More recently these historical methods have been augmented by emerging approaches to research (see table 10.5).

Meta-Analysis

Beginning in the late 1990s, meta-analysis has allowed researchers to combine findings of numerous smaller studies and draw broader conclusions. In 1997, Hattie, Marsh, Neill, and Richards conducted one of the first large-scale meta-analyses on OAE programs. Although each of the meta-analyses (cf. Neill, 2003) conducted varied slightly in focus, outcome, and sample, these studies largely supported the efficacy of outdoor and adventure education programs on a variety of outcomes. However, they caution that not all programs are efficacious and not all participants will realize gains. The major criticisms of meta-analyses stem from locating a representative population of studies and the viability of clumping a diverse set of outcomes and populations into a single analysis.

Table 10.5 Emerging Approaches to OAE Research

Approach	Description of use	Sample studies
Meta-analyses	Analyzes effects of multiple discrete studies to draw broader conclusions and explore possible patterns across studies.	Cason & Gillis, 1994; Hattie et al., 1997
Multilevel modeling	Simultaneously models effects at more than one unit of analysis such as participant and course level variables.	Russell & Sibthorp, 2004; Sibthorp et al., 2007
Mixed-methods (or multi-method) research	Uses qualitative (e.g., constructivist, inductive) data with quantitative (e.g., positivist, deductive) in consort to address related research questions in a single study.	Ewert & Yoshino, 2011; Sibthorp et al., 2008
Hierarchical value maps	Qualitative approach that describes importance of connections among attributes, consequences, and values.	Goldenberg et al., 2005; Goldenberg et al., 2010
Factorial surveys	Uses randomly generated vignettes to examine factors affecting decision making.	Galloway, 2007; Shooter et al., 2010
Experiential sampling	*In-situ* sampling of immediate conscious experience of the participant. May use either event-contingent or random approaches to sampling.	Anderson, 1994; Jones et al., 2000; Sibthorp, Schumann et al., 2011
Photo elicitation	Participants take photos of aspects of their experience and are later asked to explain details and meaning of the events, actions, and people involved in the photo.	Loeffler, 2004; Smith et al., 2010
Q-methodology	Participants are asked to rank the relative importance or relevance.	Hutson et al., 2010; Lindley, 2005

Multilevel Modeling

Another approach that has evolved over the past decade is the availability and use of multilevel modeling. This technique accounts for differences attributable to different units of analysis. For example, if a researcher is interested in the impact of Outward Bound courses on resiliency, multilevel modeling allows researchers to look at participant-level factors (e.g., their age or past experience), course-level factors (e.g., level of group cohesion or instructor rapport), and location-level factors (e.g., comparing effects of similar courses run in different geographical regions). As with all regression-based models, multilevel modeling can be used to analyze a number of different designs ranging from correlational studies to true experimental design.

Multimethod Research

The old paradigm wars of quantitative versus qualitative research are largely in the past, as most scholars now embrace multiple ways of knowing and accept the reality that there is no one best way to answer all research questions. Although quantitative, qualitative, and philosophical scholarship are all accepted and valued, the real improvement in this arena is the willingness to approach problems from inductive, deductive, and conceptual grounds simultaneously. Though a number of strictly qualitative or quantitative approaches to research remain common (e.g., case studies, interviews, pre- and posttests), some of the recent research has worked to use both qualitative and quantitative sources of evidence to draw conclusions.

Hierarchical Value Maps

This approach comes from early attempts to better understand consumer behaviors and places a premium on knowing the values that underlie decisions and behaviors. The approach typically involves asking study participants why certain attributes are important to them until the attributes lead, in turn, to consequences and, eventually, values (a process known as laddering). This linkage of attributes, consequences, and values is called a means-end chain and can be visually displayed in a hierarchical value map. Much of the work in OAE has been conducted by Goldenberg and colleagues (Goldenberg et al., 2010) and links program attributes to consequences and, ultimately values. Like most self-reporting

techniques, means-end chains and the accompanying hierarchical value maps are only as useful as the information provided by the participants. Participants must be aware of their values and able to articulate them for this approach to result in useful data.

Factorial Surveys

Factorial surveys allow situations to be manipulated through elements in vignettes. If, for example, a researcher was interested in the effect of the leadership style of an outdoor instructor on his credibility, a series of vignettes could be constructed that vary the leadership styles used and inquire about participant preferences. As the vignettes are constructed through a random process, factorial surveys represent true experimental designs and enable elements of the OAE process to be examined. However, vignettes are not truly representative of complex situations, so this approach lacks external validity.

Experiential Sampling

The experiential sample method (ESM) allows researchers to study events and times *in situ*. The strength of this approach is that it departs from the typical pretest–posttest of retrospective designs more common in OAE research. Typically, participants wear a watch set with a series of random alarms that prompt the completion of the experiential sampling form (ESF). There are also event-contingent approaches, in which ESF completion is triggered by some event (e.g., the completion of a task). This approach can provide access to data that is typically unavailable. However, experiential sampling is rather intrusive and likely affects the participants' experiences. Furthermore, the level of intrusion is a burden on the program and participants.

Photo-Elicitation

In photo-elicitation studies participants are typically given cameras and asked to take pictures of their experience. After the experience is complete, researchers interview participants regarding the rationale behind each picture in an effort to better understand the experience in the moment. Participants might explain how people in a photo were socially supportive, how a landscape was inspiring, or how a photo of the trail was taken as a prompt to recall the feeling of disorientation at a specific time. Like experiential sampling, photo-elicitation approaches provide a different window into participants' experiences. It is also somewhat burdensome and relies on accurate memory and recollection during the interview process.

Q-Methodology

The Q-methodology approach is intended to capture participants' viewpoints on a topic. This is typically done by having participants sort a series of cards into sets or piles. For example, researchers interested in participants' views of wilderness might have them sort 37 cards with wilderness-related statements, such as "pristine" and "developed." This sorting is called a Q-sort, and the results can then be analyzed through factor analysis to provide a synopsis of the participants' views of wilderness. The sorting itself is time intensive, and the validity of the findings depends largely on the representative composition of the available statements (e.g., the content of the 37 cards). If important content is omitted from the cards or is disproportionately represented, participants cannot accurately portray their views.

SUMMARY

Research in OAE remains critical to the field. Whether outcome or process, inductive or deductive, descriptive or explanatory, research provides evidence that helps communicate the importance and value of the field externally. Research evidence is also critical to *knowing,* which can improve how OAE programs are designed and implemented. Although research has progressed over the last 20 years, OAE professionals tend to note that many of the same conclusions drawn by, say, Ewert over 20 years ago remain relevant today. There remains a need for more sophisticated research designs and analytic procedures. Studies still are commonly conceptually deficient and lack the unified focus necessary to build a distinct body of knowledge.

An abundance of evidence indicates that OAE experiences are influential and developmentally relevant. These benefits are outcomes and the *raison d'etre* (reason to be) of outdoor adventure programming. However, documenting these outcomes often does little to explain how and why they have occurred. More explanatory research is needed in OAE.

Moving beyond description into explanation will prove to be as difficult as it is necessary. Explaining requires a more in-depth understanding of the related fields of psychology, sociology, and education. It will also entail the tedious tasks of formulating and testing theories.

Although theory testing and theoretical frameworks are critical as research moves forward, a more complex view of evidence is starting to unmask the processes behind OAE. When sources of contextual, experiential, and research evidence all point to specific practices, it is easier to articulate their purpose and value. Attention in both OAE and broader research indicates that practices such as reflection, autonomy, feedback, processing, and goal setting are important to creating educational experiences for program participants.

Some of the newer approaches to research appear promising. Meta-analyses, which combine the effects of multiple studies into a broad overview, have found themes that cut across OAE contexts and allow scholars to further consider certain aspects of OAE programs. Techniques such as experiential sampling, photo elicitation, hierarchical value mapping, factorial surveys, and Q-methodology have allowed different questions to be posed and informed. Multilevel modeling allows researchers to consider factors operating at nested levels of influence, thinking beyond the individual. Researchers are no longer confined to a single data source or technique; they now actively seek to triangulate findings across methods, data sources, and populations.

What is needed in OAE is the development of a body of knowledge on which future research can be grounded. This will entail moving away from the compilation of independent, unrelated studies and toward an integration of and building on past research work. Theory-based research, evidence-based practices, and new approaches and methods can all contribute to this effort.

Issues for Further Discussion

1. What research methods or approaches are most applicable to OAE?

2. If money were no object, what kind of study would be the most useful for OAE?

3. Much OAE research has been conducted on larger programs such as Outward Bound or NOLS. How relevant are these programs to other OAE programs with different program models or missions?

4. What is one topic in OAE that you remain curious about? Can you find research studies on this topic that inform your understanding?

5. Which is more important to OAE, outcome or process research? Why?

6. The most current OAE research can often be gleaned from abstracts published by OAE organizations such as the Coalition for Education in the Outdoors (www.outdooredcoalition.org) or the Association of Experiential Education's Symposium on Experiential Education Research (www.aee.org/re/seer). What topics or trends do you notice from the most recent abstracts?

Improving Research

It is always easier to condemn something than to fix it. Over the years many OAE professionals have become tired of criticism of OAE research that offers no tenable solutions. You hear the same complaints over and over: There is no control group; the sample size is not randomized; the design is weak; the OAE experience is complex and multifaceted and thus difficult to deconstruct. These criticisms are all justified, but none of them suggests a way to move research forward.

If we believe that OAE programs promote inclusion, physical activity, and personal growth,

we need data to support these conclusions. We need to show that our programs are effective and efficient. We cannot hope to advance the field much further if we continue to support the obvious or study things no one cares about.

In chapter 10 we indicated that research in OAE is often characterized as chockfull of challenges and issues that must be addressed. In this chapter we discuss how to move OAE research forward and increase both its validity and its power to identify and explain change in individual participants.

Learning Outcomes

After completing this chapter, you should be able to

- explain the three main challenges specific to OAE research;
- identify at least one solution for each of the main challenges to OAE research;
- describe possible paths to relevance; and
- name five current gaps and needs in OAE research.

ver the past 25 years, progress has been made in many of the previously identified research gaps (Ewert, 1989). For example, much work has been done on fear and anxiety in the outdoors (Drebing et al., 1987; Ewert, 1988a; 1988b), and self-efficacy has been one of the primary outcomes of interest (Probst & Koesler, 1998; Sibthorp, 2003a). Researchers have made some progress on program length and even in the order of activities (e.g., Bisson; Hattie et al., 1997; Paisley et al., 2008). Participant characteristics remain a focus area, with renewed attention on how individual participants influence adventure experiences for both their group and themselves. Model testing and verification continues to generate attention (e.g., McKenzie, 2003; Sibthorp, 2003a). But despite all this progress, significant challenges remain. Thus this chapter discusses the macrolevel challenges of OAE research and aims to offer solutions and provide a path to research relevance. We close the chapter with observations on contemporary research needs and gaps.

CHALLENGES IN OAE RESEARCH

Research in OAE is fraught with many of the same challenges evident in any type of field-based research. Many of these challenges were discussed in chapter 10, in which research reviews identified a myriad of shortcomings. In addition, challenges such as sampling, statistical power, and generalizability remain problems for all types of research. However, OAE researchers have perennially wrestled with a few major challenges that need to be addressed to move the field forward. The diversity and holistic nature of OAE programs lead to a criterion problem, difficulty with confounding variables, and numerous disparate studies rather than a productive and evolving research agenda.

Adventure programs are extremely diverse; settings, populations, missions, designs, staffs, and funding streams vary widely across programs. This diversity leads to many different curricular designs, program models, and philosophies. There is no prototypical adventure program, although many programs have developed from or emulate what can be thought of as an Outward Bound course model (see figure 5.3). The inherent differences of our programs require reliance on program-specific models and theories. Although these are well suited to evaluation and program improvement, they are often theoretically weak

and do not connect well to broader scientific theories and frameworks.

OAE experiences involve many transitions and moving parts. Though some facilities, traditions, and curricula remain relatively stable, much about the adventure environment remains in flux: Staff members vary, culture evolves, and participants change. The social and environmental contexts of these programs are often strengths, but they remain unstructured and vague. Although the social environment of an expedition is often difficult to describe, challenging to define, and resists quantitative measurement, it remains valued by most programs. Many organizations are reluctant to interfere with the valuable participant experiences their programs provide. Research can be intrusive and, for practitioners, the hassles of research often seem to outweigh the benefits.

OAE's diverse program models, goals, and objectives have defied standardized measurement, making comparisons among programs or studies difficult. Only the larger programs such as Outward Bound (OB) and the National Outdoor Leadership School (NOLS) consistently use uniform evaluation instruments. Most programs are forced to piece together disparate evaluation tools or use nothing at all. This reality makes it difficult to compare studies over time, across sessions, or between programs.

The Criterion Problem

One problem that remains at an impasse is often referred to as the criterion problem. OAE does not have a singular outcome or criterion that defines program success. For example, some groups, such as the Boy Scouts of America, use OAE to promote fitness, citizenship, and character building. Other groups promote outcomes such as diversity and tolerance through OAE. The success of these programs depends not only on what participants learn through the program but also on the intent of the program. An example is churches that use OAE to foster faith, or freshman orientation programs that use OAE to foster student retention. If such programs actually fostered independence that promoted a questioning of faith or personal awareness that encouraged students to leave church or transfer to another school, would these programs be considered successful? Without a viable criterion, it is difficult to determine either program success or which variables are most related to success. The diversity of OAE program offerings and goals make criteria for success of

OAE programs as a whole difficult to measure and hard to compare.

It is usually difficult to find a single specific measure to assess all outcomes of an OAE program unless that program is based on a specific model or theoretical basis (e.g., a program created around self-determination theory would naturally assess constructs related to motivation, competence, relatedness, and autonomy) or the outcomes are rather general in scope (e.g., a program that targets enhanced self-esteem). However, in most cases, neither of these scenarios is explicit in the program design. For example, consider the objectives generally associated with a NOLS course:

- Safety and judgment
- Leadership
- Expedition behavior
- Outdoor skills
- Environmental awareness (ethics)

The NOLS also has course-specific objectives related to courses in sailing, mountaineering, cultural immersion, and so on, which can differ depending on the type of course being offered.

Even with agreed-on definitions, it is fairly easy to see that some "off the shelf" measures are not going to cover the breadth of outcomes targeted by NOLS courses. This leaves us with two options: use a series of discrete measures initially developed for other purposes (e.g., one for leadership, one for outdoor skills) or design a custom assessment instrument. At first glance, the former of these options might seem both easier and more valid, but it implies several key assumptions:

- That the NOLS definitions (e.g., of leadership or outdoor skills) are the same operational definitions used by the designers of the previously developed measures
- That these measures are applicable to NOLS students and designed for field use
- That the approximately five measures NOLS would need to tap the content of its course objectives can be adequately compiled into a single tool that is both useful and concise

If the NOLS can meet these assumptions, then it is possible they could use existing measures. However, the first assumption is often the most difficult to meet and usually implies at least a level of instrument modification and adaptation if not an all-out custom design effort. For a more detailed discussion of instrument development in OAE, see Sibthorp (2000).

Of course, from a research perspective, simply measuring an outcome is not very helpful. So without some explicit or implicit program theory or framework for the mechanisms of fostering or creating an outcome, the program is still suffering from the age-old "black box" phenomenon (Ewert, 1989). The best programs have both a clear idea of what they are trying to achieve and a working model of how their program works to achieve this end. This entails understanding and putting into operation the constructs that explain the processes behind the outcomes. The factors involved in this processing are often tangled together and become confounded.

Confounding Variables

One of the more vexing problems associated with OAE research is confounding variables (Ewert & Sibthorp, 2009). Defined as one or more variables that obscure the effects of another variable (Vogt, 1993), confounding variables often preclude a clear understanding of the actual treatment effect. For example, suppose that on completion of a program, participants report extremely low levels of desired change for a particular variable. We might conclude that for this variable the program's treatment was highly ineffective and caused this low level of change. Confounding explanations, however, might include an exceptionally poor instructor mix, or a group that could not work together, or maybe the weather was miserable and nothing went the way it was supposed to. The question is whether the program's treatment was ineffective, or did other variables confound the outcome? Ewert and Sibthorp (2009) place confounding variables into three categories: *precursor* variables, which exert their influence prior to the start of an OAE program, *concomitant* variables, which arise during the OAE experience (e.g., weather change), and *postexperience* variables, which come into play following the experience (e.g., postcourse euphoria). Given the diversity of factors that might influence program outcomes, confounding variables will likely remain important for OAE research to address.

Lack of a Research Agenda

One of the largest challenges for OAE research remains disparate studies that do not build on each other. Graduate student theses and dissertations

Critical Thinking, Outcomes, Unintended Consequences, and OAE

Barbara Humberstone, PhD, Professor, Sociology of Sport and Outdoor Education, Department of Sport Management—Buckinghamshire New University, Buckinghamshire, UK

Despite the numerous identified positive outcomes, such as health and wellness, increased self-efficacy, and enhanced resilience, there might be unintended consequences of OAE programs. The sociologist Max Weber tells us of the unintended consequences of social and individual action, which may limit variety, restrict wellness, and constrain individuals. Thinking critically might help OAE professionals make greater sense of the complexity of learning and the situations in which this unpredictability is embedded. It might also provide educators with rich experiences of different ways of understanding and being in the world that can be of benefit to those with whom they interact.

Tolich (2012) draws attention to complex situations and the unintended outcomes that can emerge for members of an OAE experience in which independent and critical thinking of course members is encouraged. Further, Brookes (2003), an outdoor academic and safety expert witness, has highlighted the flaws in the oversimplification of traditional outdoor theory and the importance of critical engagement. Feminist outdoor adventure educators have identified the complexities and challenges when examining the construction of gendered identities in adventure (e.g., Perdersen-Gurholt, 2008). Some unintended consequences of "packaging" or rationalization of OAE experiences include standardization that can potentially provide learners with little more than fairground experiences (Loynes, 1996). Outdoor leaders should be aware of the immense prospects and outcomes provided through OAE as described in this chapter, while at the same time taking into account the inevitable unintended consequences—consequences that might enable broader program outcomes and opportunities. Uncertainty of outcome, after all, is often regarded as one of the hallmarks of the adventure experience (Becker, 2007).

As quantum mechanics has shown when researching the physical world, the different methods used to explore social and educational phenomena will uncover different facets or dimensions of those phenomena. Positivistic methodology, for the most part, might be limited in its ability to uncover the complexity of relationships between learners and teachers, individuals and groups, one environment and another, and so forth. Arguably, the use of interpretative methodologies has provided findings from a diversity of perspectives and phenomena in the outdoors, providing outdoor educators with rich alternatives and complementary narratives (Sparkes & Smith, 2012). Research narratives made accessible through autoethnographic exploration have much to offer our understanding of OAE outcomes. Humberstone (2011), Nicol (2013), and Higgins & Wattchow (2013) exemplify this well through their constructivist inquiry of water-based adventures, providing narratives that can foster proenvironmental thinking and action. Although Brown and Wattchow (2011) emphasize place-responsive pedagogy, Humberstone and Stan (2012a; 2012b) use an ethnographic approach (Stan & Humberstone, 2011) to explore well-being and outdoor pedagogy in one residential setting for primary children. This latter project takes a critical approach and uncovers a number of unintended consequences that outdoor educators should consider when making outdoor experiences available.

Much research from outside of the OAE field has highlighted the affordances of merely being in green nature or forest areas for the health and well-being of young and older people (O'Brien et al., 2011). There is the potential for much more to be gained in health and wellness benefits for participants in OAE programs when instructors pay greater attention to the natural environment and recognize the potential of unintended outcomes and consequences.

References

Becker, P. (2007). What would happen if. . . ?About the elective affinity between adventure and the *coniunctivus potentialis*. *Journal of Adventure Education and Outdoor Learning, 7*(1): 77-90.

Brookes, A. (2003). Adventure programming and the fundamental attribution error: A critique of neo-Hahnian outdoor education theory. In B. Humberstone, H. Brown, & K. Richards (Eds.), *Whose journeys? The outdoors and adventure as social and cultural phenomena* (pp. 403-422). Barrow-in-Furness, UK: Institute for Outdoor Learning.

Higgins, P., & Wattchow, B. (2013). The water of life: creative non-fiction and lived experience on an interdisciplinary canoe journey on Scotland's River Spey. *Journal of Adventure Education & Outdoor Learning, 13,* 13-18

Humberstone, B. (2011). *Embodiment and social and environmental action in nature-based sport: Spiritual spaces.* Special issue—leisure and the politics of the environment. *Journal of Leisure Studies 30*(4): 495-512

Humberstone, B., & Stan, I. (2012a). Outdoor learning: Pupils' experiences and teachers' interaction in one outdoor residential centre. *Education 3-13, International Journal of Primary, Elementary and Early Years Education,* 39(5): 529-540.

Humberstone, B. & Stan, I. (2012b). Nature in outdoor learning—authenticity or performativity? Well-being, Nature, and Outdoor Pedagogies project. *Journal of Adventure Education and Outdoor Learning, 12*(3): 183-198.

O'Brien, L., Burls, A., Bentsen, P., Hilmo, I., Holter, K., Haberling, D., Pirnat, J., Sarv, M., Vilbaste, K., & McLoughlin, J. (2011). Outdoor education, life-long learning and skills development in woodlands and green spaces: the potential links to health and well-being. In K. Nilsson, M. Sangster, C. Gallis, T. Hartig, S. de Vries, & K. Seeland. *Forests, Trees and Human Health.* Springer Publications.

Nicol, R. (2013). Returning to the richness of experience: Is autoethnography a useful approach for outdoor educators in promoting pro-environmental behaviour? *13*(1): 3-17.

Pedersen-Gurholt, K. (2008). Norwegian *friluftsliv* and the ideal of becoming an 'educated man.' *Journal of Adventure Education and Outdoor Learning, 8*(1): 55-70.

Stan, I., & Humberstone, B. (2011). An ethnography of the outdoor classroom—how teachers manage risk in the outdoors, *Education and Ethnography 6(2):* 213–228.

Sparkes, A., & Smith, B. (2008). Narrative constructionist inquiry. In J. Holstein and J. Gubrium (Eds.), *Handbook of Constructionist Research* (pp. 295-313). London/New York: The Guildford Press.

Sparkes, A., & Smith, B. (2012). Embodied research methodologies and seeking the senses in sport and physical culture. *Qualitative Research on Sport and Physical Culture Research in the Sociology of Sport, 6,* 167–190.

Tolich, M. (2012). My eye-opening midnight swim: An Outward Bound autoethnography *New Zealand Journal of Outdoor Education, 3*(1): 9-23

form the corpus of adventure-related research activity. Some of these studies are interesting and useful, but without focus and direction for a cohesive research agenda, they are not well suited to building a body of knowledge. Excluding graduate students, the number of scholars actively conducting research in OAE is minuscule. Real progress needs more effort and resources. Though it is obvious that OAE programs affect a huge number of participants each year, the other challenges so constrain research that well-resourced studies remain rare.

STRENGTHENING RESEARCH

There is no one single solution to the challenges of OAE research, but we can strengthen research by addressing the criterion problem, dealing with confounding variables, and focusing and building a better research agenda.

One option to the criterion problem is to come up with several outcome batteries that measure key outcomes of OAE programs. Examples of this approach include the Life Effectiveness Questionnaire (Neill, 2008) and the American Camp Association's Youth Outcomes Battery (ACA, 2011), which both cover a variety of common OAE outcomes. With several outcome batteries to refer to, we can select the domains of the instrument that best suits our programmatic goals and use it as a criterion relating to other variables. Such standardized batteries provide psychometric strengths with attention to the flexibility and research constraints of OAE. Over time and with increased use, the evidence of their construct validity gets further assessed, and limits and norms can be established to increase their overall utility.

Another option is to take a more inductive approach. Larger organizations with clear and defined program objectives can work to develop psychometrically valid outcome measures for

OAE experiences can be affected by so many diverse factors that confounding variables will likely remain an important issue to be addressed in OAE research.
Courtesy of Scott Schumann.

their course objectives. Of course these measures will not be widely generalizable across programs. For instance, although the NOLS values "expedition behavior," and Outward Bound values "tenacity of pursuit," the measures of these outcomes are largely program specific and targeted by particular curriculum designs. Another benefit of an inductive, customized approach is the ability to measure the same variable from different perspectives. For example, programs might move beyond reliance on self-reports to other measures such as staff reports or parent reports or even to observational measures.

Confounding variables are primarily a problem for traditional positivistic approaches to research. OAE is not the only type of program that is complex. Educational systems, ecological systems, families, and communities are all complex. The main difference between OAE and these other systems is the sophistication and scope of the studies conducted. Although the scope will only increase with increased relevance, the sophistication can improve by more actively appropriating innovative research methods, such as mixed methods studies, multilevel modeling, and experiential sampling (see chapter 10). Other emerging designs such as cluster randomized trials and data-analysis techniques such as regression discontinuity have yet to be used in OAE research, but they appear promising.

Although a unified research agenda is unrealistic, more focus and cohesion would allow the available research resources to work together. Research conducted by graduate students and faculty based on personal interests, out of convenience, or for the purpose of research as pedagogy will not advance the field. Graduate students often enter graduate programs with an interest in OAE, but without a specific research question or study in mind. Many would welcome some guidance on focusing on a topic that is relevant and needed. By aligning the energy and effort of pedagogical research studies with a grander research agenda, the OAE field can move its state of knowledge forward. Such an agenda might center on social needs or on problems and questions from practice. Either way, such an agenda will need leadership and stewardship from the key associations, organizations, and individuals in OAE.

We suggest the following reasonable and attainable steps toward increased research rigor in OAE:

- Aim for the ideal, but when compromise is necessary, make sure the compromise is not a fatal flaw for the study. For example, when a random sample of a targeted population is impossible, at least ensure that your nonrandom sample represents the population of interest. That is, be sure to match your study sample to the group of interest. If you want to know how effective a program is for teenagers, your study sample needs to be teenagers, not adults.

- Have a strong theoretical framework. A strong framework allows a study to add to a broader and more relevant body of research. Theories can be used to guide and inform thinking on how and why something is happening in our programs. And though it is true that many theories might apply to a particular situation, having *no* theory to help organize our thinking restricts our ability to explain why something is taking place, or why we are seeing change, particularly when we are trying to explain this change to others.

- Use a method that fits your research question. Just as the question should drive the method, selecting the right method is critical to providing the right answer. Although some people believe that if you cannot see a result except with statistics, then it probably does not really exist, statistics, like theories, can help organize our thinking and explanations regarding particular outcomes or observations. Ask yourself, Does this method and sample stand a good chance of giving me an answer to my question that is logical and defensible? If not, choose another approach.

- Attend to the construct validly of your measures. Reliability alone is not sufficient. Construct validity refers to the ability of an instrument or observational method to measure what it purports to measure. Confirm that you have the right instrument(s) to measure the construct of interest. For example, if theory purports that self-efficacy improves more for young people than for older adults in a particular OAE program, use questions or indicators that provide good measures of self-efficacy. After collecting the data or information, if your subjects' changes in self-efficacy are negatively correlated with age, this negative correlation is evidence that your measures are adequately able to tap the self-efficacy construct. You might, then, be able to test your study hypotheses with renewed confidence that your measures are tapping your constructs of interest in the ways you intended.

Paths to Relevance

For OAE research to be relevant, it needs connections with social issues, leadership from OAE organizations, and collaboration among practitioners and academics. By pursuing these paths and conducting rigorous research, OAE research can become more relevant to other disciplines, professional practice, and society as a whole (figure 11.1).

OAE needs to connect with compelling social issues. What do people care about? Health? Wellness? Youth development? Returning veterans? The therapeutic value of wilderness? The development of character? Social justice? Sustainability? All of these, and more. But which of these is OAE really situated to address in distinct ways, efficient ways, more effective ways than other programs can? What does OAE do that is unique?

Once establishing and connecting with a social need, a study needs to address a compelling problem for a population of interest. The design needs enough rigor (i.e., control of confounding variables) that it can provide strong evidence of the efficacy of OAE and will truly answer the research question and inform the problem. This can be achieved in one of two ways. There can be one or more large-scale grants that allow rigorous studies to be conducted. This approach, while worth pursuit, has proven difficult. It is more likely that OAE organizations will have to take on leadership roles.

Any OAE organization that wants to be a leader in the field must address issues that would benefit from research. At a minimum, this will allow researchers to align their efforts with problems birthed from the field. Better yet, organizational support should promote research that aligns with the organization's needs. This is sometimes as simple as brokering relationships between academics and practitioners. It might mean supporting the research through assistance with data collection, access to a viable sample, or a moderate level of financial support. The major organizations have the most consistent, refined, and best-articulated goals, objectives, and program models. Such programs have the consistency and culture established over years of programming, which makes for stability in their programs and insulates them from the fluctuations of a few instructors with deviating philosophies.

Empirically, the big programs such as Outward Bound, the Student Conservation Association, and the NOLS have the sample sizes necessary to tease out program components that contribute to their specified set of program outcomes. They

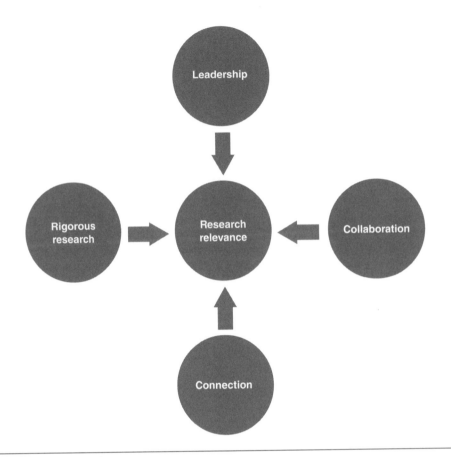

Figure 11.1 Paths to research relevance.

also have the sample sizes to control for individual instructor, group, or course differences that might confound factors established as important on smaller scales. Most important, even if these findings cannot be generalized to other programs, the large organizations can and should use these findings to refine their own programs and make changes based on data and analysis rather than on gut instinct and anecdotal evidence.

Collaboration between practice and academia is key. Practitioners tend to shun theory, yet some of the existing theories have decades of research supporting their utility in a variety of contexts and with diverse populations. In contrast, academics tend to ignore practical constraints and logistical realities common in field-based settings. Most organizations conduct some type of evaluation research. Most academics are expected to disseminate research findings to wider audiences. Organizations can benefit from the knowledge, theory, literature, and methods prioritized, prized, and valued in academic circles. Academics benefit from the practical grounding and realistic constraints of practitioners, who place a premium on the use of scholarship. If the state

of knowledge for OAE is to advance, improved dialogue and collaboration among researchers and practitioners is necessary.

There will continue to be idiosyncratic research and research that questions the status quo. Such research fills a critical role. It can shift the way scholars consider problems, methods, and approaches to the field. Such research, however, must work in partnership with other forms of scholarship; by itself, it will not build a strong body of knowledge.

Research Gaps and Needs

Although the authors of this text cannot define a research agenda for OAE, delimitating some of the notable gaps and needs in OAE research is sensible. Though the topics listed in table 11.1 represent some of the more obvious needs, it is not really the topical areas that identify gaps; it is the depth and sophistication of the research that holds the greatest potential for improvement. Gaps and needs are often not about missing scholarship—they are about missing rigorous research, lack of depth of thinking,

Table 11.1 Current Research Needs in OAE

Need	Key research needs
Evidence of sustained value	• Longitudinal studies • Transfer studies • Life-trajectory studies
Connection of OAE with contemporary social ills and issues	• Obesity and physical activity • Environmental awareness and sustainability • Potential enhancement of academic learning • Role of adventure programming in positive youth development
Professionalization of OAE	• Role of certification and accreditation in program quality • Training and retaining quality staff
Outcome research: What do programs afford?	• Only for outcomes not well examined already • Therapeutic value • Spiritual value
Process research: How do programs work?	• What elements of OAE programs make them developmental? • Which of these elements are unique to adventure programs and which are common with other developmental programs?
Conceptual and theoretical generalization: Why do programs work?	• Model and theory building and testing
Changing demographics	• What populations are best able to benefit from OAE? • How will changing demographics affect OAE?
Costs and benefits	• Do the benefits of OAE warrant the expenses (social, personal, temporal, monetary, and environmental) needed to provide them?

and nontrustworthiness of evidence. For example, although some *a priori* models have been tested via research, it is more the credibility of the tests and the degree of support that is critical to advancing knowledge.

SUMMARY

OAE research has made significant progress over the last 25 years, but many challenges remain. The criterion problem, issues with confounding variables, and the lack of a cohesive research agenda continue to constrain OAE. The criterion problem can be addressed by either instrument batteries designed and tested with OAE research or via high-quality inductive and customized approaches. Challenges from confounding variables are likely to be addressed through more comprehensive and sophisticated research designs such as cluster randomized trials or larger scale multimethod studies. To develop a research agenda and become relevant will not be easy. The process requires a combination of OAE organizational leadership, collaboration among practitioners and academics, and tying OAE to social issues. Specific research needs include such traditional issues as what OAE provides, how it works, and why it works, but to position OAE within a broader context, evidence of sustained value and the efficiency and effectiveness of OAE to influence important societal concerns are larger and more complex questions that warrant study.

W. Edwards Deming once said, "If you can't describe what you are doing as a process, you don't know what you are doing." He also said, "It is not enough to do your best; you must know what to do, and then do your best." Ultimately, research evidence is important. It improves practice, establishes relevancy, and positions OAE as a valuable field of practice. Until OAE professionals can explain what an OAE experience does and how it works, OAE will continue to operate on the periphery and be unable to garner funding and resources accessible to other programs with preventive, developmental, and rehabilitative potential.

Issues for Further Discussion

1. What major challenges exist for OAE research?
2. What solutions exist for OAE research?
3. Which social issues does OAE address more efficiently and effectively than other options?
4. Is a unified research agenda for OAE possible? Why or why not?
5. What research problems in OAE are most likely to attract large-scale funding?
6. Should OAE researchers be conducting research if no one is interested in funding it? Why or why not?

Evolving Trends and Issues

Why This Chapter Is Important

A number of trends and issues have recently presented themselves in the OAE industry. Some involve changes in types of activities, advances in technology, and new expectations among participants. For example, stand-up paddle boarding and geocaching are two relatively new activities that will require OAE to meet demands for new technologies, updated training, and fresh program offerings. Likewise, technology advances such as GPS, SPOT, and smart phones have all exerted influence on the OAE scene. OAE professionals now continually face decisions on how much technology to allow in a program or experience and how to enforce the restrictions they develop.

This is not to say that much in our field has dramatically changed. Many activities commonly associated with OAE have remained stable or even shown increased participation rates. Recreational kayaking, sea kayaking, and whitewater kayaking, for example, have shown substantial increases in number of participants between 2006 and 2013. That said, there has been an overall decrease in the number of people visiting the backcountry of many of the national parks in North America, and activities such as backpacking overnight, climbing, and scuba diving are not as popular as they once were.

The most recent data suggest that a gradual change has occurred in people's values regarding outdoor adventure and, ultimately, OAE. Obviously, understanding how and why these values are changing, as well as the implications of the changes, is critically important for OAE professionals who design and implement OAE programs.

Learning Outcomes

After completing this chapter, you should be able to

* describe and explain data trends as they relate to OAE activities;
* analyze and explain why various trends are occurring and how they might affect the field of OAE;
* discuss the impact that technology has had and is having on OAE programs;
* evaluate positions on how much technology should be allowed in OAE experiences;
* explain how people's values are changing about OAE-related program outcomes and discuss the implications of these changes; and
* predict what the near future holds for OAE.

*M*any *evolving* trends and issues within the field of OAE are affecting both users and the delivery of OAE experiences. In this chapter we will discuss four of them:

- changing levels and types of use,
- impacts of technology on outdoor recreation and adventure activities,
- changing values associated with adventure, particularly on public and other undeveloped lands, and
- consumerism and sustainability in today's interconnected economies.

CHANGING LEVELS AND TYPES OF USE

Any discussion about use levels and types of use within the context of OAE must include an understanding of the setting, the type of activity or experience being studied, and who has collected the data. For example, walking and bicycling are typically included in use levels relating to outdoor recreation and typically indicate relatively high levels of participation. This is not surprising, as many individuals walk or bike for exercise or enjoyment, although often in areas not typically associated with outdoor adventure (e.g., residential neighborhoods). Also not surprising is a general decline in the number of participants and length of participation in some forms of hunting and fishing, activities traditionally associated with outdoor recreation (Cordell, Betz, & Green, 2008). In these examples, demographics such as an aging population, urbanization, and loss of habitat likely account for much of the change that has occurred.

However, visitation rates to national parks in both the United States and Canada present an interesting case study in how land-management agencies have reacted to reduced numbers of visitors. This is important to OAE because many people seek out national parks for OAE activities. If fewer people are visiting the parks, and if they are staying for shorter durations, then it follows that OAE activity occurring at the parks has also likely (though not necessarily) decreased. Shultis and More (2011) point out that national park agencies in both Canada and the United States are concerned about decreases in visitation rates because of the underlying concern that decreases in visitation to the national parks will ultimately result in decreased public and political support for the national parks (e.g., less funding). Similar beliefs abound in other land-management agencies such as the USDA Forest Service and the various Provincial Forest Services. The decrease in visitation appears to be occurring at all three levels of use: day, frontcountry, and backcountry (Outdoor Industry Association, 2006). Selected visitation rates for both the U.S. National Park System and Parks Canada are shown in table 12.1.

Assumptions shared by both agencies for this trend of decreasing visits have focused on the following:

- decreases in visitation will lead to decreases in public and political support for parks,
- increasing use of electronic media is partially responsible for a decrease in children's use of national parks,

Table 12.1 Parks Canada and U.S. National Park Attendance in Millions

Year	Number of person visits to Canadian parks	Visits per capita	Number of person visits to U.S. national parks	Visits per capita
1984	n/a	n/a	249	1.06
1988	12	.46	282	1.15
1992	13.7	.48	275	1.07
1996	14.7	.50	266	.99
2000	16.3	.53	286	1.01
2004	12.4	.39	277	.94
2008	11.9	.36	275	.90

Data from Shultis and More 2011.

- minority visitors to the parks continue to be underrepresented, and

- off-site education efforts typically using electronic media might be effective in reconnecting with the public (Shultis & More, 2011).

Although these assumptions regarding park visitation are not automatically applicable to OAE settings, some overlap likely exists in the areas of minority participation and competition from electronic media. However, the adventure field shows a slightly different situation. That is, although participation rates for some high-end activities, such as scuba diving, have generally remained flat or decreased, data from the Outdoor Recreation Participation Report (Outdoor Foundation, 2010) point to substantial variance across adventure-based activities, as shown in figure 12.1.

The number of people participating in adventure activities does not tell the entire story, however. Another way of viewing the data is to examine the number of first-time participants (table 12.2). For example, indoor climbing has seen a significant number of first-time partici-

pants but also a sizeable number of people who have ceased participating in the activity. Indeed, if you compare the data in figure 12.1 and table 12.2, it appears that currently more people are leaving traditional climbing than are coming into the activity. Thus the number of first-time participants can be an important indicator of the growth potential of a particular activity.

Finally, in ascertaining the growth potential for a particular adventure activity it is useful to understand the generalized motives that drive first-time participants into a particular activity. Once again, borrowing from data generated in the Outdoor Recreation Participation Report (2010), first-time participation in new outdoor activities is fueled by the following factors:

- Friends and family
- Trying something new
- Bringing family or friends closer together
- Being able to exercise outdoors

Just the recognition of these factors supplies organizations with important information for developing new clientele and marketing efforts. Along with these four factors, the possibilities

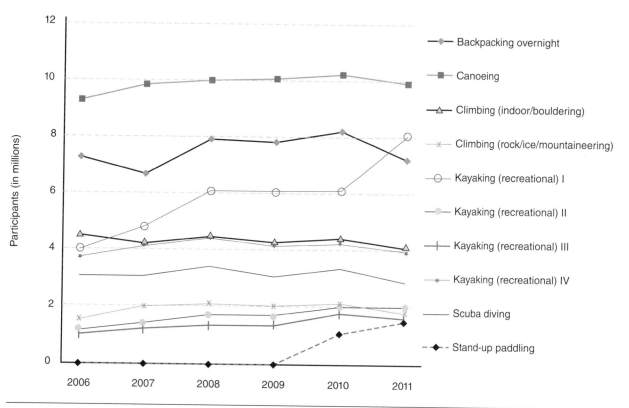

Figure 12.1 Participation in adventure-based activities.

Data from Outdoor Foundation, *Outdoor recreation participation report 2012* (Boulder, CO: The Outdoor Foundation).

in OAE settings to reduce stress and connect to nature are also likely important in attracting first-timers.

We need to take caution when interpreting participation data. First, it matters who is collecting the data and who has funded the data collection. Data collected through an industry-sponsored effort might vary from data collected via a university or nonprofit organization. For example, as shown in table 12.3, data collected several years ago from three different organizations investigating participation numbers for the same set of adventure activities show radically different results.

Second, accuracy in interpreting data might depend on how a question is asked, and even on who is asking the question. Asking the question, "Have you ever engaged in an outdoor adventure activity?" is different from asking, "How often have you engaged in an outdoor adventure activity?" The answer to the first question would typically be a *yes* or *no* response while in the second case the respondent would have to be given a time frame (e.g., last week, within the past three

Table 12.2 Number of First-Time Participants in Selected Adventure-Based Activities*

Activity	Percentage of first-time participants
Kayaking (touring)	27.3%
Kayaking (whitewater)	26.5%
Rafting	22.4%
Canoeing	14.4%
Climbing (traditional, ice, mountaineering)	18.3%
Climbing (sport, indoor, boulder)	24.4%
Backpacking	11.6%
Cross-country skiing	7.6%
Mountain biking	7.1%

*Based on a weighted sample size of 40,141 respondents.

Data from Outdoor Foundation, *Outdoor recreation participation 2012* (Boulder, CO: The Outdoor Foundation).

Table 12.3 Adventure Participation Rates (in Millions)

Activity	ORCA Study	NRSE Study	TIA
Hiking	22.7	47.8	44.8
Hiking to a summit	n/a	16.6	n/a
Orienteering	n/a	4.8	n/a
Backpacking	10.4	15.2	8.0
Backpacking to a summit	n/a	6.6	n/a
Rock climbing	4.1	17.0	7.4
Caving	n/a	27.9	5.7
Canoeing/kayaking/rafting	14	n/a	14.8
Snorkeling/scuba diving	3.2	n/a	12.4
Mountain biking	5.0	n/a	10.8

months, or within the past year). Further complicating this issue is one of precision. For example, does participation imply one day, one hour, or just one outing? What remains clear, however, and relative to the issue of participation, is that those activities requiring more skill and expertise to be successful or safe as well as higher levels of physical demands (e.g., mountaineering, caving, ice climbing) enjoy lower levels of participation then do those adventure activities that typically do not require those characteristics (e.g., backpacking or canoeing).

To further complicate matters, most projections relating to participation in OAE activities will indicate a growth in participation rates, but we are left to wonder: Is the growth a result of greater popularity of the activities, or is it simply a result of population growth? Compare the participation rates for a selected number of OAE activities from 2006 through 2011 in figure 12.1 to the population growth rates in both the United States and Canada for the same time period in figure 12.2. Clearly the population is increasing for both countries, but the same cannot be said for several OAE activities. Although somewhat simplistic, comparing the numbers of participants to actual population provides a more complete understanding of the popularity of the activities.

Finally, we should also consider how data are counted. For example, some organizations will use number of hours engaged in an activity,

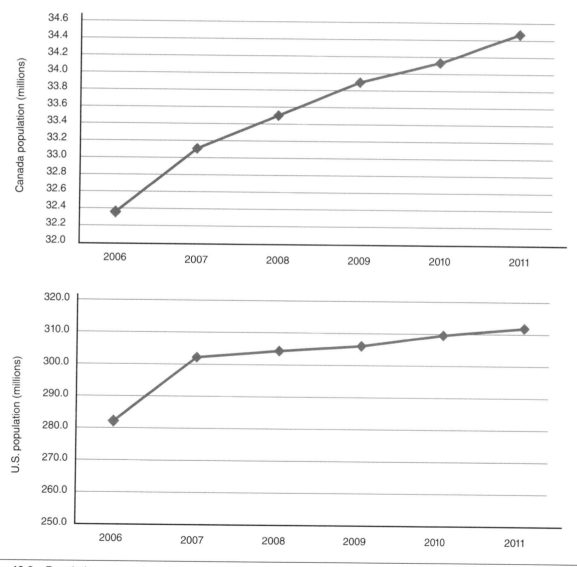

Figure 12.2 Population growth from 2006 to 2011 in Canada and the United States.

Data from Statistics Canada and the U.S. Bureau of Census.

whereas others will use any part of an hour to count as a full user day. We need to examine whether number of hours, number of outings, or frequency of participation is being used to measure participation in an activity. Clearly, if three different organizations use three different measurements, comparing the results will not tell us much.

Whatever the unit of measurement for activity participation, changes in participation levels will be dynamic because of several factors that serve to increase participation levels while others serve to decrease them. Factors that tend to increase the number of participants in outdoor adventure, and presumably OAE experiences, include the following:

- Increased selection of opportunities
- Increased visibility of opportunities
- Technological innovations and improvements
- Proliferation of training and instructional programs
- Increased exposure and visibility from media
- Search for exciting, healthy lifestyles and desired image

Conversely, factors that reduce the number of participants in outdoor adventure, and presumably OAE, include the following:

- Aging population
- Changes in demographics, such as growth of minority groups
- Concerns over safety, liability, and insurance
- Standards and levels of competence held by the staff
- Economics (cost)
- Land use restrictions implying reduced access or more complicated access procedures
- Natural resource degradation
- Level of accessibility for people with differing challenges or needs

It remains to be seen how participation rates and number of participants will change relative to OAE. Some data, however, allow us to make educated guesses about future developments in our field:

- There will be greater activity breadth but reduced depth. That is, people will become more interested in pursuing a host of adventure activities but will not necessarily pursue them in great depth or commit to them.
- An aging population will create a growing demand for facilitated access.
- How difficult is an activity to learn? How risky is it? How much time do I need to spend on this activity? How much will it cost? These sorts of questions will be increasingly asked, and also this question that is related to the first point: How committed do I need to be to successfully engage in this activity?
- Absolute numbers will remain level, although number of trips and types of trips might change. Data suggest that individuals might engage in more activities but fewer outings.
- Identifying quality programs that meet demographic trends will continue to be challenging.
- Technology will continue to replace skill and knowledge development. This trend is likely to continue. (Technology is discussed in detail in the following section.)
- The management of OAE activities and groups will become more complex with increasing competition for available permits, etc., from traditional outdoor recreation users (Ewert et al., 2006).

IMPACTS OF TECHNOLOGY

Technology plays an increasingly influential and important role in outdoor recreation and adventure. The last 10 years, in particular, have seen a virtual explosion of technological developments in the outdoors, ranging from clothes to equipment such as signaling devices and protective gear. There are five areas in which technology has played a significant role in the realm of outdoor and adventure recreation:

- access and transportation,
- comfort,
- safety,

- communication, and
- information.

Each of these areas has resulted in greater use of the outdoors, differing expectations, and changes in public policy.

For example, technology has increased access and transportation through improvements in overland travel such as snowmobiles and off-road vehicles (ORVs). These machines have allowed visitors to get further into remote areas faster and with less effort. Likewise, comfort in the outdoors has been substantially improved through lighter weight, more effective clothing, tents, boots, and so on. This reduced weight coupled with greater effectiveness has resulted in more people, within a greater age range and across ability levels, to get into extremely remote or challenging areas.

Technology has worked in two ways that relate to safety. First, improved technology has increased the level of safety available to both individuals and groups. By and large, equipment

Technology plays an increasingly influential and important role in outdoor recreation and adventure.
© Human Kinetics.

is stronger, lighter, and more versatile, though in some cases higher levels of skill and expertise is necessary to use it. For example, dive computers have essentially replaced dive tables for diving. Although reliable and extremely useful, they also require divers to understand how to use them with enough competence to capitalize on the safety features they provide.

Second, communication is the area experiencing the fastest technological growth. With the advent of GPS units, 36-mile radios, PLBs and EPIRBs (personal locator beacons and emergency position indicating radio beacons), satellite telephones, smart phone apps, and increased cellular coverage, technology now allows outdoor enthusiasts to know precisely where they are, how fast they are moving and in what direction, and how to signal for help—all at the press of a button. The potential danger of these technological advances lies in two areas. First, knowing what direction and exactly how far you need to go to reach a particular point might make you more likely to go for it, but there's no guarantee you will actually reach your destination. Ravines, canyons, mountains, steep slopes, avalanche areas, and severe weather may all conspire to make sure you don't get where you want to go. Second, technology sometimes does not work. Just as helicopters cannot always fly to your location, a GPS or handheld radio might not be in operation for a variety of reasons, such as dead batteries, remote location, or exposure to elements such as rain.

Historically, information was often obtained through word of mouth, asking the area ranger, or finding a map or brochure. Now, within the context of outdoor recreation and adventure, information is usually accessed via the Internet, automated telephone exchange, or guidebooks. Again, this ease and convenience of accessing information generally leads to increases in use, particularly in areas that have not seen much use because of their remote or difficult location.

This increased use, however, does not come without a price, namely in visitors finding themselves in situations far more challenging than their skill or knowledge levels can accommodate. Added to this, they are often in locations so remote that no one can easily get to them. Technology can also create a deceptive "bubble of safety." That is, when substituted for skill or expertise, technology can create an illusion of safety or security that allows people to become complacent, only to discover, perhaps at a critical moment, that no such safety mechanism exists

Three Key Trends

- - - - - - - - - - - - - - - - - - -

Andrew J. Bobilya, PhD—Montreat College, Montreat, North Carolina

OAE is indeed changing at a faster pace today than in previous years. Many evolving trends reflect larger societal trends facing North American cultures. Ewert's (1987) trend analysis included emphasis on accountability, evaluation and documentation, certification of instructors, restrictions on land and water use, overall program growth, and others. Ewert (1995) further identified demographic and participation changes that would influence outdoor and adventure-based programs. Attarian (2001) examined Ewert's predicted trends and discussed their influence on OAE programs, confirming many of Ewert's (1987) trends. Bobilya, Holman, Lindley, and McAvoy (2010) more recently identified the following trends: cultural diversity and changing demographics, increasing older adult population, nature-deficit disorder, public land access challenges, professionalization of outdoor leaders, and program outcome accountability. Many of the trends and issues presented in this chapter are similar to those identified in these previous trends studies. The following three trends are highlighted because they involve the unique human element of OAE programming, namely the participants and instructors. A close understanding of the changes in the human dimension of OAE will inform our responses to all other important trends.

Diversity and Changing Participant Demographics

Many programs have seen change in the demographics of the participants they serve over the past few decades. This has resulted in a mismatch between staff, who have long histories with these programs and participants, who are increasingly diverse. Thus, often program staff are not representative of the clientele they serve. Studies by Wright and Tolan (2009) and Orren and Werner (2007) also suggest a need to focus more attention on diversity in adventure programming. Questions include, What can we do to better adapt to and serve the people who are representative of our communities? How can OAE programs attract and retain qualified staff who are representative of the people the program is trying to serve?

The recent change in cultural diversity within our communities and the lack of representative participants and staff is an important and growing trend that OAE must address.

Overcertified and Underexperienced Leaders

Leaders are a critical component of OAE programs (Kalisch, 1999; Sibthorp, Furman, Paisley, Gookin, & Schumann, 2011). However, OAE program administrators have noticed two recent issues in the preparation of leaders. The first is a deficit of multiday expedition leadership experience, and the second is a proliferation of technical skills but lack of interpersonal skills. Today's OAE leaders seem to be good technicians but less strong in the area of social skills. This trend might result in leaders who do not possess the interpersonal skills required to inspire participants or to engage alongside participants during an adventure experience (Bobilya et al., 2010). The future of OAE programs depends largely on having competent, experienced instructors who can connect with participants, monitor their safety, and inspire them.

Nature Deficit Disorder

Finally, the combination of increased urbanization, parental concern for child safety, and use of technology is resulting in young people who have not developed a positive view of outdoor activities (Louv, 2008). A challenge for OAE staff will be engaging children who have limited experience with the outdoors to participate in their programs. It is also in the OAE field's interest to introduce these potential participants to the outdoors, thereby helping create a citizenry that values natural spaces. Research has shown that experiences in nature as a child can influence an adult's proenvironmental behavior (Chawla, 1998; Chawla & Cushing, 2007; Ewert, Place, & Sibthorp, 2005). If children are not having experiences that promote proenvironmental behavior, how will they learn to care about protecting their natural spaces?

The trends discussed in this chapter, and elaborated on here, are currently having an impact on

OAE programs and should be seriously considered. These programs have a unique opportunity to strengthen their position as meaningful contributors to the health, education, and character development of participants. However, if they are going to succeed, programs must reach out to their increasingly diverse community members, hire and develop qualified staff, and captivate a generation that has been nature deprived.

References

Attarian, A. (2001). Trends in outdoor adventure education. *Journal of Experiential Education, 24*(3): 141-149.

Bobilya, A., Holman, T., Lindley, B. McAvoy, L. (2010). Developing trends and issues in U.S. outdoor and adventure-based experiential education programming. *Journal of Outdoor Recreation, Education and Leadership 2* (3): 301-321.

Chawla, L. (1998). Significant life experiences revisited: A review of research on sources of environmental sensitivity. *Journal of Environmental Education, 29* (3): 11-21.

Chawla, L., & Cushing, D. (2007). Education for strategic environmental behavior. *Environmental Education Research, 13*, 437-452.

Ewert, A. (1987). Outdoor adventure recreation: A trend analysis. *Journal of Leisure Research, 5*(2): 56-57.

Ewert, A. (1995). Current trends in risk recreation: The impacts of technology, demographics, and related variables. In J. Thompson, D. Lime, B. Gartner, & W. Sames (Comps.), *Proceedings of the Fourth International Outdoor and Tourism Trends Symposium and the 1995 Natural- Recreation Resource Planning Conference* (pp. 60-64). St. Paul, MN: University of Minnesota College of Natural Resources and Minnesota Extension Service.

Ewert, A., Place, G., & Sibthorp, J. (2005). Early-life outdoor experiences and an individual's environmental attitudes. *Leisure Sciences, 27*(3): 225-239.

Kalisch, K. (1999). *The role of the instructor in the Outward Bound educational process.* Kearney, NE: Morris.

Louv, R. (2008). *Last child in the woods: Saving our children from nature-deficit disorder.* Chapel Hill, NC: Algonquin.

Orren, P., & Werner, P. (2007). Effects of brief wilderness programs in relation to adolescents' race. *Journal of Experiential Education, 30*(2): 117-133.

Sibthorp, J., Furman, N., Paisley, K., Gookin, J., & Schumann, S. (2011). Mechanisms of learning transfer in adventure education: Qualitative results from the NOLS transfer survey. *Journal of Experiential Education, 34*(2): 109-126.

Wright, A. & Tolan, J. (2009). Prejudice reduction through shared adventure: A qualitative outcome assessment of a multicultural education class. *Journal of Experiential Education, 32*(2): 137-154.

(Ewert & Shultis, 1999). For example, an avalanche beacon can be a lifesaver, but no beacon ever prevented an avalanche from occurring, and if you are buried by one, your chances of survival are automatically decreased by 50 percent.

In sum, technology has contributed a number of benefits to OAE activities and participants. It has increased comfort and safety, improved access, enhanced communication, and enlarged the information base from which we make decisions. It has also been known to create illusions of safety and might create a different set of expectations in relation to outdoor settings. Underskilled participants can find themselves in situations that require search and rescue (SAR) or other forms of assistance from managing or government agencies. In such cases, technology serves to *increase* demands on the environment and land resources rather than decreasing them.

CHANGING VALUES

When Mt. Everest was first successfully climbed by Tenzing Norgay and Sir Edmund Hillary on May 29, 1953, Everest was considered the premier climbing objective throughout the world and a great deal of value was placed on reaching the top, often for patriotic reasons. As of the 2013 season, there have been approximately 5,100 recorded ascents to the summit with over 220 recorded fatalities. Not surprisingly, people's motivations for making the climb are quite diverse, but Everest has now been climbed by people who are blind, amputees, wheelchair users, the very young, and older adults (80 years+), many of whom have used the services of commercial outfitters and guides. Buckley (2000) has made the point that as the number of guiding and outfitting organizations increases, the remaining wilderness and under-explored areas on Earth continues to shrink. We will discuss this issue in greater detail toward the end of the chapter.

The original values commonly associated with outdoor recreation and adventure activities, such as personal challenge, self-identity, teamwork, image, and setting (Ewert et al., 2010), have expanded to include health and wellness issues. More specifically, there is a growing awareness that outdoor activities can alleviate many health-related problems, including stress, obesity, imbalance, cardiovascular and respiratory conditions, and attention deficit hyperactivity disorder (ADHD) (Godbey, 2009). Some positive effects of outdoor activity on health disorders are listed in table 12.4.

Associated with the values related to health benefits is the need for public policy to consider the importance of providing space and resources for people to engage in outdoor recreation and adventure-based opportunities. Although much of the attention devoted to public outdoor recreation resources is directed to national parks and forests, a study by Roper indicated that only 32 percent and 28 percent of Americans have visited a national park or national forest, respectively. Thus, the opportunity to provide settings that allow for enhanced individual health through outdoor recreation and adventure will increasingly lie in the provision of municipal and regional locations. For example, the National Association of State Park Directors report that state parks play an important role in the recreation lives of a significant number of citizens (Godbey, 2009).

CONSUMERISM

Outdoor adventure recreationists underwent an impressive change in the years between World War II and the 1980s. Not so long ago outdoor adventure was predominantly associated with hunting, fishing, and otherwise "living off the land." Particularly over the last half century, the popularity of wilderness exploration, development of equipment that makes new adventure-seeking behaviors possible, and a shift in cultural values regarding interaction with nature has forged a new majority in outdoor adventure recreation. What it means to be an "outdoorsman" has come a long way. Lean-tos and canvas have been replaced by waterproof nylon tents. Where once were fires and spits are now camp stoves. Wool was replaced by fleece and other synthetics. Pemican and beef jerky have been replaced by energy bars and dehydrated premade meals. What all these changes have in common is that they have both grown out of and contribute to consumerism, which has had an enormous effect on outdoor recreation and adventure. Considering that many people associate consumerism with materialism, it might seem ironic that consumerism and the minimal-impact movement in outdoor adventure recreation have historically gone hand in hand.

This irony is not lost on OAE professionals, who recognize underlying contradictions in the so-called improvements that have contributed to the surge in the outdoor recreation movement. Many of the people who champion

Table 12.4   The Effect of Outdoor Recreation and Adventure on Selected Health-Related Disorders

Health-related disorders	Effects of outdoor recreation and adventure
Stress	Rejuvenation from indoor environments Reduction of negative moods Reduction of self-reported levels of stress
Obesity	Increased physical activity Increased enjoyment through physical activity
Children's health	Reduced levels of obesity through increases in physical activity Reduced incidence of type-2 diabetes
Attention deficit hyperactivity disorder	Reduced symptoms of ADHD Reduction in nonactive spectator activities such as TV Reduced need for medication

environmental and ecological causes such as minimal-impact hiking in the name of "leaving nothing but footprints" are the same people who have fueled the tidal wave of consumerism that has washed over most of North America. Although their halogen camp stoves and nylon tents do reduce the immediate impact on a site, which at first look makes them seem eco-friendly, these objects can hardly be considered environmentally benign. Many camp stoves are made of metals that had to be mined, processed, molded, and assembled, more than likely at various points on the planet, and nylon is, of course, made from petroleum. Both were created in various markets, some of which might not be favorable to the individuals engaged in producing them, so it would be foolhardy to expect a camp stove or nylon tent to exist without a trace on both planet and livelihood, though it might be difficult to believe this while held in one's hand. All that said, these products do allow a certain level of environmental interaction to occur without using the natural resources at one's immediate disposal, and multiplied through many users they likely provide some security within a natural landscape.

Despite the ethical complexity inherent in the equipment used for outdoor adventure pursuits, business is booming. Nearly half of all people in North America participate in outdoor adventure recreation in some form, and roughly one quarter of those people anticipate annual increases in equipment and travel expenditures to continue pursuing adventure activities (Outdoor Foundation, 2010). Not taking into account the popularity of such brands as The North Face or Patagonia among nonoutdoor adventurers, we are still looking at a multimillion dollar industry, many of whom find a ready market as a relatively recent historical dependence on petroleum for technical clothing and fabric is shifting toward sustainable resources such as wool, bamboo, and recycled material.

FUTURE CHALLENGES

Despite the popularity of both recreational and educational experiences through an outdoor adventure setting, a number of issues are still in need of answers and resolution. Because this book has focused on the research and theoretical side of OAE, we shall stay within that context in our discussion of these concerns.

The Power of Adventure

One reason OAE is popular is its ability to change people. Whether that change be in sense of achievement, resilience, empowerment, restoration, or other variables, OAE programs and experiences generally involve a mix of activities, instruction, and reflection that provide a mechanism to "change" an individual, usually in positive ways. Juxtaposed to this, programs have a concern over liability and legal action if a participant is injured or otherwise suffers a loss. As a result of this concern, there has been a long-term tendency to "water down" many of the experiences to make them safer and less risky. If this truly is happening, what is the result of this diminished experience? Can experiences that are less adventurous achieve the same outcomes as those that are genuinely adventurous? Can more sophisticated reflection and processing of an experience result in the same outcomes, or other outcomes that are equally valuable, even though the activity itself might be less demanding? The answers to these and similar questions within the OAE setting remain in the future.

Multidimensional Impacts and Transfer of Learning

Most OAE programs follow a fairly linear progression of events that looks something like this:

1. Participants arrive
2. Debriefings and processing events occur
3. Participants depart to "use" their new skills, behaviors, and abilities

Two issues come to mind. First, are there ways that the engagement phase of the experience can be strengthened and made more efficacious? As it stands, the primary experience point tends to be the participant's actual engagement with the activity. Although these engagements are often powerful, the OAE field tends to over rely on high-impact activities such as rock climbing or rafting in addition to placing a heavy emphasis on reflection and processing to further add value to the experience. But what happens when participants have already experienced rock climbing or other impact activities through a previous program or event (as is increasingly the case)? Is the overall outcome of the program diminished?

Second, with few exceptions, once participants complete a program there is generally little

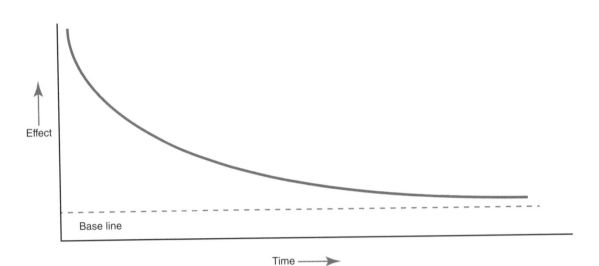

Figure 12.3 Trends analysis of level of effect over time.

follow-up. Thus the level of change experienced by the end of the OAE program tends to diminish over time. As shown in figure 12.3, this diminishment, or downward trend, is asymptotic in that it tends to level out almost to baseline as time progresses.

The diminishment of the effect of OAE programs we witness is similar to other types of training and interventions that lack a follow-up process. Thus the question arises, What would constitute an effective and logistically feasible follow-up or "booster" process? For example, can the technique of participants writing a letter to themselves (often used by OAE instructors) be modified to provide a more powerful impact on the durability of the learning experienced during the course? Developing ways to enhance the durability of the positive effects often experienced in OAE programs will be increasingly important for OAE professionals in the future.

Economics

What role does economics play in the provisioning of OAE and outdoor adventure activities? As mentioned earlier in the chapter, the number of organizations such as commercial tour operators, guide businesses, and outfitters continues to grow. A decade ago, Cloutier (2003) made a point that has since only become more apparent: that OAE and businesses offering adventure activities to clients are becoming more professional and, in many cases, profitable. Similarly, Ewert and Jamieson (2003) and others have made an increasingly strong link between OAE experi-

ences and adventure tourism. Not surprisingly, accompanying this growth is a growing interest in instituting best-practice environment management (BPEM), including minimal-impact and environmental interpretations (Buckley, 2000). There is also an increasing awareness of the growing size and magnitude of the total economic value associated with OAE and related areas (Mallett, 1998; Wilks & Page, 2003).

Although data specific to the OAE field is difficult to generate, the related field of outdoor recreation offers a growing data base. The numbers are somewhat staggering, but note they are primarily generated by the outdoor recreation industry. For example, the Bureau of Economic Analysis, using 2010 data on personal consumption expenditures, estimates that out of the seven major personal expenditures such as motor vehicles, financial services, outpatient health care, and household utilities, outdoor recreation was the third highest ($646 billion), just behind financial services and insurance ($780 billion) and outpatient health care ($767 billion). The expenditures in outdoor recreation occur in two primary ways: equipment and travel. In the OAE case, a third category can be added, namely the cost of the course itself. Moreover, it is estimated that the $646 billion spent in 2010 ($120.7 billion in product sales and $524.8 billion in travel-related spending) resulted in over 6.1 million direct jobs and $80 billion in federal, state, and local tax revenue (Outdoor Industry Association, 2011). Relative to these jobs, employment in a variety of areas is a direct result of interest and involvement in both outdoor recreation and outdoor adventure, and include opportunities in marketing, inventory, customer service, product conception and development, and manufacturing. In addition, according to Bureau of Labor Statistics in 2007, more jobs were generated in outdoor recreation than in any other sector, including oil and gas, information, education, transportation, construction, and finance. Keep in mind that while these data are directed toward outdoor recreation, many of these expenditures are a direct result of involvement in the outdoor adventure area (tents, climbing gear, kayaks, etc.).

In addition to the often hidden input of OAE to the economy are contributions that occur through the ripple effect, which is a measure of total economic contribution effected by bringing a final product (such as an OAE course) to the market. When taking into account the ripple effect, overall impact to the economy from outdoor recreation and related areas, such as OAE, dramatically increase. For example, direct participant spending for outdoor recreation is currently estimated to be around $645 billion. When the total contribution, or ripple effect, is considered, that spending grows to $1.6 trillion dollars. Similarly, the number of jobs directly supporting outdoor recreation is estimated to be around 6 million, but when the ripple effect is factored in that number grows to over 12 million jobs resulting from outdoor recreation (Outdoor Industry, 2010). Even localized impacts can be significant. For example, in an earlier work, Ewert (1996) found that mountain climbers going through the staging area of Talkeetna, Alaska, contributed over $4 million dollars to the local economy. And that was in 1996; the number is undoubtedly larger now.

Evidence

Much of the information presented in this chapter has obvious implications for the design and implementation phases of OAE. The evidence phase is less obvious but still important. We feel relatively confident about the participant and economic data, notwithstanding our concern that those data often come from industry. Making the connection between outdoor recreation data and implications to OAE can be more problematic. That is, however, the nature of our body of evidence in the OAE field, with respect to emerging trends and issues. The evidence and research surrounding the issue of technology is still in the development stage, with a great deal known about what people use but much less known about

what this contributes to their overall experience. Evidence in the area of changing values is also in a developmental stage but perhaps offers the greatest vitality in terms of interesting research questions and tantalizing implications for the future. As Moisey and McCool (2001, p. 347) have pointed out, the question remains to be answered whether the economic development in areas such as OAE will coincide with the development of a shared meaning regarding what constitutes a high-quality OAE experience.

SUMMARY

Like all professions, OAE is not immune to change and adaptations; in fact, in many ways, it embraces and encourages change. Not surprisingly, many of these changes occur at the design, implementation, and evidence phases, as we have discussed. Although somewhat dependent on the activity, trend analyses show a consistent increase for many of the activities associated with OAE, certainly exceeding those of many of the more traditional activities and experiences linked to outdoor recreation. These trends include variations in both level of use and type of use. For example, data suggest that hunting is decreasing in popularity, whereas kayaking is substantially increasing.

OAE is not, however, isolated from other external trends. For example, it remains to be seen how or if decreases in visitation rates to the national parks in the United States and Canada will affect the OAE scene. Another potential indicator of use and popularity are first-time user data. In this case, the data suggest that roughly a quarter of participants in an OAE activity are first-time users, many of whom are introduced to an activity such as rock climbing or kayaking for the first time as a participant in an OAE program. To the extent that these first-time users translate into regular, long-term participants will, in part, be determined by the efficacy and methods used in OAE programs.

Another significant and evolving trend is the use and availability of technology, which continues to progress at a rapid pace. Though providing great assistance at times, technology can also create a "bubble of safety" in which participants feel safe or connected even when their link to the outside world has become extremely precarious.

Finally, we have discussed a number of challenging issues related to evolving trends in OAE. For example, as more people participate in OAE programs, will the effectiveness be the same the next time they engage in an OAE experience? Also, in what ways and to what extent will OAE programs and activities contribute to the overall economy? Should OAE practitioners even be concerned about that issue? Finally, will our research methods and ability to collect evidence supporting OAE evolve at a rate sufficient to demonstrate the efficacy and importance of OAE programs?

Needless to say, there are many questions and fewer answers relating to these and other issues. What we do know is that OAE as a profession, educational method, and lifestyle continues to be increasingly attractive to millions of citizens. As conditions change economically, politically, and demographically, OAE appears poised to continue to grow.

Issues for Further Discussion

1. What are some of the driving forces underlying changes in participation rates?

2. What role should technology play in the OAE experience? How would you enforce technology-related rules that you set as an OAE instructor? For example, how would you enforce a no-cell phone rule?

3. What current empirical trends suggest growth in OAE programs and activities?

4. There is a growing expectation that use of location determination tools, such as the SPOT, will increase safety and emergency response time. How should the OAE industry respond to these expectations?

5. How have changes in consumer habits over the last half century affected OAE and outdoor adventure in general? What have been your personal experiences with changes in equipment and clothing used in the OAE setting?

References and Bibliography

Abraham. H. (1970). *Psychological aspects of stress.* Springfield, IL: Charles C Thomas.

Adams, W. (1970). *Survival training: Its effects on the self-concept and selected personality factors of emotionally disturbed adolescents.* Dissertation Abstracts International, 1970-71, 31: p. 388B.

Ajzen, I. (1988). *Attitudes, personality, and behavior.* Chicago, IL: Dorsey Press.

Albert, D., Chein, J., & Steinberg, L. (2013). The teenage brain: Peer influences on adolescent decision making. *Current Directions in Psychological Science, 22*(2): 114-120.

Alexandris, K., Kouthouris, C., & Girgolas, G. (2007). Investigating the relationship among motivation, negotiation, and alpine skiing participation. *Journal of Leisure Research, 39*(4): 648-667.

Allen, S. (1980a). Risk recreation: Some psychological bases of attraction. *Dissertation Abstracts International, 41*(4): 1766.

Allen. S. (1980b). Risk recreation: A literature review and conceptual model. In J. Meier, T. Morash, & G. Wellon (Eds.), *High Adventure Outdoor Pursuits* (pp. 52-81). Salt Lake City, UT: Brighton Publishing.

American Camp Association (2005). Directions: Youth development outcomes of the camp experience. http://www.acacamps.org/research/enhance/directions. (Retrieved December 30, 2010.)

American Camp Association. (2007). *Programming for positive youth development.* Martinsville, IN: American Camp Association.

American Camp Association. (2011). *Camp youth outcome battery: Measuring developmental outcomes in youth programs* (2nd ed.). Martinsville, IN: American Camp Association.

Anderson, L. (1994). *Outdoor adventure recreation and social integration: A social-psychological perspective.* (Unpublished doctoral dissertation). University of Minnesota.

Anderson, L., & Krathwohl, D., et al. (2000). *A taxonomy for learning, teaching, and assessing: A revision of Bloom's taxonomy of educational objectives.* Boston: Allyn & Bacon.

Anderson, L., Schleien S., McAvoy, L., Lais, G. & Seligman, D. (1997). Creating positive change through an integrated outdoor adventure program. *Therapeutic Recreation Journal, 31*(4): 214-229.

Arnett, J. (2009). Emerging adulthood: Learning and development during the first stage of adulthood. In M. Smith & N. DeFrates-Densch (Eds.), *Handbook of Research on Adult Learning and Development.* New York: Routledge.

Armitage, C., & Conner, M. (2000). Social cognition models and health behavior: A structured review. *Psychology and Health, 15*(2): 173-189.

Atchley, R.A., Strayer, D.L., and Atchley, P. (2012). Creativity in the wild: Improving creative reasoning through immersion in natural settings. *PLoS ONE* 7(12): e51474. doi: 10.1371/journal.pone.0051474.

Bacon, S. (1983). *The conscious use of metaphor in Outward Bound.* Denver, CO: Outward Bound.

Baldwin, C., Persing, J., & Magnuson, D. (2004). The role of theory, research, and evaluation in adventure education. *Journal of Experiential Education, 26*(3): 167-183.

Bandura, A. (1977). Self-efficacy: Toward a unifying theory of behavioral change. *Psychological Review, 84*(2): 191-215.

Bandura, A. (1982). Self-efficacy mechanism in human agency. *American Psychologist, 37*(2): 122-147.

Bandura, A. (1995). Exercise of personal and collective efficacy in changing societies. In A. Bandura (Ed.), *Self-efficacy in changing societies* (pp. 1-45). New York: Cambridge University Press.

Bandura, A. (1997). *Self efficacy: The exercise of control.* New York: W.H. Freeman and Company.

Barcus, C., & Bergeson, R. (1972). Survival training and mental health: A review. *Therapeutic Recreation Journal, 6*(1): 3-8.

Bardwell, L. (1992). *A bigger piece of the puzzle: The restorative experience and outdoor education.* Paper presented at the Coalition for Education in the Outdoors: Research Symposium Proceedings (pp. 15-20), Bradford Woods, IN. January 17-19, 1992.

Barrett, J., & Greenaway, R. (1995). *Why Adventure? The role of outdoor adventure in young people's personal and social development.* Foundation for Outdoor Adventure: Coventry, UK.

Bechtel, A. (1972). A behavioral comparison of urban and small town environments. In A. Berstein, Wilderness as a Therapeutic Behavior Setting, *Therapeutic Recreation Journal, 4,* 160.

Berlyne, D. (1960). *Conflict, arousal and curiosity.* New York: McGraw-Hill.

Bertolami, C. (1981). *Effects of a wilderness program on self-esteem and locus of control orientations of young adults.* ERIC Report No. 266 928.

Bialeschki, M., & Sibthorp, J. Celebrating the camp experience through eighty years of camp research. Invited paper. *Taproot: A Journal of Outdoor Education*, 20(2): 13-24.

Bickman, L., & Rog, D. (2009). *Applied social research methods* (2nd Ed.). Thousand Oaks, CA: Sage Publications.

Bird, F., & Germain, G. (1992). *Practical loss control leadership*, Loganville, GA: International Loss Control Institute.

Bixler, R., Carlisle, C., Hammitt, W., & Floyd, M. (1994). Observed fears and discomforts among urban students on field trips to wildland areas. *Journal of Environmental Education, 26*(1): 24-33.

Black, B. (1983). The effect of an outdoor experiential adventure program on the development of dynamic balance and spatial veering for the visually impaired adolescent. *Therapeutic Recreation Journal, 17*(3): 39-49.

Blanchard, J., Strong, M., & Ford, P. (2007). *Leadership and administration of outdoor pursuits* (3rd Ed.). State College, PA: Venture.

Blanchard-Fields, F., & Kalinauskas, A. (2009). Challenges for the current status of adult development theories: A new century of progress. In M. Smith & N. Defrates-Densch (Eds.), *Handbook of research on adult learning and development* (pp. 3-33). New York: Routledge.

Bloom, B., Engelhart, M., Furst, E., Hill, W., & Krathwohl, D. (1956). *Taxonomy of educational objectives: The classification of educational goals; Handbook I: Cognitive Domain.* New York: Longmans Green.

Bobilya, A., McAvoy, L., & Kalisch, K. (2005). The power of the instructor in the solo experience: An empirical study and some non-empirical questions. *Journal of Adventure Education and Outdoor Learning, 5*(1): 35-50.

Bobilya, A., Holman, T., Lindley, B., & McAvoy, L. (2010). Developing trends and issues in U.S outdoor and adventure-based programming. *Journal of Outdoor Recreation, Education, and Leadership, 2*(3): 301-321.

Borstelman, L. (1970). *Psychological readiness for and change associated with the Outward Bound program.* Morganton, NC: North Carolina Outward Bound School. Mimeographed. 9 pgs.

Breivik, G. (1996). Personality, sensation-seeking, and risk-taking among Everest climbers. *International Journal of Sport Psychology, 27*(3): 308-320.

Breunig, M., O'Connell, T., Todd, S., Young, A., Anderson, L. & Anderson, D. (2008). Psychological sense of community and group cohesion on wilderness trips. *Journal of Experiential Education, 30*(3): 258-261.

Bronfenbrenner, U., & Morris, P. (1998). The ecology of developmental processes. In R. Lerner (Ed.), *Theoretical Models of Human Development* (5th ed.), Vol. 1, pp. 993-1027. New York: Wiley and Sons.

Bronfenbrenner, U. (Ed.). (2005). *Making human beings humans: Bioecological perspectives on human development.* Thousand Oaks, CA: Sage Publications.

Brown, K., Cozby, P., Kee, D., & Worden, P. (1999). The scientific view. In *Research Methods in Human Development* (pp.1-11). Mountain View, CA: Mayfield Publishing Company.

Brown, B., & Larson, J. (2009). Peer relationships in adolescence. In R. Lerner & L. Steinberg (Eds.), *Handbook of adolescent psychology* (3rd ed.), Vol. 2, pp. 74-103. New York: Wiley.

Bryan, H. (1979). *Conflict in the great outdoors.* Bureau of Public Administration. Sociological Studies No. 4. Tuscaloosa: University of Alabama.

Buckley, R. (2000). Neat trends: Current issues in nature, eco- and adventure tourism. *International Journal of Tourism Research, 2*(6): 437-444.

Buckley, R. (2012). Rush as a key motivation in skilled adventure tourism: Resolving the risk recreation paradox. *Tourism Management, 33*(4): 961-970.

Burke, J. (1985). *The day the universe changed.* Boston: Little, Brown.

Burton, L. (1981). *A critical analysis and review of the research on Outward Bound and related programs.* Dissertation Abstracts International, 42: p. 1581 B.

Carlson, J., & Evans, K. (2001). Whose choice is it? Contemplating challenge-by-choice and diverse-abilities. *Journal of Experiential Education, 24*(1): 58-63.

Carney, R. (1971). *Risk-taking behavior.* Springfield, IL: Charles C Thomas.

Cason, D., & Gillis, H. (1994). A meta-analysis of outdoor adventure programming with adolescents. *Journal of Experiential Education, 17*(1): 40-47.

Caspi, A. (1998). Personality development across the life course. In W. Damon & N. Eisenberg (Eds.), *Handbook of child psychology: Social, emotional, and personality development* (5th ed.), Vol. 3. New York: Wiley & Sons.

Cattell, R. (1968). Trait-view theory of perturbations in ratings and self-ratings (L[BR]- and Q-data): Its application to obtaining pure trait score estimates in questionnaires. *Psychological Review, 75*(2):95-113.

Celsi, R., Rose, R., & Leigh, T. (1993). An exploration of high-risk leisure consumption through skydiving. *Journal of Consumer Research, 20*(1): 1-21.

Cherry, L. (1978). On the real benefits of eustress. *Psychology Today*, March, pp. 60-70.

Clawson, M., & Knetsch, J. (1966). *Economics of outdoor recreation*. Baltimore: Johns Hopkins University Press.

Clifford, E., & Clifford, M. (1967). Self-concepts before and after survival training. *British Journal of Social and Clinical Psychology, 6*(4): 241-248.

Cloutier, R. (2003). The business of adventure tourism. In: S. Hudson (Ed.). *Sport and Adventure Tourism* (pp. 241-272). New York: Haworth Press, Inc.

Cober, L. (1972). *A personality factor study of participants in high risk sports*. (Unpublished master's thesis). Pennsylvania State University.

Coble, T., Selin, S., & Erickson, B. (2003). Hiking alone: Understanding fear, negotiation strategies, and leisure experience. *Journal of Leisure Research, 35*(1): 1-22.

Colan, N. (1986). *Outward Bound: An annotated bibliography, 1976-1985*. Denver: Colorado Outward Bound.

Collins, R., Paisley, K., Sibthorp, J., & Gookin, J. (2010). Black and white thinkers and colorful problems: Intellectual differentiation in experiential education [Abstract]. *Journal of Experiential Education, 33*(4): 416-420.

Collins, R., Paisley, K., Sibthorp, J., & Gookin, J. (2012). Black and white thinkers and colorful problems: Understanding student thinking in outdoor education. *Journal of Outdoor Recreation, Education, and Leadership, 4*(2): 11-24.

Collins, R., Sibthorp, J., Gookin, J., & Schumann, S. (2012). The role and importance of program quality in outdoor adventure programs for youth: Examining program quality indicators as predictors of outcome achievement among NOLS participants. *Research in Outdoor Education, 11*: 28-46.

Cordell, H., Betz, C., & Green, G. (2008). Nature-based outdoor recreation trends and wilderness. *International Journal of Wilderness, 14*(2): 7-9, 13.

Craik, K. (1986). Personality research methods: An historical perspective. *Journal of Personality, 54*(1): 18-51.

Crandall, R. (1980). Motivations for leisure. *Journal of Leisure Research, 12*(1): 45-54.

Crane, D., Hattie, J., & Houghton, S. (1997). Goal setting and the adventure experience. *Australian Journal of Psychology, 49*(1): 6-13.

Creyer, E., Ross, W., & Evers, D. (2003). Risky recreation: An exploration of factors influencing the likelihood of participation and the effects of experience. *Leisure Studies, 22*(3): 239-253.

Crompton, J., & Sellar, C. (1981). A review of the literature: Do outdoor education experiences contribute to positive development in the affective domain? *Journal of Environmental Education, 12*(4): pp. 21-29.

Csikszentmihalyi, M. (1975). *Beyond boredom and anxiety*. San Francisco: Jossey-Bass.

Csíkszentmihályi, M. (1990). *Flow: The psychology of optimal experience*. New York: Harper and Row.

Csikszentmihalyi, M. (1997). *Finding flow: The psychology of engagement with everyday life*. New York: Basic Books.

Csikszentmihalyi, M., & Csikszentmihalyi, I. S. (1990). Adventure and the flow experience. In J. Miles & S. Priest (Eds.), *Adventure Education* (pp. 149-156). State College, PA: Venture.

Csikszentmihalyi, M., Larson, R., & Prescott, S. (1977). The ecology of adolescent activity and experience. *Journal of Youth and Adolescence, 6*(3): 281-294.

D'Amato, L., & Krasny, M. (2011). Outdoor adventure education: Applying transformative learning theory to understanding instrumental learning and personal growth in environmental education. *The Journal of Environmental Education (42)*4: 237-254.

Daniel, B. (2007). Life significance of a spiritually oriented, Outward Bound type wilderness expedition [Abstract]. *Journal of Experiential Education, 29*(3): 386-389.

Deci, E., & Ryan, R. (2002). Overview of self-determination theory: An organismic dialectical perspective. In E. Deci & R. Ryan (Eds.), *Handbook of self-determination research* (pp. 3-33). Rochester, NY: University of Rochester Press.

Deep-River Jim (1937). *Wilderness trail book*. Boston: Open Road Publishing Company.

Delle Fave, A., Bassi, M., & Massimini, F. (2003). Quality of experience and risk perception in high altitude rock climbing. *Journal of Applied Sport Psychology, 15*(1): 82-98.

Demirhan, G. (2005). Mountaineers' risk perception in outdoor-adventure sports: A study of sex and sports experience. *Perceptual and Motor Skills, 100*(300c): 1155-1160.

Dewey, J. (1938). *Experience and education*. New York: Touchstone.

DiRenzo, G. (Ed.). (1967). *Concepts, theory, and explanation in the behavioral sciences*. New York: Random House.

Donaldson, G., & Donaldson, L. (1958). Outdoor education: A definition. *Journal of Physical Education, Recreation, and Dance, 29*(17): 17, 63.

Donaldson, G., & Donaldson, L. (1968). *In outdoor education: A book of readings.* Minneapolis, MN: Burgess.

Doublet, S. (2000). *The stress myth.* Chesterfield, MO: The Science and Humanities Press.

Dozier, R. (1998). *Fear itself: The origin and nature of the powerful emotion that shapes our lives and our world.* New York: St. Martin's Press.

Drebing, C., Willis, S., & Genet, B. (1987). Anxiety and the Outward Bound process, *Journal of Experiential Education, 10*(2): 17-21.

Driskell, J., Johnston, J., & Salas, E. (2001). Does stress training generalize to novel settings? *Human Factors: The Journal of the Human Factors and Ergonomics Society, 43*(1): 99.

Driver, B., & Brown, P. (1987). Probable personal benefits of outdoor recreation. In *Proceedings: President's Commission on Americans Outdoors,* 1987, Washington, DC: U.S. Government Printing Office.

Driver, B., & Rosenthal, D. (1982). *Measuring and improvement effectiveness of public outdoor recreation programs.* USDA Forest Service: USDI Bureau of Land Management and George Washington University.

Driver, B., & Tocher, R. (1970). Toward a behavioral interpretation of recreational engagements with implications for planning. In B. Driver (Ed.), *Elements of Outdoor Recreation,* pp. 9-31. Ann Arbor, MI: University of Michigan Microfilms.

Duerden, M., Widmer, M., Taniguchi, S., & McCoy, J. (2009). Adventures in identity development: The impact of a two-week adventure program on adolescent identity development. *Identity: An International Journal of Theory and Research, 9*(4): 341-359

Durlak, J., & Weissberg, R. (2007). *The impact of after-school programs that promote personal and social skills.* Chicago: Collaborative for Academic, Social, and Emotional Learning.

Dustin, D., & McAvoy, L. (1982). The decline and fall of quality recreation opportunities and environments. *Environmental Ethics, 4*(1): 49-57.

Eells, E. (1986). *A history of organized camping: The first 100 years.* Martinsville, IN: American Camping Association.

Elderhostel. (2007). Mental stimulation and lifelong learning activities in the 55+ population. http://www.roadscholar.org/research/lifelong-learning/LifelongLearning55.pdf (Retrieved August 1, 2012.)

Elkins, D., Hedstrom, L., Hughes, L., Leaf, J., & Saunders, C. (1988). Toward a humanistic-phenomenological spirituality: Definition, description, and measurement. *Journal of Humanistic Psychology, 28*(4): 5–18.

Ellis, M. J. (1973). *Why people play.* Englewood Cliffs, NJ: Prentice-Hall, Inc.

Emerson, L. & Golins, G. (Eds.). (n.d) *Workbook on Adventure Based Education.* Denver, CO: Colorado Outward Bound.

Epstein, S. (1976). Anxiety, arousal, and the self-concept. In I. Sarason & C. Spielberger (Eds.), *Stress and Anxiety,* (Vol 3.). Washington, DC: Hemisphere Publishing Corporation.

Estes, C., & Ewert, A. (1988). Enhancing mixed-gender programming: Considerations for experiential educators. *The Bradford Papers Annual, 3,* 34-43.

Evans, C., & Dion, L. (1991). Group cohesion and performance: A meta-analysis. *Small Group Research, 22,* 175–186.

Evans, N., Forney, D., & Guido-DiBrito, F. (1998). *Student development in college.* San Francisco: Jossey-Bass.

Ewert, A. (1983). *Outdoor adventure and self-concept: A research analysis.* (Unpublished doctoral dissertation). University of Oregon.

Ewert, A. (1985a). Identifying fears in the outdoor environment. In *Proceedings Southeastern Recreation Research.* Athens, GA: University of Georgia Institute for Behavioral Research.

Ewert, A. (1985b). Why people climb: The relationship of participant motivations and experience level in mountaineering. *Journal of Leisure Research, 17*(3): 241-249.

Ewert, A. (1985c). Risk recreation: Trends and issues. *Trends, 22*(3): 4-9.

Ewert, A. (1986). The therapeutic modification of fear through outdoor recreation activities. *Bradford Papers Annual, 1,* pp. 1-10.

Ewert, A. (1987a). Values, benefits and consequences in outdoor adventure recreation. In *Proceedings: President's Commission on Americans Outdoors,* U.S. Government Printing Office.

Ewert, A. (1987b). Research in outdoor adventure recreation: Analysis and overview. *The Bradford Papers, 2,* pp. 15-28.

Ewert, A. (1988a). Reduction of trait anxiety through participation in Outward Bound. *Leisure Sciences, 10*(2): 107-117.

Ewert, A. (1988b). The identification and modification of situational fears associated with outdoor recreation. *Journal of Leisure Research, 20*(2): 106-117.

Ewert, A. (1989). *Outdoor adventure pursuits: Foundations, models, and theories.* Columbus, OH: Horizons Publishing.

Ewert, A. (1994). Playing the edge: Motivation and risk taking in a high altitude wilderness-like environment. *Environment and Behavior, 26*(1): 3-24.

Ewert, A. (1996). Gateways to adventure tourism: The economic impacts of mountaineering on one portal community. *Tourism Analysis, 1,* 59-63.

Ewert, A., Attarian, A., Hollenhorst, S., Russell, K., & Voight, A. (2006). Evolving adventure pursuits on public lands: Emerging challenges for management and public policy. *Journal of Park and Recreation Administration, 24*(2): 125-140.

Ewert, A., & Garvey, D. (2007). The philosophy and theory of adventure education. In D. Prouty, J. Panicucci, & R. Collinson (Eds.). *Adventure Education: Theory and Applications* (pp. 19-32). Champaign, IL: Human Kinetics.

Ewert, A., Gilbertson, K., & Luo, Y. C. (2012). *Motive identification and fluidity in adventure recreation.* Presentation at the National Recreation and Park Association Convention, October 16-18, 2012, Anaheim, CA.

Ewert, A., & Hollenhorst, S. (1989). Testing the adventure model: Empirical support for a model of risk recreation participation. *Journal of Leisure Research, 21*(2): 124-139.

Ewert, A., & Jamieson, L. (2003). Current status and future directions in the adventure tourism industry. In. J. Wilks, & S. Page (Eds.), *Managing tourist health and safety in the new millennium* (pp. 67-83). Boston: Pergamon.

Ewert, A., & McAvoy, L. (2000). The effects of wilderness settings on organized groups: A state of the knowledge paper. *USDA Forest Service Proceedings, 3,* 13-26.

Ewert, A., Overholt, J., Voight, A., & Wang, C. (2011). Understanding the transformative aspects of the wilderness and protected lands experience upon human health. In: Watson, A., Murrieta-Saldivar, J., & McBride, B. (Eds.). Proceedings: RMRS-P-64, 225: pp. 140-146. Fort Collins, CO: Department of Agriculture, Forest Service, Rocky Mountain Research Station. Presented at: *Science and Stewardship to Protect and Sustain Wilderness Values: Ninth World Wilderness Congress Symposium,* Merida, Yucatan, Mexico.

Ewert, A., Shellman, A., Yoshino, A., & Gilbertson, K. (2008). The development of a conceptual framework of motivations for participation in adventure recreation activities. *Book of Abstracts of the 12th Canadian Congress on Leisure Research,* Concordia University, Montreal, Quebec, Canada, May 13-16, 2008, pp. 127-130.

Ewert, A., & Shultis, J. (1999). Technology and backcountry recreation: Boon to recreation or bust for management? *Journal of Physical Education, Recreation and Dance, 70*(8): 23-31.

Ewert, A., & Sibthorp, J. (2009). Creating outcomes through experiential education: The challenge of confounding variables. *Journal of Experiential Education, 31*(3): 376-389.

Ewert, A., & Voight, A. (2007). *Environment-based activities to enhance physical activity: A conceptual model.* Presentation at the Diversity in Physical Activity and Health: Measurement and Research Issues and Challenges Conference, The Cooper Institute, Dallas Texas, October 18-21.

Ewert, A., & Voight, A. (2012). The role of adventure education in enhancing health-related variables. *The International Journal of Health, Wellness, and Society, 2*(1): 75-88.

Ewert, A., & Wu, G. (2007). Two faces of outdoor adventure leadership: Educational adventure programs and guided trips. *Journal of Wilderness Education Association, 18*(1): 12-18.

Ewert, A., & Yoshino, A. (2011). The influence of short-term adventure-based experiences on levels of resilience. *Journal of Adventure Education and Outdoor Learnin, 11*(1): 35-50.

Farley, F. (1986). The big T in personality. *Psychology Today, 20*(5): 44-52.

Fave, A., Bassi, M., & Massimini, F. (2003). Quality of experience and risk perception in high-altitude rock climbing. *Journal of Applied Sport Psychology, 15*(1): 82-98.

Felder, R, & Silverman, L. (1988). Learning and teaching styles in engineering education. *Engineering Education, 78*(7): 674–681. www.ncsu.edu/felder-public/Papers/LS-1988.pdf (Retrieved July 1, 2012.)

Felsten, G. (2009). Where to take a study break on the college campus: An attention restoration theory perspective. *Journal of Environmental Psychology, 29*(1): 160-167.

Festeu, D. (2002). Motivational factors that influence students' participation in outdoor activities. *Journal of Adventure Education and Outdoor Learning, 2*(1): 43-54.

Fishbein, M., & Ajzen, I. (1975). *Belief, attitude, intention, and behavior: An introduction to theory and research.* Reading, MA.: Addison-Wesley.

Fitzgerald, R. (Trans.) (1963). *The Odyssey.* New York: Doubleday.

Flamer, A. (1995). Developmental analysis of control beliefs. In A. Bandura (Ed.), *Self-efficacy in changing societies* (pp. 69-113). New York: Cambridge University Press.

Ford, D. & Lerner, R. (1992). *Developmental systems theory: An integrative approach.* Newbury Park, CA: Sage Publications.

Fredrickson, B. (2001). The role of positive emotions in positive psychology: The broaden-and-build theory of positive emotions. *American Psychologist, 56*(3): 218-226.

Fridhandler, B. (1986). Conceptual note on state, trait, and the state-trait distinction. *Journal of Personal and Social Psychology*, 50(1): 169-174.

Frigden, J. & Hinkelman, B. (1977). *Recreation behavior and environmental congruence*. Paper presented at the NRPA Research Symposium National Recreation and Park Association, Las Vegas, NV.

Fry, S., & Heubeck, B. (1998). The effects of personality and situational variables on mood states during Outward Bound wilderness courses: An exploration. *Personality and Individual Differences*, 24(5): 649-659.

Galloway, S. (2000). Assessment in wilderness orientation programs: Efforts to improve college student retention. *Journal of Experiential Education*, 23(2): 75-84.

Galloway, S. (2007). Experience and medical decision-making in outdoor leaders. *Journal of Experiential Education*, 30(2): 99-116.

Galloway, S. (2012). Recreation specialization among New Zealand river recreation users: A multiactivity study of specialization and site preferences. *Leisure Sciences*, 34(3): 256-271.

Gambone, M., Klem, A., & Connell, J. (2002). *Finding out what matters for youth: Testing key links in a community action framework for youth development*. Philadelphia, PA: Youth Development Strategies, Inc. and Institute for Research and Reform in Education.

Gardner, H. (1993). *Multiple intelligences: The theory in practice*. New York: Basic Books.

Gass, M. (2007). Dealing with issues of program effectiveness, cost benefit analysis, and treatment fidelity: The development of the NATSAP Research and Development Network. *Journal of Therapeutic Schools and Programs*, 2(1): 8-24.

Gass, M. (2008). *Cost effectiveness of the behavior management through adventure program for male offenders in residential treatment* [Abstract]. Bradford Woods, IN: Coalition for Education in the Outdoor Biennial Research Symposium Book of Abstracts.

Gass, M., Garvey, D., & Sugerman, D. (2003). The long-term effects of a first-year student wilderness orientation program. *Journal of Experiential Education*, 26(1): 30-40.

Gass, M., & Priest, S. (2006). The effectiveness of metaphoric facilitation styles in corporate adventure training (CAT) programs. *Journal of Experiential Education*, 29(1): 78-94.

Gassner, M., & Russell K. (2008). Relative impact of course components at Outward Bound Singapore: A retrospective study of long-term outcomes. *Journal of Adventure Education and Outdoor Learning*, 8(2): 133-156.

Gaston, D., Plouffe, M., & Chinsky, J. (1978). *An empirical investigation of a wilderness adventure program for teenagers: the Connecticut Wilderness School*. ERIC Report No. ED 178 250.

Gaver, W. (1991). Technology affordances. In S. Robertson, G. Olson, & J. Olson (Eds.), *Human Factors in Computing Systems Conference*. Symposium conducted in New Orleans, LA.

George, R. (1979). *Learning survival self-sufficiency skills and participating in a solo camping experience related to self-concept*. Dissertation Abstracts International, 40, p. 106A.

Gibson, J. (1979). *The ecological approach to visual perception*. Boston, MA: Houghton Mifflin.

Giedd, J., Blumenthal, J., Jeffries, N., Castellanos, F., Liu, H., et al. (1999). Brain development during childhood and adolescence: A longitudinal MRI study. *Nature Neuroscience*, 2(10): 861-863.

Gilbertson, K., Bates, T., McLaughlin, T., & Ewert, A. (2006). *Outdoor education: Methods and strategies*. Champaign, IL: Human Kinetics.

Glancy, M. (1986). Participant observation in the recreation setting. *Journal of Leisure Research*, 18(2): 59-80.

Glass, J., & Benshoff, J. (2002). Facilitating group cohesion among adolescents through challenge course experiences. *The Journal of Experiential Education*, 25(2): 268-277.

Godbey, G. (2009). *Outdoor recreation, health, and wellness: Understanding and enhancing the relationship*. (RFF DP 09-21). Washington, DC: Resources for the Future.

Goldenberg, M., McAvoy, L., & Kenosky, D. (2005). Outcomes from the components of an Outward Bound experience. *Journal of Experiential Education*, 28(2): 123-146.

Goldenberg, M., Soule, K., Cummings, J., & Pronsolino, D. (2010). Longitudinal participant outcomes associated with Outward Bound and National Outdoor Leadership School: A means-end investigation. *Research in Outdoor Education*, 10, 57-73.

Gookin, J. (2011). *Development of a psychometric scale to measure challenge (stress) type and intensity in wilderness education students*. (Unpublished doctoral dissertation). Prescott College, Prescott, AZ.

Gookin, J., Sibthorp, J., & Paisley, K. (2012). *Measurement of challenge (stress) type and intensity in wilderness education students*. Abstracts from the Coalition for Education in the Outdoor eleventh Biennial Research Symposium (pp. 16-18), Martinsville, IN.

Gray, J. (1974). *The psychology of fear and stress*. New York: McGraw-Hill.

Green, G., Kleiber, D., & Tarrant, M. (2000). The effect of an adventure-based recreation program on development of resiliency in low-income minority youth. *Journal of Park and Recreation Administration, 18*(3): 76-97.

Griffin, J., & LeDuc, J. (2009). Out of the fish tank: The Impact of adventure programs as a catalyst for spiritual growth. *Leisure/Loisir, 33*, 197-215.

Haas, G., Driver, B., & Brown, P. (1980). Measuring wilderness recreation experiences. In *Proceedings of the Wilderness Psychology Group Annual Conference, pp. 20-40*. Durham, NH: University of New Hampshire.

Hackensmith, C. (1966). *History of physical education*. New York: Harper and Row.

Hackman, J. (1970). Tasks and task performance in research on stress. In J. McGraph (Ed.), *Social and Psychological Factors in Stress* (pp. 202-237). New York: Holt Rinehart & Winston.

Hamilton, L. (1981). The changing face of American mountaineering. *Review of Sport and Leisure, 6*(1): 15-36.

Hammerton, M., & Tickner, A. (1968). An investigation into the effects of stress upon skilled performance. *Ergonomics, 12*(6): 851- 855.

Hammitt, W. (1982). Psychological dimensions and functions of wilderness solitude. In F. Boteler (Ed.), *Wilderness Psychology Group*, pp. 50-60. Morgantown, WV: West Virginia University.

Hamonko, M., McIntosh, S., Schimelpfenig T., & Leemon, D. (2010). Injuries related to hiking with a pack during national outdoor leadership school courses: A risk factor analysis. *Wilderness & Environmental Medicine, 22*, 2–6.

Hampton, N. (2000). Self-efficacy and quality of life in people with spinal cord injuries in China. *Rehabilitation Counseling Bulletin, 43*(2): 66-74.

Han, K-T. (2001). A review: Theories of restorative environments. *Journal of Therapeutic Horticulture, 12*, 30-43.

Haras, K., Bunting, C., & Witt, P. (2006). Meaningful involvement opportunities in ropes course programs. *Journal of Leisure Research, 38*(3): 339-363.

Harrow, A. (1972). *A taxonomy of the psychomotor domain*. New York: David McKay Co.

Hartig, T., Mang, M., & Evans, G. (1991). Restorative effects of natural environment experience. *Environment and Behavior, 23*(1): 3-26.

Hattie, J., Marsh, H., Neill, J., & Richards, G. (1997). Adventure education and Outward Bound: Out-of-class experiences that make a lasting difference. *Review of Educational Research, 67*(1): 43-87.

Hauck, P. (1975). *Overcoming worry and fear*. Philadelphia: Westminster Press.

Heaps, R., & Thorstenson, C. (1974). Self-concept changes immediately and one year after survival training. *Therapeutic Recreation Journal, 8*(2): 60-63.

Heintzman, P. (2010). Nature-based recreation and spirituality: A complex relationship. *Leisure Sciences, 32*(1): 72-89.

Henderson, K., & Bialeschki, D. (2010). *Evaluating leisure services: Making enlightened decision* (3rd ed.). State College, PA: Venture.

Hinton, J., Twilley, D., & Mittelstaedt, R. (2006). An investigation of self-efficacy in a freshman wilderness experience program. In: K. Paisley, L. McAvoy, Shooter, W., & J. Bochniak (Eds.), *Research in Outdoor Education* (Vol. 8), pp. 105-118. Cortland, NY: Coalition for Education in the Outdoors.

Hitzhusen, G. (2005). Understanding the role of spirituality and theology in outdoor environmental education: A mixed-method characterization of 12 Christian and Jewish outdoor programs. *Research in Outdoor Education, 7*, 39-56.

Hoare, C. (2009). Models of adult development in Bronfenbrenner's bioecological theory and Erikson's biopsychosocial life stage theory: Moving to a more complete three-model view. In M. Smith & N. DeFrates-Densch (Eds.), *Handbook of Research on Adult Learning and Development* (pp. 68-102). New York: Routledge, Taylor & Francis.

Holden, T. (2005). The impacts of satellite phone technology on a North Carolina Outward Bound experience. In K. Paisley, A. Young, C. Bunting, & K. Bloom (Eds.), *Research in Outdoor Education: Vol. 7*. Coalition for Education in the Outdoors Seventh Biennial Research Symposium (pp. 52-57). Cortland: State University of New York College.

Holly, J., McIntosh, S., Schimelpfenig, T., & Leemon, D. (2010). *Prevalence of high altitude illness on national outdoor leadership school adventure courses*. Abstracts from Wilderness Medical Society, 2011 Winter Scientific Conference, p. 190.

Holman, T., & McAvoy, L. (2005). Transferring benefits of participation in an integrated wilderness adventure program to daily life [Abstract]. *Journal of Experiential Education, 27*(3): 322-325.

Hopkins, D., & Putnam, R. (1993). *Personal growth through adventure*. London: David Fulton.

Huberman, J. (1968). *A Psychological study of participants in high-risk sports. PhD dissertation.* University of British Columbia.

Hunt, J. (1965). Intrinsic motivation and its role in psychological development. In D. Levine (Ed.), *Nebraska Symposium on Motivation* (Vol. 13.), pp. 189-282. Lincoln: University of Nebraska Press.

Hutson, G., Montgomery, D., & Caneday, L. (2010). Perceptions of outdoor recreation professionals toward place meanings in natural environments: A Q-method inquiry. *Journal of Leisure Research, 42*(3): 417-442.

Iso-Ahola, S. (1980). *The social psychology of leisure and recreation.* Dubuque, IA: Wm. C. Brown.

Iwasaki, Y. (2006). Counteracting stress through leisure coping: A prospective health study. *Psychology, Health, & Medicine, 11*(2): 209-220.

James, P., Leach, R., Kalamara, E., & Shayeghi. (2001). The worldwide obesity epidemic. *Obesity Research, 9,* 228–233.

James, T. (1980). *Education at the edge.* Denver, CO: Colorado Outward Bound.

Jones, C., Hollenhorst, S., Perna, F., & Selin, S. (2000). Validation of the flow theory in an on-site whitewater kayaking setting. *Journal of Leisure Research, 32*(2): 247-261.

Jones, G. (1964). A *history of the vikings.* Cambridge: Oxford University Press.

Kalisch, K., Bobilya, A., & Daniel, B. (2011). The Outward Bound solo: A study of participants' perceptions. *Journal of Experiential Education, 34*(1): 1-18.

Kane, M., & Trochim, W. (2006). *Concept mapping for planning and evaluation.* Thousand Oaks, CA: Sage.

Kanters, M., Bristol, D., & Attarian, A. (2002). The effects of outdoor experiential training on perceptions of college stress. *Journal of Experiential Education, 25*(2): 257-367.

Kaplan, R. (1984). Wilderness perception and psychological benefits: An analysis of a continuing program. *Leisure Sciences, 6*(3), 271-290.

Kaplan, S. (1995). The restorative benefits of nature: Toward an integrative framework. *Journal of Environmental Psychology, 15*(3): 169-182.

Kaplan, S. (2001). The restorative environment: Nature and human experience. In M. DeHart & J. Brown (Eds.), *Horticultural therapy: A guide for all seasons* (pp. 8-11). St Louis, MO: National Garden Clubs.

Kaplan, S. & Berman, M. (2010). Directed attention as a common resource for executive functioning and self-regulation. *Perspectives on Psychological Science 5*(1): 43.

Kaplan, S., & Kaplan, R. (1989). *The experience of nature: A psychological perspective.* Cambridge, MA: Cambridge University Press.

Kaplan, R., & Kaplan, S. (2011). Well-being, reasonableness, and the natural environment. *Applied Psychology: Health and Well-Being, 3*(3): 304-321.

Kaplan, S., & Talbot, J. (1983). Psychological Benefits of a Wilderness Experience. In J. Altman & J. Wohlwill (Eds.), *Behavior and the natural environment,* pp. 163-204. New York: Plenum.

Kellert, S. (1998). *A national study of outdoor wilderness experience.* Washington, DC: Island Press.

Kelly, F., & Baer, D. (1968). *Outward Bound: An alternative to institutionalization for adolescent delinquent boys.* Boston, MA: Fandel Press.

Kelly, F., & Baer, D. (1969). Jesness inventory and self-concept measures for delinquents before and after participation in Outward Bound. *Psychological Reports, 25,* 719-724.

Kelly, F., & Baer, D. (1971). Physical challenges as a treatment for delinquency. *Crime and Delinquency, 17,* 437-445.

Kephart, H. (1917). *Camping and Woodcraft.* New York: Macmillan.

Kiewa, J. (1994). Self-control: The key to adventure? Towards a model of the adventure experience. *Women & Therapy, 15*(3/4): 29-41.

Kitchener, K.S. (1990). The reflective judgment model: Ten years of research. In M. Commons & C. Armon, et al. (Eds.), *Adult Development Vol. 2. Models and Methods in the Study of Adolescent and Adult Thought.* New York: Praeger.

Klausner, S. (Ed.). (1968). *Why man takes chances.* New York: Anchor Books.

Kleinman, G. (1984). *The attractive enemy.* Paper presented at Chautauqua Lecture Series. Chautauqua, NY.

Knopf, R., & Lime, D. (1984). *A recreation manager's guide to understanding river use and users.* USDA Forest Service General Technical Report WO-38.

Knowles, M., Holton, E., & Swanson, R. (1998). *The adult learner: The definitive classic in adult education and human resource development.* Houston, TX: Gulf Publishing Company.

Kohlberg, L. (1984). *The psychology of moral development: The nature and validity of moral stages.* San Francisco: Harper & Row.

Kolb, D. (1984). *Experiential Learning.* Upper Saddle River, NJ: Prentice Hall.

Kraft, R. (1985). Towards a theory of experiential learning. In R. Kraft (Ed.). *The Theory of Experiential Education,* pp. 4-85. Boulder, CO: Association for Experiential Education.

Kraiger, K., Ford, J., & Salas, E. (1993). Application of cognitive, skill-based, and affective theories of learning outcomes to new methods of training evaluation. *Journal of Applied Psychology, 78*(2): 311-328.

Krathwohl, D., Bloom, B., & Masia, B. (1964). *Taxonomy of educational objectives: Handbook II: Affective domain.* New York: David McKay Co.

Kraus, R. & Allen, L. (1998). *Research & evaluation in recreation, parks, & leisure studies.* Boston: Allyn and Bacon.

Lacey, P. (Ed.) (1978). *Great Adventures that changed the world*. Pleasantville, NY: Readers Digest Association, Inc.

Lambert, M. (1978). Reported self-concept and self-actualizing: Value changes as a function of academic classes with wilderness experience. *Perceptual and Motor Skills, 46*, 1035-1040.

LaPage, W. (1983). Recreation resource management for visitor satisfaction. In S. Lieber & D. Fesenmaier (Eds.), *Recreation Planning and Management*. State College, PA: Venture.

Lazarus, R. & Cohen, J. (1977). Environmental stress. In I. Altman & J. Wohlwill (Eds.), *Human Behavior and the Environment: Current Theory and Research* (pp. 90-127). New York: Plenum.

Lazarus, R. & Folkman, S. (1984). *Stress, appraisal, and coping*. New York: Springer.

Leberman, S., & Martin, A. (2004). Enhancing transfer of learning through post-course reflection. *Journal of Adventure Education and Outdoor Learning, 4*(2): 173-184.

Leemon, D. (2008). Adventure program risk management report. *Proceedings, Wilderness Risk Management Conference*, Jackson, WY.

Leonard, R., Wexler, A., Siri, W., & Bower, D. (1956). *Belaying the leader*. San Francisco: Sierra Club.

Levitt, E. (1980). *The psychology of anxiety*. Hillsdale, NJ: Lawrence Erlbaum Associates.

Lida, M. (1975). Adventure orientated programs: A review of research. In *Research in Camping and Environmental Education*. Proceedings from the National Research Workshop, Pennsylvania State University.

Lieberman, G. & Hoody, L. (2002). *Closing the achievement gap. Using the environment as an integrating context for learning*. Poway, CA: Science Wizards.

Lindeman, E. (1961). *The meaning of adult education*. Montreal, QC: Harvest House.

Lindley, B. (2005). The influence of a wilderness experience program on students' attitudes towards wilderness. (Unpublished doctoral dissertation). University of Minnesota.

Loeffler, T. (2004). A photo elicitation study of the meanings of outdoor adventure experiences. *Journal of Leisure Research, 36*(4): 536-556.

Love, P., & Guthrie, V. (1999). Perry's intellectual scheme. *New Directions for Student Services, 88*, 5-15.

Lowenstein, D. (1975). *Wilderness adventure programs: An activity profile*. ERIC Report No. ED 127 102.

Lyng, S. (Ed.) (2005). *Edgework: The sociology of risk-taking*. New York: Routledge.

Mallett, J. (1998). *Plenary address*. Seventh World Congress on Adventure Travel and Ecotourism, Quito, Ecuador.

Mannell, R., & Kleiber, D. (1997). *A social psychology of leisure*. State College, PA: Venture.

Mannell, R., Walker, G., & Kleiber, D. (2011). *A social psychology of leisure* (2nd ed.). State College, PA: Venture.

Manning, R. (1986). *Studies in outdoor recreation*. Corvallis, OR: Oregon State University.

Manning, R. (1999). *Studies in outdoor recreation* (2nd ed.). Corvallis, OR: Oregon State University Press.

Manning, R. (2011). *Studies in outdoor recreation* (3rd ed.). Corvallis, OR: Oregon State University Press.

Market Opinion Research (1986). *Participation in outdoor recreation among American adults and the motivations which drive participation*. New York: National Geographical Society.

Marsh, P. (2008). Backcountry adventure as spiritual development: A means-end study. *Journal of Experiential Education, 30*(3): 290-293.

Marsh, H., & Richards, G. (1988). The Outward Bound bridging course for low-achieving high school males: Effect on academic achievement and multidimensional self-concepts. *Australian Journal of Psychology, 40*(3): 281-298.

Marsh, H., & Richards, G. (1989). A test of bipolar and androgyny perspectives of masculinity and femininity: The effect of participation in an Outward Bound program. *Journal of Personality, 57*(1): 115-138.

Marsh, H., Richards, G., & Barnes, J. (1986). Multidimensional self-concepts: The effect of participation in an Outward Bound program. *Journal of Personality and Social Psychology, 50*(1): 195-204.

Marsh, H., Richards, G., & Barnes, J. (1987). Multidimensional self-concepts: A long term follow-up of the effects of participation in an Outward Bound program. *Personality and Social Psychology Bulletin, 12*(4): 475-492.

Martin, B., Cashel, C., Wagstaff, M., & Breunig, M. (2006). *Outdoor leadership: Theory and practice*. Champaign, IL: Human Kinetics.

Martin, P., & Priest, S. (1986). Understanding the adventure experience. *Journal of Adventure Education, 3*(1): 18-21.

Maslow, A. (1943). A theory of human motivation. *Psychological Review, 50*(4): 370- 396.

Mattews, B. (1976). *Adventure education and self-concept—an annotated bibliography with appendix*. ERIC Report ED 160 287.

Mazze, S. (2006). *Beyond wilderness: Outdoor education and the transfer of environmental ethics*

(Unpublished master's thesis). University of Oregon.

McGowan, M. (1986). Self-efficacy: Operationalizing challenge education. *Bradford Papers Annual, 1*, pp. 65-69.

McIntyre, N., & Roggenbuck, J. W. (1998). Nature/person transactions during an outdoor adventure experience: A multi-phasic analysis. *Journal of Leisure Research, 30*(4): 401-422.

McKenzie, M. (2003). Beyond "The Outward Bound Process:" Rethinking student learning. *Journal of Experiential Education, 26*(1): 8-23.

McKibben, B. (1989). *The end of nature.* New York: Random House.

McMillan, D. & Chavis, D. (1986). Sense of community: A definition and theory. *Journal of Community Psychology, 14*(1): 6-23.

Meier, J. (1977). *Risk recreation: Explorations and implications.* Paper delivered at the Congress for Recreation and Parks. Las Vegas, NV.

Meier, J., Morash, T., & Welton, G. (1987). *High-adventure outdoor pursuits: organization and leadership.* Columbus, OH: Publishing Horizons.

Metcalfe, J. (1976). *Adventure programming.* Austin, TX: National Educational Laboratory Publishing.

Mezirow, J. (1995). Transformation theory of adult learning. In M. Welton (Ed.). (1995). *In defense of the lifeworld.* Albany, NY: State University of New York Press.

Miles, J., & Priest, S. (1990). *Adventure programming.* State College, PA: Venture.

Miles, J., & Priest, S. (Eds.). (1999). *Adventure programming.* State College, PA: Venture.

Miner, J. L., & Boldt, J. (1981) *Outward Bound U.S.A.: Learning through experience in adventure-based education.* New York, NY: William Morrow.

Mitchell, R. (1983). *Mountain experience: The psychology and sociology of adventure.* Chicago: The University of Chicago Press.

Mitchell, H. & Mitchell, M. (1988). *A study of aspects of self-concept over a two-year period: Possible effects of an intervening Outward Bound course.* Nelson, New Zealand: Mitchell Research.

Mitten, D. (1992). Empowering girls and women in the outdoors. *Journal of Physical Education, Recreation and Dance, 63*(2): 56-60.

Mitten, D. (1994). Ethical considerations in adventure therapy: A feminist critique. *Wilderness therapy for women: The power of adventure,* 55-84.

Mitten, D. (2009). Under our noses: The healing power of nature. *Taproot Journal 19*(1): 20-26.

Moisey, R., & McCool, S. (2001). Sustainable tourism in the 21st Century: Lessons from the past; challenges to the address. In S. McCool & R. Moisey (Eds.), *Tourism, Recreation, and Sustainability* (pp. 343-352). Wallingford, UK: CABI Publishing.

Moore, R., & Driver, B. (2005). *Introduction to outdoor recreation: Providing and maintaining natural resource-based opportunities.* State College, PA: Venture.

Moote, G., & Wodarski, J. (1997). The acquisition of life skills through adventure based activities and programs: A review of the literature. *Adolescence, 32*(125): 143-167.

Morgan, C., & Stevens, C. A. (2008). Changes in perceptions of risk and competence among beginning scuba divers. *Journal of Risk Research, 11*(8): 951-966.

Morse, W. (1957). An interdisciplinary therapeutic camp. *Journal of Social Issues, 13*(1): 3-14.

Mortlock, C. (1983). *Adventure education and outdoor pursuits.* Keswick, England: Ferguson.

Moses, D. (1968). *Improving academic performance.* Provo, UT: Brigham Young University.

Moses, D., & Peterson, D. (1970). *Academic achievement helps programs.* Provo, UT: Brigham Young University.

Murphy, J. F. (1975). *Recreation and Leisure Services: A Humanistic perspective.* Dubuque, IA: William C. Brown.

Murphy, J. F. (1981). *Concepts of leisure* (2d ed). Englewood Cliffs, NJ: Prentice-Hall.

Murray-Webster, R., & Hillson, D. (2008). *Managing group risk attitude.* Hampshire, UK: Gower Publishing, Ltd.

Nash, R. (1967). *Wilderness and the American Mind.* New Haven, CT: Yale University Press.

National Research Council. (2002). *Community programs to promote youth development.* Washington, DC: National Academy Press.

Neill, J. (2008). *Enhancing life effectiveness: The impacts of outdoor education Programs* (Unpublished doctoral dissertation). University of Western Sydney, Sydney, Australia.

Neill, J., & Dias, K. (2001). Adventure education and resilience: The double-edged sword. *Journal of Adventure Education and Outdoor Learning, 1*(2): 35-42.

Nelson, N., & Martin, W. (1976). *Project BACSTOP evaluation report. 1974-1975.* ERIC Report No. ED 198 992.

Neuman, W. (2007). *Basics of social research: Qualitative and quantitative approaches* (2nd ed.). Boston: Pearson.

Newton, A. (Ed.) (1968). *Travel and travelers of the middle ages.* London: Barnes and Noble.

Nold, J. (1978). *Profiles in adventure.* Staff Development Paper, 21 pages. Denver, CO: Colorado Outward Bound.

Norling, J., & Sibthorp, J. (2006). A survey of experiential education outcomes and evaluation strategies: Reanalysis and condensed reporting. *Horizons,* July, 14-18.

Norman, D. (1988). *The psychology of everyday things.* New York: Basic Books.

Noyce, W. (1958). *The springs of adventure.* New York: The World Publishing Company.

Nurenberg, S. (1985). Psychological development of borderline adolescents in wilderness therapy. *Dissertation Abstracts International, 46*(11): 3488A.

Nye, R. (1976). The influence of an Outward Bound program on the self-concept of the participants. *Dissertation Abstracts International, 37,* 142A.

Ocobock, C., & Gookin, J. (2011). *Energy demands of wilderness education students.* Abstracts from the Coalition for Education in the Outdoor eleventh Biennial Research Symposium (p. 16-18), Martinsville, IN.

O'Connell, T. (2010). The effects of age, gender, and level of experience on motivation to sea kayak. *Journal of Adventure Education and Outdoor Learning, 10*(1): 51-66.

O'Connor, C. (1971). Study of personality needs involved in selection of specific leisure interest groups. *Dissertation Abstracts International, 31*(II -A): 5865.

Oettington, G. (1995). Cross cultural perspectives on self-efficacy. In A. Bandura (Ed.), *Self-efficacy in changing societies* (pp. 149-176). Cambridge, MA: Cambridge University Press.

Olpin, M., & Hesson, M. (2007). *Stress management for life: A research-based experiential approach.* Belmont, CA: Thomson.

Outdoor Foundation. (2010). *Outdoor recreation participation report, 2010.* Boulder, CO: The Outdoor Foundation

Paisley, K., Furman, N., Sibthorp, J., & Gookin, J. (2008). Student learning in outdoor education: A case study from the National Outdoor Leadership School. *Journal of Experiential Education, 30*(3): 201-222.

Paxton, T., & McAvoy, L. (1998). Self-efficacy and adventure programs: Transferring outcomes to everyday life. In K. Fox, L. McAvoy, M. Bialeschki, A. Young, S. Ryan, and R. Johnson (Eds.), *Coalition for Education in the Outdoors Fourth Research Symposium Proceedings.* (pp. 32-39). Cortland, New York: CEO.

Perry, W. (1999). *Forms of ethical and intellectual development in the college years: A scheme.* San Francisco, CA: Jossey-Bass.

Petrie, A., Collins, W. & Solomon, P. (1958). Pain sensitivity, sensory deprivation, and susceptibility to satiation. *Science, 12*(1): 45-54.

Petzoldt, P. (1974). *The Wilderness Handbook.* New York: W W. Norton and Company.

Pintrich, P., & Schunk, D. (1996). *Motivation in education: Theory, research, and applications.* Englewood Cliffs, NJ: Merrill.

Pittman, K., Irby, M., Tolman, J., Yohalem, N., & Ferber, T. (2003). *Preventing problems, promoting development, encouraging engagement: Competing priorities or inseparable goals?* Based on K. Pittman, & M. Irby (1996). Preventing Problems or Promoting Development? Washington, DC: The Forum for Youth Investment, Impact Strategies, Inc. Available online at www.forum-fyi.org.

Pollack, R. (1976). *An annotated bibliography of the literature and research on Outward Bound and related programs.* ERIC Report No. 171 476.

Potts, V. (1974). *Project BACSTOP evaluation report, 1973-1974.* Battle Creek, MI: Michigan Department of Education, Battle Creek Public Schools.

Powell, F., & Verner, J. (1982). Anxiety and performance relationships in first-time parachutists. *Journal of Sport Psychology, 4*(2): 184–188.

President's Commission on Americans Outdoors [P.C.A.0.]. (1986). *Americans Outdoors, The Legacy, The Challenge.* Washington, DC: Island Press.

Priest, S. (1986). Redefining outdoor education: A matter of many relationships. *Journal of Environmental Education 17*(3): 13-15.

Priest, S. (1999). The adventure experience paradigm. In: J. Miles & S. Priest (Eds.), *Adventure Programming* (pp. 159-168). State College, PA: Venture.

Priest, S., & Gass, M. (2005). *Effective leadership in adventure programming* (2nd ed.). Champaign, IL: Human Kinetics.

Prochaska, J., DiClemente, C, & Norcross, J. (1992). In search of how people change: Applications to addictive behaviors. *American Psychology, 47*(9): 1102-1114.

Propst, D., & Koesler, R. (1998). Bandura goes outdoors: Role of self-efficacy in the outdoor leadership development process. *Leisure Sciences, 20,* 319-344.

Prouty, D. (2007). Introduction to adventure education. In D. Prouty, J. Panicucci, & R. Collinson (Eds.), *Adventure Education: Theory and Applications* (pp. 3-17). Champaign, IL: Human Kinetics.

Prouty, D., Panicucci, J., & Collinson, R. (Eds.). (2007). *Adventure education: Theory and applications.* Champaign, IL: Human Kinetics.

Puddy, R., & Wilkins, N. (2011). *Understanding evidence part 1: Best available research evidence. A Guide to the continuum of evidence of effectiveness.* Atlanta, GA: Centers for Disease Control and Prevention.

Rachman, S. (1974). *The meanings of fear.* Baltimore, MD: Penguin Books.

Rachman, S. (1978). *Fear and courage.* San Francisco: W. H. Freeman and Company.

Ratner, S. (1975). Animal's defenses fighting in predator-prey relations. In: P. Pliner, L. Krames, & J. Alloway (Eds.), *Advances* in *the Study* of *Communication and Affect,* Vol. 2, *Non-Verbal Communication* of *Aggression.*

Reinharz, S. (1979). *Social science.* San Francisco: Jossey-Bass.

Resnik, H., & Reuben, H. (1975) *Emergency psychiatric care.* Bowie, MA: Charles Press Publishers.

Rhoades, J. (1972). The problem of individual change in Outward Bound: An applicaton of change and transfer theory. (Unpublished PhD Dissertation). University of Massachusetts.

Richtel, M. (2010). Outdoors and out of reach, studying the brain. *The New York Times,* August 15. http://www.nytimes.com/2010/08/16/technology/16brain.html. (Retrieved July 31, 2013.)

Rickinson, M., Dillon, J., Teamey, K., Morris, M., Choi, M., Sanders, D., & Benefield, P. (2004). *A review of research on outdoor learning.* Shrewsbury, UK: National Foundation for Educational Research and King's College London.

Rigby, C., Deci, E., Patrick, B., & Ryan, R. (1992). Beyond intrinsic-extrinsic dichotomy: Self-determination in motivation and learning. *Motivation and Emotion, 16*(3): 135-185.

Robb, G., & Ewert, A. (1987). Risk recreation and persons with disabilities. *Therapeutic Recreation Journal, 21*(1): 58-69.

Robbins, S. (1976). Outdoor wilderness survival and its psychological and sociological effects upon students in changing human behavior. *Dissertation Abstracts International, 37,* 1473A.

Roberts, A., & Camasso, M. (1991). Juvenile offender treatment programs and cost benefit. *Juvenile and Family Court Journal, 42*(1): 37-45.

Roberts, D. (1985). The growth of adventure travel. In *1000 Adventures: with Tales of Discovery.* New York: Harmony Books.

Robinson, D. (1992a). The risk recreation experience: Subjective state dimensions and the transferability of benefits. *Journal of Applied Recreation Research, 17*(1): 12-36.

Robinson, D. (1992b). The risk-sport process: An alternative approach for humanistic physical education. *Quest (National Association for Physical Education in Higher Education), 44*(1): 88-104.

Roland, C., & Havens, M. (1981). An introduction to adventure: A sequential approach to challenging activities with persons who are disabled. Loretto, MN: The Vinland National Center.

Rossi, P., Freeman, H., & Lipsey, M. (2004). *Evaluation: A systematic approach* (6th ed.). Thousand Oaks, CA: Sage Publishing.

Rossman, B., & Ulehla, J. (1977). Psychological reward values associated with wilderness use: A functional reinforcement approach. *Environment and Behavior, 9*(1): 41-66.

Ruddell, J., & Shinew, K. (2006). The socialization process for women with physical disabilities: The impact of agents and agencies in the introduction to an elite sport. *Journal of Leisure Research, 38*(3): 421-444.

Russell, K. (2006). *Examining substance use frequency and depressive symptom outcome in a sample of outdoor behavioral healthcare participants* (Research Report No 1). Minneapolis, MN: Outdoor Behavioral Healthcare Research Cooperative College of Education and Human Development, University of Minnesota.

Russell, K., & Sibthorp, J. (2004). Hierarchical data structures in adventure education and therapy. *Journal of Experiential Education 27*(2): 176-190.

Ryan, R., & Deci, E. (2000a). Self-determination theory and the facilitation of intrinsic motivation, social development, and well-being. *American Psychologist, 55*(1): 68-78.

Ryan, R., & Deci, E. (2000b). Intrinsic and extrinsic motivations: Classical definitions and new directions. *Contemporary Educational Psychology, 25*(1): 54-67.

Sackett, D., Rosenberg, W., Gray, J., Haynes, R., & Richardson, S. (1996). Evidence based medicine: What it is and what it isn't. *British Medical Journal, 312,* 71-72.

Sameroff, A. (2010). A unified theory of development: A dialectic integration of nature and nurture. *Child Development, 81*(1): 6-22.

Sammet, K. (2010). Relationships matter: Adolescent girls and relational development in adventure education. *Journal of Experiential Education, 33*(2): 151-165.

Schiraldi, G. (2000). *The post-traumatic stress disorder sourcebook.* McGraw-Hill: New York.

Schraer, H. (1954). Survival education: A survey of trends in survival education in certain public schools and teacher training institutions and a detailed study of the elements of survival education found in the programs of the Boy Scouts and Girl Scouts of America. *Dissertation Abstracts International: 14*(1): 966.

Schreyer, R., & Knopf, R. (1984). The dynamics of change in outdoor recreation environments—some equity issues. *Journal of Park and Recreation Administration, 2*(1): 9-19.

Schreyer, R., & White, R. (1979). A conceptual model of high-risk recreation. *American Society of Civil Engineers: Conference on Recreation Planning and Development*, New York, NY.

Schroder, K. (2004). Coping competence as predictor and moderator of depression among chronic disease patients. *Journal of Behavioral Medicine, 27*(2): 123-145.

Schumann, S., Paisley, K., Sibthorp, J., & Gookin, J. (2009). Instructor influences on student learning at NOLS. *Journal of Outdoor Recreation and Education Leadership, 1*(1): 15-37.

Schunk, D. (2004). *Learning theories: An educational perspective* (4th ed). Upper Saddle River, NJ: Pearson.

Scott, D. (1974). *Big wall climbing.* New York: Oxford University Press.

Sears, G. (1920). *Woodcraft.* New York: Forest and Stream Publishing.

Seipp, B. (1991). Anxiety and academic performance: A meta-analysis of findings. *Anxiety Research, 4*(1): 27-41.

Seton, E. (1912). *The book of woodcraft.* Garden City, NY: Garden City Publishing Co.

Severin, T. (1978). *The Brendan voyage.* New York: McGraw-Hill.

Seyle, H. (1950). *The psychology and pathology of exposure* to *stress.* Montreal, Canada: ACTA Publishers.

Seyle, H. (1976). Forty years of stress research: Principal remaining problems and misconceptions. *Canadian Medical Association Journal, 15*(1): 53-56.

Sharp, L. (1947). Basic considerations in outdoor and camping education. *The Bulletin of the National Association of Secondary-School Principals*. Washington, DC: The Department of Secondary Education of the National Education Association,

Sheard, M., & Golby, J. (2006). The efficacy of an Outdoor Adventure Education curriculum on selected aspects of positive psychological development. *Journal of Experiential Education, 29*(2): 187-209.

Shellman, A. (2009). *Empowerment and resilience: A multi-method approach to understanding processes and outcomes of adventure education program experiences* (Doctoral dissertation). Available from ProQuest Dissertations and Theses database.

Shellman, A. (2011). Fostering resilience through outdoor education. *Taproot: A Journal of Outdoor Education, 20*(1), 4-11.

Shooter, W., Paisley, K., & Sibthorp, J. (2010). Trust development in outdoor leadership. *Journal of Experiential Education, 33*(3): 189-207.

Shooter, W., Paisley, K., & Sibthorp, J. (2012). Fostering trust in outdoor leaders: The role of personal attributes. *Journal of Experiential Education, 35*(1): 222-237.

Shore, A. (1977). *Outward Bound: A reference volume.* New York: Topp Litho.

Shorey, P. (Trans.) (1953). Plato's *The Republic.* Cambridge, MA: Loeb Classical Library, Harvard University Press.

Shultis, J., & More, T. (2011). American and Canadian national park agency responses to declining visitation. *Journal of Leisure Research, 43*(1): 110-133.

Sibthorp, J. (2003a). An empirical look at Walsh and Golins' adventure education process model: Relationships between antecedent factors, perceptions of characteristics of an adventure education experience, and changes in self-efficacy. *Journal of Leisure Research, 35*(1): 80-106.

Sibthorp, J. (2003b). Learning transferable skills through adventure education: The role of an authentic process. *Journal of Adventure Education and Outdoor Learning, 3*(2): 145-157.

Sibthorp, J., & Arthur-Banning, S. (2004). Developing life effectiveness through adventure education: The roles of participant expectations, perceptions of empowerment, and learning relevance. *Journal of Experiential Education 27*(1): 32-50.

Sibthorp, J., Furman, N., Paisley, K., Schumann, S., & Gookin, J. (2011). Mechanisms of learning transfer in adventure education: Qualitative results from the NOLS transfer survey. *Journal of Experiential Education. 34*(2): 109-118.

Sibthorp, J., Paisley, K., & Gookin, J. (2007). Exploring participant development through adventure-based recreation programming: A model from the National Outdoor Leadership School. *Leisure Sciences, 29*(1): 1-18.

Sibthorp, J., Paisley, K., Furman, N., & Gookin, J. (2008). Long-term impacts attributed to participation in adventure education: Preliminary findings from NOLS. *Research in Outdoor Education, 9*, 86-102.

Sibthorp, J., Schumann, S., Gookin, J., Baynes, S., Paisley, K., & Rathunde, K. (2010). Experiential education and lifelong learning: Examining optimal engagement in college students [Abstract]. *Journal of Experiential Education, 33*(4): 388-392.

Sinnott, J. (2009). Cognitive development as the dance of adaptive transformation: Neo-Piagetian perspectives on adult cognitive development. In M. Smith & N. DeFrates-Densch (Eds.),

Handbook of research on adult learning and development (pp. 103–134). New York: Routledge/ Taylor & Francis

Skidelsky, R. (1969). *English progressive schools.* Middlesex, England: Penguin.

Slanger, E., & Rudestam, E. (1997). Motivation and disinhibition in high risk sports: Sensation seeking and self-efficacy. *Journal of Research in Personality, 31*, 355-374.

SlawSki, C. (1981). *Social psychological theories: A comparative handbook for students.* Glenview, IL: Scott, Foresman and Company.

Slovic, P. (1972). Information processing, situation specificity, and the generality of risk-taking behavior. *Journal of Personality and Social Psychology, 22*(1): 128-134.

Slovic, P. (2006). *The perception of risk.* London: Earthscan

Slovic, P. (2010). *The feeling of risk.* London: Earthscan.

Smith, C., Strand, S., & Bunting, C. (2002). The influence of challenge course participation on moral and ethical reasoning. *Journal of Experiential Education, 25*(2): 278-280.

Smith, E., Steel, G., & Gidlow, B. (2010). The temporary community: Student experiences of school-based outdoor education programmes. *Journal of Experiential Education, 33*(2): 136-150.

Smith, S., & Ng, D. (1982). *Perspectives on the nature of leisure research.* Waterloo, Canada: University of Waterloo Press.

Smith, T. (1982). Self-concept, special populations and outdoor therapy. In G. Robb (Ed.) *The Bradford Papers, 2,* 1-15.

Smith, T. (1985a). Outdoor therapy: Dangling ropes and solid foundations. In G. Robb, & P. Hamilton (Eds.), *The Bradford Papers, 5,* 63-68.

Smith, T. (1985b). Issues in challenge education. In G. Robb and E. Hamilton (Eds.), *Issues in Challenge Education and Adventure Programming.* Bradford Woods: Indiana University Press.

Somerville, L. (2013). The teenage brain: Sensitivity to social evaluation. *Current Directions in Psychological Science, 22*(2): 121-127.

Staley, F. (1979). *The research, evaluation and measurement dragons in outdoor education.* Paper presented at the National Outdoor Education Association Meeting, Lake Placid, NY.

Stefansson, V. (1950). *Arctic manual.* New York: Macmillan.

Stegner, W. (1961). The wilderness idea. In P. Brower (Ed.) *America's Living Heritage,* pp. 97-102. San Francisco: Sierra Club.

Stemba, B., & Bisson, C. (Eds.) (2009). *Teaching adventure education theory: Best practices.* Champaign, IL: Human Kinetics.

Stich, T. (1983). Experiential therapy for psychiatric patients. *Journal of Experiential Education, 5*(3): 23-30.

Stogner, J. (1978). The effects of a wilderness experience on self-concept and academic performance. *Dissertation Abstracts International, 39,* 4704A.

Stringer, L., & McAvoy, L. (1992). The need for something different: Spirituality and wilderness adventure. *Journal of Experiential Education, 15*(1): 13–21.

Stromberg, R. W (1969). *A history of western civilization.* Homewood, IL: The Dorsey Press.

Swarbrooke, J., Beard, C., Leckie, S., & Pomfret, G. (2003). *Adventure tourism: The new frontier.* Oxford: Butterworth Heinmann.

Sugerman, D. (2001). Motivations of older adults to participate in outdoor adventure experiences. *Journal of Adventure Education and Outdoor Learning, 1*(2): 21-33.

Talbot, J., & Kaplan, S. (1986). Perspectives on wilderness: Re-examining the value of extended wilderness experiences. *Journal of Environmental Psychology, 6*(3): 177-188.

Tanner, J., Arnett, J., & Leis, J. (2009). Emerging adulthood: Learning and development during the first stage of adulthood. In M. Smith & N. DeFrates-Densch (Eds.), *Handbook of research on adult learning and development* (pp. 34-67). New York: Routledge/ Taylor & Francis.

Templin, G. (n.d.). The element of stress. In L. Emerson & G. Gollins (Eds.), *Workbook on adventure based education.* Denver, CO: Outward Bound.

Tennant, M. (2006). *Psychology and adult learning.* New York: Routledge.

Thapa, B., Confer, J., & Mendelson, J. (2004). *Trip motivations among water-based recreationists.* www.metla.fi/julkaisut/workingpapers/2004/ mwp002-30.pdf. (Retrieved February 2, 2008.)

Thelen, E., & Smith, L.B. (2006). Dynamic systems theories. In W. Damon & R. Lerner (Eds.), *Handbook of child psychology* (258-312). *Volume 1, Theoretical Models of Human Development* (6th ed.).

Theobald, W. (1979). *Evaluation of recreation and park programs.* New York: John Wiley and Sons.

Thomas, S. (Comp.) (1985). *Adventure education: A bibliography.* Amherst, NY: Institute on Classroom Management and School Discipline at State University of New York at Buffalo.

Thomas, G., Potter, T., & Allison, P. (2009). A tale of three journals: A study of papers published in AJOE, JAEOL, and JEE between 1998 and 2007. *Australian Journal of Outdoor Education, 13*(1): 16-29.

Thompson, D. (2009). A brief history of research and theory on adult learning and cognition. In M. Smith & N. DeFrates-Densch (Eds.), *Handbook of Research on Adult Learning and Development*. New York: Routledge.

Tinsley, H., & Johnson, T. (1984). A preliminary taxonomy of leisure activities. *Journal of Leisure Research, 16*(3): 234-244.

Tinsley, H., & Kass, R. (1979). The latent structure of the need satisfying properties of leisure activities. *Journal of Leisure Research, 11*(4): 278-291.

Todd, S., Anderson, L., Young, A., & Anderson, D. (2002). The relationship of motivation factors to level of development in outdoor adventure recreationists. *Research in Outdoor Education, 6*, 124-138.

Turner, J. (2002). From woodcraft to 'leave no trace': Wilderness, consumerism, and environmentalism in twentieth-century America. *Environmental History, 7*(3): 462-484.

Ulrich, R., (1984). View through a window may influence recovery from surgery. *Science, 224*(4647): 420-421.

Ulrich, R. (1987). Aesthetic and affective responses to natural environment. In I. Altman & J. Wohlwill (Eds.), *Behavior in the Natural Environment* (pp. 85-125). New York: Plenum Press.

Ulrich, R., Simons, R., Losito, B., Fiorito, E., Miles, M., & Zelson, M. (1991). Stress recovery during exposure to natural and urban environments. *Journal of Environmental Psychology, 11*(3): 201-230.

Vancouver, J., & Kendall, L. (2006). When self-efficacy negatively relates to motivation and performance in a learning context. *Journal of Applied Psychology, 91*(5): 1146–1153.

Vancouver, J., Thompson, C., Tischner, E., & Putka, D. (2002). Two studies examining the negative effect of self-efficacy on performance. *Journal of Applied Psychology, 87*(3): 506–516.

Vander Wilt, R., & Klocke, R. (1971). Self-actualization of females in an experimental orientation program. *National Association of Women's Deans and Counselors Journal, 34*(3): 125-129.

Van Doren, C., & Hodges, L. (1975). *America's park and recreation heritage*. Washington, DC: U.S. Government Printing Office.

Vogl, R., and Vogl, S. (1974). *Outdoor education and its contributions to environmental quality: A research analysis*. Austin, TX: National Educational Laboratory Publishers, Inc.

Vogt, W. (1993). *Dictionary of statistics and methodology*. Newbury Park, CA: SAGE Publications.

Vygotsky, L. (1978). *Mind and society: The development of higher psychological processes*. Cambridge, MA: Harvard University Press.

Wagstaff, M., & Attarian, A. (2009). *Technical skills for adventure programming: A curriculum guide*. Champaign, IL: Human Kinetics.

Walsh, V., & Golins, G. (1976). *The exploration of the Outward Bound process*. Denver, CO: Outward Bound Publications.

Webb, E., Campbell, D., Schwartz, R., & Sechrest, L. (1966). *Unobtrusive measures: Nonreactive research in the social sciences*. Chicago: Rand McNally.

Weiner, B. (1985). An attributional theory of achievement, motivation, and emotion. *Psychological Review, 92*(4): 548-573.

Weiner, B. (1992). *Human motivation: Metaphors, theories, and research*. Newbury Park, CA: Sage Publications.

Wells, M., Widmer, M., & McCoy, J. (2004). Grubs and grasshoppers: Challenge-based recreation and the collective efficacy of families with at-risk youth. *Family Relations, 53*(3): 326-333.

Wetmore, R. (1972). The influence of Outward Bound school experience on the self-concept of adolescent boys. *Dissertation Abstracts International, 33*(1): 498A.

Whisman, S., & Hollenhorst, S. (1998). A path model of whitewater boating satisfaction on the Cheat River of West Virginia. *Environmental Management, 22*(1): 109-117.

Whitacre, J. (2011). *Assessing the relationship between participant risk-taking through adventure recreation and propensity for risk-taking in everyday life*. (Unpublished master's thesis.) Indiana University, December, 2011.

White, R. (1959). Motivation reconsidered: The concept of competence. *Psychological Review, 66*(5): 297-333.

Whymper, E. (1981;1871). *Scrambles amongst the Alps: In the years 1860-1869*. [Reprint.] Berkeley, CA: Ten Speed Press.

Wilder, R. (1977). EEl: A survival tool. *Parks and Recreation, 12*(8): 22-24, 50-51.

Wildland Research Center. University of California. (1962). *Wilderness and recreation—A report on resources, values, and problems*. ORRRC Report No. 3 Washington, DC. U.S. Government Printing Office.

Wilks, J., & Page, S. (Eds.), (2003). *Managing tourist health and safety in the new millennium*. Boston: Pergamon.

Williams, K., & Bond, M. (2002). The roles of self-efficacy, outcome expectancies and social support in the self-care behaviors of diabetes. *Psychology, Health & Medicine, 7*(2): 127-141.

Wilson, R. (1981). *Inside Outward Bound*. Charlotte, NC: The East Woods Press.

Witt, P., & Caldwell, L. (2005). *Recreation and youth development*. State College, PA: Venture.

Wolfe, B., & Samdahl, D. (2005). Challenging assumptions: Examining fundamental beliefs that shape challenge course programming and research. *Journal of Experiential Education, 28*(1): 25-43.

Wright, A. (1982). *Therapeutic potential of the Outward Bound process: An evaluation of a treatment program for juvenile delinquents.* (Unpublished doctoral dissertation). Pennsylvania State University.

Yenser, S. (1972). *Personal and interpersonal effects of outdoor survival.* (Unpublished master's thesis). Brigham Young University.

Yerkes, R., & Dodson, J. (1908). The relation of strength of stimulus to rapidity of habit-formation. *Journal of Comparative and Neurological Psychology, 18*(5): 459-482.

Young, R. (1983). Toward an understanding of wilderness participation. *Leisure Sciences, 5*(4): 339-357.

Young, R., & Crandall, R. (1984). Wilderness use and self-actualization. *Journal of Leisure Research, 16*(2): 149-160.

Zajonc, R. B. (1980). Feeling and thinking: Preferences need no inferences. *American Psychologist, 35*(2): 151-175.

Zuckerman, M. (1971). Dimensions of sensation-seeking. *Journal of Consulting and Clinical Psychology, 36*(1): 45-52.

Zuckerman, M. (1979). *Sensation seeking: Beyond the optimal level of arousal.* Hillsdale, NJ: Lawrence Erlbaum.

Zuckerman, M. (1985). Biological foundations of the sensation-seeking temperament. In: J. Strelau, F. Farley, & A. Gale (Eds.), *The Biological Bases of Personality and Behavior* (pp 97 – 113). Washington, DC. Hemisphere.

Zweig, P. (1974). *The adventurer: The fate of adventure in the western world.* New York: Basic Books.

Index

Note: The f and t following page numbers refer to figures and tables, respectively.

About the Authors

Alan Ewert, PhD, is a distinguished and titled professor at Indiana University. He holds the Patricia and Joel Meier Endowed Chair in Outdoor Leadership and served as the editor of the *Journal of Experiential Education*. He was the 1996 recipient of the Reynold E. Carlson Award for Distinction in Outdoor Environmental Education; the 2002 recipient of the J.B. Nash Scholar Award through the American Association for Leisure and Recreation; the 2005 recipient of the Julian W. Smith Award through the American Alliance for Health, Physical Education, Recreation and Dance; and the 2013 Association of Experiential Education's Distinguished Researcher. A prolific scholar, Ewert has published articles in a variety of journals and books related to outdoor leadership and recreation. He continues his professional service through numerous venues, including his status as a fellow and past president of the Academy of Leisure Sciences and one of the founding editors of the *International Journal of Wilderness*. Dr. Ewert also serves as a course director and instructor for Outward Bound and the Wilderness Education Association.

Jim Sibthorp, PhD, is associate professor and the coordinator of Adventure and Outdoor Programs in the department of parks, recreation and tourism at the University of Utah. He has written numerous publications in adventure-based programming and outdoor adventure education. Much of his current research stems from partnerships with the National Outdoor Leadership School (NOLS) and the American Camp Association. He has served the profession in many ways, including as co-chair of the NRPA Leisure Research Symposium, an editorial advisor for the *Journal of Experiential Education*, and an associate editor of *Leisure Sciences* and *Research in Outdoor Education*. He served on the research committees for Outward Bound and the Coalition for Education in the Outdoors. He is an active field instructor with NOLS, and he has received numerous awards, including Indiana University's Eppley Alumni Award and the University of Utah College of Health Distinguished Mentor Award for his work with graduate students.